Honk -
AUTHOR
04/05/2011

"Everyone should read this real-life story and discover what really went on behind the scenes in the making of these championship title fights. Hank includes all the people and the political, social and economic happenings that made up the golden era of the heavyweight title. This book tells it all. I was there, I lived it and Hank has captured it all in this accurate retelling of the unbelievable story that was the best boxing the world has ever seen."

—Gene Kilroy, Business Advisor to Muhammad Ali

"This book is gonna shake up the world of boxing. It is full of shit that people have not heard before. Most people have no idea what it takes to put a fight together. Hank is the real deal and the way he tells this story... you cannot put the book down. And lemme tell ya dis, dis guy wouda been nowhere if it wasn't fa me. Ha-ha-ha..."

—Tommy Gallagher, Trainer,
1959 Golden Gloves welter-weight champ,
Owner, Gallagher's Gym of Champions,
ESPN's The Contender

"The insight into this angle of Ali is truly unsurpassed."

—Dr. Scott Weiss, trainer, consultant to the USOC,
author of *Confusing the Enemy: The Cus D'Amato Story*

"Hank Schwartz ROCKS! I only knew pieces of this story before I read this book. I laughed, I cried, I was blown away. Whether you are into boxing or not, this book is a grabber from the first paragraph."

—Tim Morehouse, US Olympic Fencer, Silver Medal
blogger @ http://timmorehouse.wordpress.com/

From the Corners of the Ring
To the Corners of the Earth
The Adventure Behind the Champions

Hank Schwartz

Foreword by Smokin' Joe Frazier

CIVCOM

CIVCOM INC. PUBLISHERS
CIVCOM, Inc., P.O. Box 935, Valley Stream NY 11582-0935

© 2009-2010 Henry (Hank) Schwartz. All rights reserved.

No part of this publication may be reproduced and distributed and/or transmitted by any means and in any form or language or by any electronic, film or mechanical means or stored in any database or retrieval system without the prior written permission of the publisher.

From the Corners of the Ring, To the Corners of the Earth -The Adventure Behind the Champions is a personal memoir that has been written from my recollection of the events reported. These events took place during an exciting segment of my life at which time I was acting as an engineer, entrepreneur, and television producer using the growing satellite technologies to broadcast live television throughout the world.

No part of this manuscript contains any intentional false or misleading statement. Memory-based recollections are supported by primary sources in the form of executed documents, public records, news stories and taped interviews. No statement in this manuscript is intended to create a malicious or libelous statement. The events described in this manuscript and my participation in them, are a matter of historical fact and involve both public figures and private persons. In a few limited circumstances I have changed the names of minor players to protect their privacy. I have retold these incidents to the best of my personal recollection.

ISBN: 978-1-61623-359-4

Book design by Naomi Hui

Printed in the United States of America.
Signature Book Printing, www.sbpbooks.com

To my lovely wife Constance who traveled with me many times to various countries where she supported my business, social, governmental and technical exploits which enabled me to participate in a Golden Era of heavyweight boxing.

ACKNOWLEDGEMENTS

The author wants to express his gratitude to **THE ICTUS INITIATIVE** editorial team who played a significant part in the success of the text structure.

Kudos to Naomi Hui, Michael Rechtman, and Marty Hager for special insights and critical analysis of the manuscript.

CONTENTS

DEDICATION	i
ACKNOWLEDGEMENTS	iii
FOREWORD BY SMOKIN' JOE FRAZIER	xi
CAST OF CHARACTERS	xv

PROLOGUE

THE INTERSECTION OF TECHNOLOGY AND MYTHOLOGY

1

PART ONE

ALI-MAC FOSTER IN TOKYO

9

PART TWO

FOREMAN-FRAZIER IN JAMAICA

1. The Call from Alex	21
2. Meeting at the Sour Sop	24
3. The Jamaican Welcoming Committee	30
4. A View From the Roof	35
5. We Have A Deal	42
6. One in the Hand is Worth Two in the Bush	45
7. An OK From the UK	48
8. The Gang's All Here	52
9. The Stony Hill Hotel	56

10. A Labor Stand-off	61
11. A Tour of the Blue Mountains	66
12. A Night on the Town	72
13. Shot At in the Chevy	77
14. "Down Goes Frazier!"	81

PART THREE
FOREMAN-ROMAN IN JAPAN

1. Who the Hell is Don King?	91
2. Benihana's Bentley and Blondes	96
3. A Bromance Begins	100
4. A Matter of the Mind	104
5. Watermelon at the Victory Banquet	110
6. Touring Kyoto with Muhammad Ali	112

PART FOUR
FOREMAN-NORTON IN VENEZUELA

1. A New Vice president	119
2. Forming Telemedia de Panama	123
3. Signing Norton	128
4. A Briefcase for Foreman	133
5. Bringing the Fight to Caracas	144
6. Ali-Foreman: We Can Do This!	149
7. A Walk in the Parking Lot	154
8. A Stay of Execution	160
9. The Financing Fails	170
10. Achtung! A Trip to Paris	174

11. A Brawl at Barclays	178
12. George in a Funk	184
13. Kneed an Excuse	193
14. Norton Goes Down in 2	196
15. Getting the Hell Out of Caracas	200

PART FIVE
THE RUMBLE ON THE ROPES: ALI-FOREMAN IN ZAIRE

1. George Gets a Dog, Ali Bolts	209
2. An Architectural Ruin	217
3. Press Party at the Rainbow Room	221
4. No Prob-lem in Kinshasa	226
5. A Meeting in the Slammer	229
6. A Banger Before Bail	234
7. Ali Arrives in Zaire	237
8. Diego Flies in First Class, George is a Pain in the Ass	241
9. Live with Howard Cosell	248
10. Whirlybird Jitters	254
11. Stayin' Alive	261
12. Across the Table from Mobutu	264
13. Don Sells Lemonade, While I Work on the Lemons	269
14. Failure is Not an Option	273
15. The Flip of a Switch at the Weigh-In	281
16. "Just Another Day in the Gym"	289
17. The Rain Comes	295
18. Dancing with the Watusi	298

PART SIX
THE POWER SHIFT: BOXING BECOMES KING

1. A Visit from the Treasury — 309
2. Ali Defends his Title — 312
3. Hank Defends His Title — 319
4. Ali-Bugner in Kuala Lampur — 329
5. The Thrilla in Manila — 335
6. The Thrilla is Gone — 338
7. Stepping on Imelda's Shoe (she has more) — 345

PART SEVEN
THE FINAL ROUND

1. Regina v. Henry Schwartz — 351
2. Evicted from 30 Rock — 359
3. Ali's Last Hurrah — 361

EPILOGUE
THESE PRECIOUS HANDS
369

ABOUT THE AUTHORS — 375

FOREWORD
By Smokin' Joe Frazier

The Golden Era of heavyweight boxing was that frantic period during the 1970's and early 80's characterized by the rivalry for the heavyweight title between myself, Muhammad Ali, and George Foreman. Even while it was happening, we knew it was something special, it was history, and we were part of it. We were the actors and the ring was the stage on which this drama was set—this three-way battle that raged among us. This book tells this exciting story and captures my own real life memories of winning and losing the heavyweight boxing championship title.

Being the heavyweight champion of the world is a thrill beyond any experience you can imagine. I was a participant in what is still described as the greatest boxing rivalry in the history of the sport. Hank Schwartz provided the previously-missing piece that enabled our thrills and our rivalries to be a part of the life of the fan. You were able to watch the action, voice your opinions and passionately defend your position because you could experience for yourself all that was unfolding as it happened.

It was the first time in the history of the sport when the fans could see the fight from the perspective in the ring. Fans worldwide could see up close the impact of each blow of a pounding glove and its effect. They could see and feel blood dripping down the side of my face and see the gradual swelling around my eye as the rounds progressed. They could experience the force of my left hook as it put Ali on the canvas. They could hear the verbal blows thrown by Muhammad, garbled through his mouth guard, even while the ref was telling us to play nice. Hank Schwartz-innovated advances in video production and satellite distribution of the live TV picture made this possible. He figured out how to make all the electronic devices talk to each other.

Many other people have written about parts of this story. But in this intriguing book, Hank Schwartz tells it from his very unusual perspective that will capture the imagination of boxing fans. He watched most of these fights on a wall of television monitors in his TV studio buried in the insides of a poorly designed sports arenas while you sat on the sofa in your living room watching me do battle with my opponent.

Hank tells the story of how he went into making these fights happen. The "real life" adventure behind the champions. It is a story that I would not have wanted to live any other way. Hank's story tells it as it happened from the center of the ring, seen through the camera lens with dramatic lighting and TV camerawork. Hank explains the details surrounding these fights. He scheduled our travel, took care of the press corps, and arbitrated our disputes making sure we were comfortable. In many cases, he was the one who got the "job done" including the media hype that kept fans on the edge of their seats. Hank has given us all a glimpse of the blood, sweat, and tears that went into getting two fighters in the ring and a live color picture on your TV set.

The fight mob is a funny brotherhood of men—and a few women—who have made their lifelong living from the sport of boxing. Those of us who have survived all the body slams, upper cuts, and yes, even the left hooks that life has dealt us are a loose fraternity held together by the glue that you will never understand if you haven't lived it. The glue forms a stronger bond between some of us than others, but no one from this world will ever deny the strength of the hold it has on us.

Hank Schwartz is a full-fledged member of the fight mob. He earned his membership because of his imaginative approach to communications technology and because he was one of the best damn fight promoters in the business. When Hank Schwartz was running the show, everyone got a fair shake. Hank is part of the glue that held us all together during the Golden Era. We've had our issues and we've acted out on the international stage. We've suffered in different ways and experienced some long-standing pain. But we all have had the great privilege of living one hell of a life—in and out of the boxing ring.

Hank tells his story. He went a few rounds with the unpredictable summons of third-world dictators and the sometimes irrational demands of heavyweight champions. But at the final bell Hank won by unanimous decision. He had a clever way of working from the neutral corner.

All of us in the fight mob owe a debt of gratitude to Hank Schwartz for this book telling the story of his contribution to the Golden Era of boxing. I thank him for being a significant factor in the strength of the bond that held us all together then, and in keeping the legend alive now. It was a glorious time to be a heavyweight champion. The shimmer of the gold that distinguishes our era would not be as lustrous if it were not for Hank Schwartz.

—Joe Frazier
Philadelphia, PA
April 2010

CAST OF CHARACTERS

Hank Schwartz – I grew up in Brooklyn. A stint in the military during World War II exposed me to groundbreaking new approaches to video communications. A Bachelor of Electrical Engineering degree from Brooklyn Polytechnic gave me the background to think differently about the way television signals were developed and transmitted. Eventually, I figured out some clever ways to apply microwave and satellite technology that revolutionized the way sports fans were able to experience prizefighting in real time from anywhere in the world.

By 1971, my career was focused on the distribution of sports and political events. My company was hired to install new microwave systems to broadcast television signals so that heavyweight championship fights could be seen on major television networks and in selected movie theaters in the U.S. and other developed countries around the world. Fight promoters had long since learned that there was far more money to be made by selling the television rights to championship fights than could ever be made through arena ticket sales. By the time Muhammad Ali fought Jerry Quarry and Oscar Bonevena, Video Techniques had hit its stride and was considered the industry leader in the use of television distribution technologies.

Heavyweight Champions

Muhammad Ali – Born Cassius Clay on January 17, 1942 in Louisville, KY. He capped off an impressive amateur career by winning the gold medal in the light heavyweight division at the 1960 Olympics in Rome. In 1964, he won the coveted heavyweight championship title in Miami, FL by defeating Sonny Liston, despite 7 to 1 odds against him. Before he took his stand against induction into the Army, Cassius Clay joined the Nation of Islam and changed his name to Muhammad Ali. He explained his refusal to serve in the military by stating that "the war [in Vietnam] is against the teachings of the Holy Quoran. I am not trying to dodge the draft—we are not supposed to take part in no wars." On April 28, 1967, the New York State Athletic Commission suspended Ali's boxing license and thereby stripped him of the heavyweight title. Other state boxing commissions soon followed suit and the dethroned champion was not allowed to fight anywhere in the United States until 1970. On June 28, 1971, after a lengthy court battle, the U.S. Supreme Court ruled that Ali had been unjustly denied his boxing license.

George Foreman – Born January 10, 1949 in Marshall, TX, Foreman grew up a troubled youth in a poor neighborhood in Houston. Foreman, who was prone to instigating fistfights, got his start in boxing when a trainer broke up one of his brawls. The powerful, hulking young fighter set his sights on the heavyweight title and turned professional the year after winning the gold medal in the heavyweight division at the 1968 Olympics in Mexico City. Foreman was undefeated (37-0 with an intimidating 34 KOs) leading up to his fight with the favored Joe Frazier in 1973.

George Foreman lost his heavyweight title to Ali in 1974 and got out of boxing in 1977. While away from boxing, Foreman found religion and became a preacher in Houston. He returned to boxing ten years later and in 1994, the thundering Foreman reclaimed the title, becoming the oldest heavyweight champion in the history of boxing at the age of 45. From there he became a successful entrepreneur, showing off his new-found teddy bear charm as the spokesperson for "George Foreman's Lean Mean Grilling Machine."

Joe Frazier – Born January 12, 1944 in Beaufort, SC, "Smokin' Joe" was considerably shorter than his counterparts but made up for his height with an aggressive and brutal style that included his signature left hook. He won the gold medal in the heavyweight division at the 1964 Olympics in Tokyo and turned professional the following year. After Ali was stripped of the heavyweight title, the undefeated Frazier became the "undisputed" champion in 1970 when he defeated Jimmy Ellis. He earned the title the next year when he knocked out Ali in "The Fight of the Century."

After losing his third fight to Ali, Smokin' Joe Frazier faced Foreman at the Nassau Coliseum in Long Island in 1976. This time Frazier withstood Foreman's blows until the fifth round, when he was knocked out. Frazier attempted a comeback in 1981, but this lasted for only one fight, resulting in a TKO in ten rounds at the hands of Floyd "Jumbo" Cummings.

Challengers

Trevor Berbick – Ended Ali's career by winning with a unanimous decision

Joe Bugner – Hungarian-born, British boxer who lost to Ali twice by decision, the second of which was for the heavyweight title in Kuala Lumpur

Floyd "Jumbo" Cummings – Ended Frazier's comeback with a TKO in 10 rounds

Mac Foster – Former sparring partner of Ali; fought Ali in Tokyo

Ken Norton – Charismatic fighter who challenged Foreman for the heavyweight title in Caracas; broke Ali's jaw in the second round of a fight he would win by decision

Jose "King" Roman – Intimidated contender who fought Foreman for the heavyweight title in Tokyo

Leon Spinks – Upstart fighter who defeated Ali to win the heavyweight title by split-decision; lost the title to Ali seven months later

Chuck Wepner – Fought Ali for the heavyweight title in Cleveland; his gutsy performance against the superior Ali supposedly inspired the movie "Rocky"

Video Techniques

Juan Berrara – Cameraman

John Bull – Hank's Queen's Counsel in London

Connie – Hank's wife

Hank's Angels – Karen, Helen, Casey, Dolly

Don King – VP of Video Techniques; head of Don King Productions

Anthony Leader – Hank's solicitor

Mike – Cameraman

Jack Murphy – Head of Hank's production team

Mike Russo – helps Don King find his NY house and office

Milt Shermett – Hank's attorney

Fight Personnel

Steve Bomse – Foreman's attorney who appeared at Hank's trial

Bundini – controversial member of Ali's entourage

Al Braverman – Trainer for Wepner and Roman

Zack Clayton – Referee for the Rumble in the Jungle; former Harlem Globetrotter

Diego – Foreman's white German Shepherd

Mickey Duff – Bugner's manager

Angelo Dundee – Ali's trainer

Leroy Jackson – Foreman's business manager

Gene Kilroy – Ali's business manager

Archie Moore – Foreman's trainer

Dr. Ferdie Pacheco – Ali's doctor

Carlos Padilla – Referee for the Thrilla in Manila

Arthur Rivkin – Norton's business manager

Dick Sadler – Foreman's manager/trainer; former lightweight boxer from 1932-42

Andy Smith – Bugner's trainer

Raymond Velazquez – Executive of the World Boxing Council

Promoters

Bob Arum – Fight promoter in U.S. with an interest in Frazier

Jarvis Astaire – Fight promoter in London

John Daly – President of Hemdale Films based out of London; investor in the Rumble in the Jungle

Don Elbaum – Fight manager/promoter; introduced Don King to Hank

Ted Francis – Jack Solomons' technical guy

Jerry Perenchio – Fight promoter in U.S.

Richard Saul – Fight distributor in the U.K. for InstantVision; sued Hank after losing money on Foreman-Norton fight

Jack Solomons – British fight promoter backed by Ladbroke

John Stutter – Attorney for Hemdale Films

Alex Valdez – Peruvian dealmaker and financier

Public Relations

Murray Goodman – PR consultant with close ties to the boxing community

Bobby Goodman – PR consultant and son of Murray

Bill Caplan – Foreman's PR man

Shelly Saltman – PR consultant

Media

Roone Arledge – Representative of ABC Sports

Howard Cosell – Legendary sports broadcaster

Reg Gutteridge – British boxing journalist, signed for Hank's bail

Jerry Izenberg – Sports journalist for the New Jersey *Star-Ledger*

Dick Young – Sports journalist for *New York Daily News*

Nation Of Islam

John Ali – National secretary for the Nation of Islam

Elijah Muhammad – Leader of the Nation of Islam from 1934 until his death in 1975

Herbert Muhammad – Ali's manager; son of Elijah Muhammad

Jamaica

Paul Fitzritson – Attorney representing the Jamaican government

John Hall – Prime Minister Manley's right hand man

Norman Manley – Prime minister of Jamaica

Max and Yolanda – Eccentric husband and wife couple who owned The Stony Hill Hotel

Japan

Rocky Aioki – Founder of Benihana restaurants; fight announcer

Bob Cummings – Connie's Mind Dynamics teacher; helped coach Roman

Venezuela

Aldomero Romero – Representative of the Venezuelan government, manager of the stadium

Zaire

Cinga – Engineer for Mai 20 Stadium

Henry Clark – Foreman's sparring partner

Raymond Nicolet – Representative for Mobutu's Swiss-based company, Risnelia Investment

Mandunga Bula Nyati – Foreign minister of Zaire

Captain Unyon Pewu – Manager of the Mai 20 Stadium

Mobutu Sese Seko – President of Zaire

Shango – Goddess of weather

Tshimpumpu – Head of telecommunications in Zaire
Fred Weymar – Business advisor to Zaire

Malaysia

Mike Ong Phoot Aun – Representative for Tinj Dunla Sendirian Berhad, the Malaysian based company that promoted the fight in Kuala Lumpur

Philippines

Ferdinand Marcos – President of the Philippines
Imelda Marcos – First Lady of the Philippines

PROLOGUE

THE INTERSECTION OF TECHNOLOGY AND MYTHOLOGY

ALI-FRAZIER I:
THE FIGHT OF THE CENTURY

Madison Square Garden, March 8, 1971

Muhammad Ali sits slumped in the corner of the ring. His chest is heaving and sweat is dripping from his face onto his body, down his arms, spotting his now-filthy red trunks. A left hook sent Ali to the canvas in the final round. His gloved hands hang between his thighs as he tries to breathe normally. Arthur Mercante, the referee, signaled the end of the fight. It will be decided by the judges. If the decision is for Ali, he will regain the heavyweight title after a three-year absence from the ring.

He waits for the announcement of the judges' decision while staring at the dead zone between his feet. Ali looks across the ring at Joe Frazier. Frazier's corner men have circled round him and thrown his robe over his shoulders. Ali spits his mouth guard to Angelo Dundee, his trainer. A pool of perspiration accumulates beneath his stool. Ali sits alone. He waits.

He takes a deep breath. He waits.

Mercante crosses the ring and lifts Frazier's arm in the air. 20,000 fans erupt. It is the first defeat of Muhammad Ali's professional career. The decision against him is unanimous.

I remove the headphones and sign off the live broadcast from Madison Square Garden.

BELIEVING IN MUHAMMAD ALI

March 22, 1971

The door was closed because I was reviewing a contract to film and broadcast a sporting event outside New York in an arena I had never seen before. This is always risky and I wanted to think through all the possible obstacles to transmission of a clean, clear picture delivered from an outdoor stadium not designed to accommodate television cameras.

My phone rang and a voice whispered, "Muhammad Ali is here to see you."

Ali and I had met during the video production of several of his fights. My company, Video Techniques, had been hired by the Garden management to broadcast ring action to closed-circuit locations in theaters around the country.

"Well, send him in," I whispered back as I reached for the door into the only other room in my suite.

Muhammad Ali sat down beside me at my desk because there was no place else to sit in my cramped office on West 55th Street in New York City.

"How's the jaw? The swelling seems to have gone down," I asked, shocked once again by his ability to recover virtually overnight.

"Oh I'm pretty Hank... ain't I pretty?"

We relived the fight round by round. Then we discussed all the glamorous celebrities that were in the audience... and Diana Ross's velvet hot pants.

He hit my right shoulder after each statement he made with a soft knuckled blow that hurt like hell. "I really should have won the decision over that ugly gorilla."

That day when Muhammad Ali dropped by to visit, he convinced me that he would regain the heavyweight title. He sprinkled in details about his past and speculated on his future in that inimitable mix of rhyme and eloquence that can only be described as "Ali speak". He did not reclaim the title that night in Madison Square Garden, but he was by no means defeated. Toward the end of our conversation, he stopped throwing punches at my shoulder and quietly sang into my ear, "I'm coming back, Hank. You better believe it."

Anyone who ever met Muhammad Ali knew that you couldn't doubt him. I believed he would make it back to the top. I also believed that I had a role in helping him get there.

PART 1

ALI-MAC FOSTER IN TOKYO

March 15, 1972

It took me fourteen hours to fly from JFK to Tokyo's Haneda Airport. When I landed I felt tired as hell in spite of the fact that I drank tea all the way instead of the sake that was offered every twenty minutes to the first class passengers who spent the extra money to ride up front.

I moved through the Japanese customs line and handed my new passport to the customs agent, who was standing on a stool. I guessed that the agent was impressed when he viewed the unusual stamp on my visa's first page. This special visa allowed me to enter and leave Japan anytime I wanted during the next four years.

He looked carefully at each page of my passport. He didn't ask and I didn't explain how I managed to get the ambassador in Washington to arrange the four-year visa enabling me to work on projects in Japan.

The agent seemed unhappy, mumbling to himself in Japanese. I did not speak the language but I was sure he was saying to himself, "No American can do things better than a Japanese engineer, especially here in Tokyo."

Finally the agent smiled broadly as he held the stamp high and brought it down on my passport with a loud thump. I was reminded of scenes in old WWII films in which the Japanese failed to come out on top against the American invasion. This agent, with his toothy smile and officious stamp, seemed determined to compensate for the loss right there at the counter. He wanted me to know that he controlled when and how this American entered his country.

As we finished our exchange and I walked past the agent, his mumbling became clear and I heard him say, "Ali, Ali, Ali." The agent guessed I had something to do with the boxing match that was about to take place. Muhammad Ali had already arrived. With his winning smile, his colorful vocabulary, and his poetic musings, Ali was adored by the Japanese people.

I turned back without smiling at the agent, and signaled to him that I was indeed there because of the Ali-Mac Foster fight.

The next smiling agent, responsible for the exploration of my luggage, also seemed curious as to why I was there on a four-year visa. I watched him lift, shake, and turn over every article of clothing in my suitcase. I wanted to explain to him the contents of my bag was harmless and that I was there because very few Asian engineers knew anything about the new microwave and satellite technologies that were necessary to broadcast the fight back to the United States. I would liked to have told him that my company specialized in these technologies and the worldwide distribution of political and sporting events. I was responsible for the television broadcast and for improving the picture quality so that it was clear of the "falling snow" that normally plagued such programming.

Having cleared Japanese customs, I was greeted in the lobby by a group of four executives from Japan's ITV. This Japanese television network had hired me to advise their production crew on the new communications technology, which they had not yet mastered, in order to distribute the fight around the world. Our conversation progressed in choppy little fragments of English as we bowed and smiled and tried to be cordial. I kept saying "Thank you" to each statement because I didn't know what else to say.

After bowing and greeting each other according to traditional Japanese custom, the five of us squeezed into a small car manufactured by an automobile company I had never heard of before. I watched my single carry-on bag and attaché case get sandwiched in between the three executives in the back seat. The car had no trunk. The thin fenders sank close to the road as we all piled in.

"Mr. Schwartz, we go to have some, how do you say in English, 'dinner?'" one of the executives said. "And then we will take you to your hotel, which we made ready for you."

The pleasantries continued uncomfortably between me and the four executives as we drove slowly to the restaurant. The driver was highly skilled at dodging bicyclists and an astonishing number of pedestrians who, making no distinction between sidewalk and road, walked carelessly in the streets. Finally we arrived at a large, elegant building beautifully lit and surrounded by artful landscaping.

The restaurant did not have a valet parking service, so one of the executives stayed with the car to make sure that my suitcase, the tires, and the car itself would not disappear. There seemed to be a good chance that if the car were left alone, a reasonably strong thief could pick it up and make off with all three.

We entered the restaurant and, after more bowing and smiling, were led to a beautifully appointed table that was low to the floor and surrounded by pillows. I watched the executives settle easily on the low cushions and realized I was expected to do the same. I clumsily sat down but found it difficult to cross my legs under the table and position myself so that I could fit into the space available. I am 5'11" and folding my legs to fit under the table was a challenge. There was no one else over five feet tall in the restaurant.

I noticed there were no male waiters, only enticingly-dressed Japanese girls. At first my knees were bothering the hell out of me. But I discovered I was more comfortable after about a dozen sakes, served by a pretty waitress who massaged my neck and other body parts. I wished my cameraman was there to preserve the moment.

After a while I could no longer remember who I was with, what I was eating, or why I had been brought here directly from the Haneda Airport.

When it was time to leave, three waitresses had to help me up. I staggered outside, still chatting with the executives, thinking everything I said was perfectly hilarious. Fortunately, the little car remained parked in front of the restaurant, with my luggage still in it. It was 1 a.m. local time and the frantic bicyclists and pedestrians had disappeared. We piled back into the car and took a slow drive through the empty streets.

Suddenly the lampposts that lined the road started to swing back and forth. I wondered, how much sake had I drunk? With a screeching jolt, the driver jammed on the brakes and stopped the car between two swinging streetlights.

"What the hell is going on?" I yelled at the driver as the car started to shake.

"*Ah so*, Mr. Schwartz, we are having a little earthquake."

The fuzzy buzz of the sake instantly vaporized and gave way to terror. I had never been in or near an earthquake before. I had flown for 14 hours, eaten strange food, drunk large quantities of high-alcohol content rice wine, and I was at the end of my tolerance. I surrendered to fear.

A lamppost noisily crashed to the street, barely missing the car. Then, as suddenly as it had begun, the swaying stopped. In an instant, everyone in the car started laughing and talking at the same time in nervous relief. The car took off at top speed, given the weight of its cargo, and landed at the entrance to my hotel. I was thankful to have arrived in one piece.

I went directly to my suite and picked up the phone to call my wife Connie, back home in New York.

"Can't you connect me to the number I gave you in the United States?" I was finding out how difficult it was to maneuver through Japan's telephone communication link. I chuckled thinking how shocked newly arrived Americans must be when they try to phone back to the good old U.S. of A.

"*Ah so*. We have your corrections." I assumed that the operator meant "connection" and I was happy to finally hear Connie's voice on the other end of the line.

"Hello Connie!" I shouted with relief.

"Is that you?" she asked, clearly glad to hear my voice.

"Yeah, what time is it in New York?"

"It's only 12:30 in the afternoon here. What time is it in Tokyo?"

"The time difference is crazy. It's 1:30 in the morning here, about thirteen hours ahead of you." I knew that I was slurring when I spoke and sounded like I was more than a little woozy—which happened to be perfectly accurate.

I had undressed while the operator struggled to complete the call and now stood naked, looking into a mirror mounted on the wall. I focused on my reflection while still feeling the vertigo effect of the earthquake and the sake. It seemed as if I was swaying left to right and I decided that I would not tell Connie the full story about the earthquake.

"I just got here and I am getting settled in the hotel. Everything's fine." I also decided not to disclose the full details about my first restaurant experience in Tokyo, knowing that it would not sit too well at home.

"Everything alright?" Connie asked.

"*Ah so.* It was a perfect flight and perfect night." We both laughed. I said goodbye and got into bed.

Despite my exhaustion, my mind was spinning and I could not get to sleep. I kept thinking about the importance of this fight as Muhammad Ali pursued his quest to regain the heavyweight title. Ali was going to fight Mac Foster, his old sparring partner, the following morning—April 1, 1972.

The production of the Ali-Frazier fight had opened the door for Video Techniques to become an advisor to the Japanese Television Network. My job was to oversee the TV camera positions and advise them on how to create exciting camera shots from various angles within the arena. I was sure that Video Techniques could deliver this boxing event to the world over the newly-developed international communications networks via the mechanical birds flying around the equator, also known as satellites.

I quickly learned, however, that trying to advise the Japanese TV director was a no-win situation. Either he didn't understand English or he didn't want to hear my advice in any language. Suggestions I made as to where to place camera platforms and lighting structures were ignored. My advice went in one ear and out the other.

The broadcast of Ali's easy victory over Mac Foster was totally uninteresting, despite going the full fifteen rounds. The Japanese crew did not take advantage of any of the modern production techniques that would have made the program exciting and memorable. All things considered, our broadcast from Madison Square Garden had gone a hell of a lot better than this one from Tokyo.

In spite of all the bad camera work and disconnected clips that could not be stitched together to produce a coherent program, I got the fight distributed worldwide. Fight fans around the globe were able to see Ali "float like a butterfly and sting like a bee," in many cases for the first time. This first live broadcast from Japan was adequate but, in my opinion, needed a lot of improvement.

It took another fourteen hours to fly back to New York and this time I drank the sake; it facilitates the creative process, I have learned. I had a lot of time to think about what had gone wrong and to consider what we needed to do in the future to produce a better live television event.

I realized a blue floor canvas should be used in the ring in the future instead of a white one, because the white reflected light upward and washed out Ali's dancing feet. Many technical details like this were flying through my head. The broadcast of the Tokyo fight had been a tremendous learning experience, if nothing else. My brain was working in overdrive, analyzing all the various elements that would make a live sporting event more exciting. If we could make it more "real" for the viewer, the program was more saleable. It occurred to me that if I could package together all the technical services, including well-equipped television production, a communication infrastructure able to reach the newer satellites, and proper site selection, then I could change everything. I knew how to produce great live television. By the time I got back to New York I had reinvented the business model of my company and I knew Video Techniques was headed in the direction of championship boxing.

PART 2

FOREMAN-FRAZIER IN JAMAICA

CHAPTER 1
THE CALL FROM ALEX

Fall, 1972

I was thrilled to get out of Tokyo so I could stop worrying about the next earthquake. Connie was delighted to see me home and I was happy to be back no worse for wear. My Angels were also glad to see me alive and well. My lovely and loyal office staff had acquired the moniker "Hank's Angels" as they had become increasingly indispensable through the years. These women helped me with all the technical, networking, sales, and marketing decisions in addition to completing general administrative duties. From the one large desk they shared in the front room of my office suite, the Angels kept me afloat by doing a little bit of everything.

The Video Techniques office was located on West 55th Street in Manhattan and consisted of two cramped rooms on the top floor of an old building that was buried half way down the street from Fifth Avenue. Karen, my right-hand Angel, along with Helen, Casey, and Dolly, were always smartly dressed, upholding the fashionable image of the neighborhood. Toward the end of one of my first days back in New York, Karen called over from her office, "Hank, there's someone on the phone who's insisting to talk to you."

I looked up from my paperwork and asked, "Who is it?"

"This is the third time he's called today and each time you said you were too busy. He sounds like a foreigner to me."

I was trying to get out of the office so I could be home for dinner at a decent hour but I was curious to know why this guy was so persistent. "Let me take the call so I can get him off my back." I reached for the extension but hesitated and called over to Karen, "Do we owe him any money?"

Karen walked into my office and smiled. "We owe everybody money, Hank, but most of them don't bother you." I picked up the receiver.

"May I help you?"

"Is this Henry Schvartz?" the man asked, speaking in a thick accent. "My name is Alex."

"Yeah, but everyone calls me Hank. Nobody uses the Schvartz part. That last part is actually Schwartz. I'm guessing you speak German?" I hoped this was going to be a quick phone conversation.

"Schvartz…Hank… I think that I'm as Jewish as you are. My family is from Peru and I speak six languages, so I can put any spin on it you want. I am an agent for the government of Jamaica. Jamaica wants to build up its image around the world as a tourist mecca. They hope to do a major boxing championship to increase the visibility of their country." Alex sounded like he could be sweating on the other side of the line. I heard tension in his voice.

Alex took a big breath. "Anyway, let's forget about that right now. Let's talk about a contract for a championship fight that I got signed by Joe Frazier to kick the shit out of George Foreman."

I wondered who the hell I was talking to and how the hell he had found out about us. Video Techniques had been involved in the sports side of the communications business only for a few years. Just a handful of people in technical television and the sports industry knew about my company as a result of our broadcasting fights from Madison Square Garden.

"So what's your name again?"

"I'm Alex Valdez and someone at Madison Square Garden told me you can convince the Jamaican politicians that Video Techniques can televise and broadcast a championship fight live from Kingston around the world."

I knew there were challenges to doing business in Jamaica because of the high crime rate and the anti-government stance of the general population. The socio-economic issues and general distrust of business transactions would make it difficult to work in such a politically-unstable environment. *Is this guy on the other end of the phone for real?*

"Listen buddy, I don't want to miss my dinner tonight. Where are you anyway?"

"I'm going for a meeting at the Sour Sop Bar and Restaurant in the Bronx and I would like you to join me there," Alex said.

"To do what?" I was ready for a quiet evening with Connie. I could not believe this joker. But then I had one of those gut-level signals that occasionally come to me at pivotal moments in my life. I knew that I needed to see the face behind the voice. Perhaps this could be a viable business opportunity for Video Techniques. I was silent for about thirty seconds. "Where is this place and how do I get there?"

CHAPTER 2
MEETING AT THE SOUR SOP

By the time I arrived at the Sour Sop and introduced myself to the table, an agreement in principle had been reached.

Alex Valdez had gotten there more than an hour ahead of me. He had directed the cab to the shabby Bronx neighborhood and then to the unmarked doorway which served as the entrance to the unofficial Jamaican consulate, named after the infamous island rum drink. The smell of marijuana overwhelmed him as he tried to distinguish faces but could really only see the fiery red glow of smoldering joints that littered the tables throughout the room.

Alex had been sent to New York City by a business associate in Spain. When he walked into the Sour Sop he knew only the name of the person he was looking for. Alex made his way to the bar.

"*Señor*, what is the best Jamaican rum that you have here?"

The bartender looked at him and snarled, "C'mon man—what are you doing here? You sent here by Bacardi to test the rums sold in this bar?"

Alex smiled. "*Señor*, do you also serve the Bacardi rums that come from Puerto Rico or do you carry brands only from the country of Jamaica?"

"Man, I asked you what you're doing here." The frown disappeared from the bartender's face. Alex moved his left hand into his jacket pocket, giving the impression that he might be carrying a pistol.

A fairly large rum drink appeared in front of Alex and he became more comfortable as he sipped from the frosty glass. He again scanned the bar area and the tables in the back. He turned back to the bartender.

"*Señor*, do any of your friends here go by the name of Fitzritson, Paul Fitzritson?"

The bartender yelled in a high pitched Jamaican slang the equivalent of, "Boss, someone here to see you."

A well-dressed man pushed away from a crowded table in the back of the bar. Alex tried to distinguish the man's features, but the marijuana smoke was too thick.

Paul motioned to Alex to come have a seat. "Over here, Mr. Valdez." Alex picked up his drink and carried it toward the table where Paul was sitting. Paul was a tall, light-skinned, very attractive young man. He did not look like he fit in with the other men huddled around the small tables that were too close to each other in the bar area. Paul was the attorney who represented the government of Jamaica and was key to making the deal work.

"Hello, Mr. Valdez. We've been told that you have arranged a heavyweight championship fight between George Foreman and Joe Frazier. We are very interested in having this fight take place in Kingston, Jamaica."

Alex interrupted, "*Señor* Paul, why in hell did you set up a meeting with me and my associate in such a place? Pardon me for saying so, but this is a filthy shitty joint!"

Paul smiled and leaned back in his chair, shifting his long legs under the table. "Funding by the government and support from local politicians are what makes this world work. Look around this 'shitty joint.' These are the people who are in a position to make this event go forward, or not."

As Paul alluded to the financial realities known on the street, but rarely stated openly, two shabbily dressed locals sitting nearby—close enough to hear—approached the table. Alex's hand went back into his left jacket pocket.

"Hold on, Alex." Paul smiled again and held his hand out in a calming gesture as the men approached. Alex was not comfortable.

Paul motioned to the bartender, who brought over a glass of French wine and set it in front of Alex.

"Alex, let me introduce you to two of our government's funding sources. These sources will support the letters of credit or cash that is needed. The four of us will work everything out so we can hold the Frazier-Foreman fight in Kingston."

"Hello, *Señor* Valdez," one of the locals said in a soft voice. "Our names are not important. We will arrange to have the funds available for the championship fight." It was apparent that these seeming low-lifes were part of Paul Fitzritson's team.

"Alex, did you bring copies of the contracts with Frazier and Foreman?"

Alex had calmed down and was studying Paul's face and checking out the moneymen. All three were smiling and relaxed. Alex took his left hand out of his pocket and reached inside his vest. He laid the papers on the table—the agreements with Joe Frazier and George Foreman. Both contracts specified that they were ready, willing, and able to fight for the title at any site both fighters agreed to.

For the next hour the men conducted a sophisticated negotiation involving millions of dollars. Everyone at the table was an experienced dealmaker. The discussion resulted in a commitment to produce the first championship boxing event ever to take place on the island of Jamaica, paid for by the government.

I had made my way to the Bronx via subway. I had to inquire several times before I was able to get any of the locals to give me the straight story as to the location of our meeting place. I decided to keep a low profile for the first few minutes so I could scope out the joint and decide if I wanted to stick around. It was almost impossible to see anything through the thick cloud of smoke that engulfed the barroom. I surveyed the occupants of the bar stools and easily concluded none of them was Alex. I ordered a Jack Daniels and walked to the back, thinking I could assess the players at the clusters of little round tables more easily from the far end of the room. I quickly narrowed the possibilities to two groups of men. Both groups appeared to be conducting business transactions. The first was examining the contents of small plastic bags and tasting small samples as the bag was passed around the table. The second group was looking at documents and pointing to provisions as they seemed to reach a consensus among themselves.

I kept my eye on the group with the papers for the length of time it took me to finish my drink. I placed my empty glass on a round tray near the kitchen door and walked over to the table. I was fairly certain Alex was the guy with his hand in the pocket of his jacket. I was not clear who the guy in the suit across from him was, but it was obvious he was the power broker.

I dragged a chair over from a neighboring table and made eye contact with Alex. He extended his hand as I sat down and no further introductions were made. I listened as the final aspects of the deal were hammered out with the money men.

"Gentlemen, I'm Hank Schwartz," I said when they reached a pause in the negotiations. I reached across the table to shake hands with the power broker. Alex made the introductions and the conversation continued as if there had been no interruption.

"Hank, there is a meeting tomorrow morning in the National Stadium in Kingston; we need you there," Paul Fitzritson told me. "Prime Minister Manley and John Hall, his chief-of-staff, will be there, as well as the rest of the government board needed to approve the contracts and arrange full funding for the event."

"Why the hell do you need me there?" I asked. Alex had apparently briefed them on my background.

"Before the government puts the money on the table, we have to be certain that somebody can produce a live televised event and broadcast it internationally from our stadium. I must admit the stadium is in need of a few repairs and modernization," Paul explained. "We need someone at the meeting who can assure the members of the board that our vision is possible. Our goal is to create a positive image for Jamaica's tourism business. We have experienced serious setbacks in the last couple of years." Fitzritson spoke quietly over the noise and I began to like his cool, intelligent approach to the situation.

Alex had finished several drinks but his mind was still sharp. "Do I understand you have to get the deal approved by the government board—the National Sports Ltd.?"

I was still not clear on Alex's role in the transaction or how he became involved with the Jamaican government. I did not understand how they would pay the fighters. I was not even sure I was dealing with a person in a position to make a binding agreement. I would have felt more comfortable if Alex's accent had been from Brooklyn.

"You want me to come down tomorrow morning and meet with the government to see whether my company can provide some communication services?"

"Hank, it would be *schlecht* if we can't get the fight broadcast out of Jamaica," Alex said. He was throwing in some Yiddish statements to focus me on the problems we could be facing with National Sports Ltd. and so that he would not be understood by Paul and his moneymen.

"I'll have you on a first-class flight in the morning and in front of the board at two in the afternoon. You're to look over everything in the stadium and see what you can do down there," Paul stated without smiling. I knew Paul must have dealt with Jewish businessmen before, because Alex's Yiddish had caused him to become more serious.

I went to the bar, ordered another Jack Daniels, and motioned to Alex to join me. "Alex, before I get on any airplanes, I have some questions. First of all, are you nuts?"

He just looked at me and said nothing. "Secondly, I am not sure what your role is in this transaction. You and I do not have a deal—are you expecting a percentage of anything I earn…. if my company gets a contract? And third, is this deal legit? How do you know these people are for real? I mean look at the financiers for god's sake!"

"*Si… Oui… Da* and yes… the ticket will be waiting for you at the airline counter at JFK." Alex appeared to have a firm commitment, which caused my confidence that he knew what he was doing to steadily rise. We were both quiet for the next sixty seconds.

I stared into my drink and tried to convince myself that Alex Valdez was not some whack job trying to convince me the fight contracts with Frazier and Foreman were real.

"Schvartz, are you still with me?" Alex had been looking at my face while I was staring into my Jack Daniels.

"If you're for real and this deal is legit, I can find a way to shoot this fight and get it out of the stadium. If you're not some nut… or trying to do a deal with one of my competitors who don't know what the hell they are doing…" I hesitated one last moment. "I'll see you at the hotel that you will arrange for me in Jamaica."

CHAPTER 3
THE JAMAICAN WELCOMING COMMITTEE

As I boarded the plane to Kingston I asked myself whether I was on the precipice of something big or if I was headed down another yellow brick road to what might have been. At least I was comfortable in first class on the Jamaica Airlines' "big yellow bird."

The breakfast was lousy, even if it was in first class. There was no Jack Daniels. The airline served only Jamaican rum, which did not sit too well with me at 8 a.m. But the flight did have beautiful dark Caribbean girls with short skirts and lovely legs. I could not help but think that Jamaica might be a great place to host a championship fight in the hopes of drawing fans from around the world.

As I proceeded through immigration, the customs agent asked, without looking at me "Are you here as a tourist?" His stamp was poised and ready to approve my passport.

I watched his face as I said, "No, I've been invited here by Prime Minister Manley to see if we can broadcast a championship prize fight from Kingston's Stadium."

His head snapped up. He gave me a big wide smile and said, "Man, you are crazy. That stadium is in bad shape!" Thump. The passport was stamped. This trip already appeared to be going better than my visit to Tokyo. As I walked toward the exit, I heard him laughing with the other customs agents behind me. "Man, dat guy must be *bandulu*... ha ha... he want to do soomting in dat ol' stadium. Ha ha." I knew that *bandulu* meant "nuts" in Jamaican lingo. Maybe it wasn't going as well as I thought. I continued walking and the customs doors closed behind me. I was on Jamaican soil.

Jamaica advertised itself as a lush, beautiful island, but in 1972 it was still struggling with lawlessness in the streets. I found out later that Jamaica has one of the world's highest murder rates. Bad publicity and threatening news stories jeopardized the tourism industry. These thoughts caused me concern as I walked over to get a taxi.

"Taxi? Hey brother, over here. What hotel do I take you to?" a driver shouted. Then, in a softer voice, the driver said, "Hey, white brother, would you like a little ganja? I can buy some for you just a little drive up the road."

"No, black brother," I replied. "Just drive me over to the Kingston Stadium. Drop me off there and wait."

The taxi driver looked at me and asked, "You want to pay me with US dollars?"

"Yup."

"You gonna pay me with green dollars US?"

"Yup."

"I get you there in five minutes but I ain't gonna wait for ya."

I glared at the driver. "Now listen, brother, I'm not gonna stay there too long. I'm gonna need a driver for the rest of the day. I'm gonna give you ten dollars when we get there and I'll give you another ten dollars when you take me to the Hilton Hotel. If we ain't gonna do it that way, I'm gonna open the door and get out of this lousy taxi and get that other cabby over there."

There was silence for about ten seconds. "OK white brother, my name is Joshua. I ain't workin' for this fuckin' government but I'll be your driver today. Give me the ten green now."

We roared out of the Palisadoes Airport. I hoped he was driving to the Stadium. It's a wonder we didn't smash into one of the other cars or bicycles we swerved to avoid. I prayed that I would not be killed in the first hour I arrived in this screwed-up country. The driver parked the taxi a full block and a half away from the stadium. I looked out the window and asked why we had stopped.

"Mon, this is as far as I go. Those are all government soldiers over there and they're keeping people out of the stadium."

"Why?"

"Mon, I told you it's the fuckin' government. I ain't going any closer than this."

I wanted the taxi to wait for me because I wasn't comfortable with the military squadron in front of the stadium. I assumed that the government officials were meeting in a conference room and needed military protection. This deepened my level of discomfort. I was sure that Joshua would split with my ten bucks so I gave him a stern look. "Now remember, I told you to wait for me. It shouldn't take me more than a half hour to an hour." I saw the concern on his face as he checked out the armed guards.

"Sure man. I'm gonna be here waitin' for ya," he assured me. I got out of the taxi and ducked under the yellow tape that ran around the entryway of the stadium. The young soldiers that had been assigned to monitor the front gate were leaning against trees and looked as if they had been enjoying a smoke.

"Hey mon, what are you doing? You can't come in here," a soldier shouted while he shifted his rifle off his shoulder and looked me over.

"I've been invited to a meeting with Prime Minister Manley. I need to look over the stadium before we meet." I was scheduled to meet with him at 2:00. I was early.

"What's your name?"

"Use one of your big radio units and tell your prime minister that Henry Schwartz is here from Video Techniques in New York."

A lot of fast talk went back and forth over what looked like old mobile radio equipment from World War I. Eventually two soldiers loaded me into a Jeep and drove me through the stadium's front gate. It looked as if I was being taken into custody. Out of the corner of my eye, I saw Joshua make a sharp U-turn and take off with my ten US dollars.

The soldiers had been assigned by Manley to take me wherever I was supposed to be. Hopefully they would stay with me while I investigated the stadium.

"Beautiful country you have here…" I said, trying to break the ice. It was hot.

The soldiers relaxed when they found out why I was going into the stadium. They now seemed to understand that I was on good terms with their government.

I stepped into the interior of the stadium to assess the situation. Although the arrangement was not optimum, I could tell in a second it would be workable. The middle of the stadium was large enough to install the boxing ring with ample space for VIP seating to accommodate government officials and high-priced ticket buyers. I decided where we would put the television cameras. We would have to build a complete television studio in a very short period of time. The ring would be fully illuminated from towered lights over the ring with additional lights mounted around the stadium. I needed to figure out how to transmit the television signal out of the stadium and up to the satellites.

"Hey brothers, do you guys know where JAMINTEL, the telephone company is?" The security detail was immediately back on the radio.

"I need to get over to JAMINTEL now. Tell your commanding

officer that I am demanding that you take me over there before I meet with the prime minister." The radio discussion resumed.

"Alright mon, we'll drive you over there but we've got to stay with you and bring you back here in time for the meeting."

An older military Jeep pulled up and I was ushered into the back seat. Apparently two new soldiers had been assigned to me for the trip to the telephone company. They also looked like they had enjoyed a smoke.

CHAPTER 4

A VIEW FROM THE ROOF

The JAMINTEL building was fairly modern and looked like it was equipped to reach INTELSAT's international satellite network. In order to broadcast the fight, I needed to send the live signal from the stadium to the JAMINTEL building. When their telephone-based studio received the video transmission, they would send the program to the international satellite through an uplink. Finally, the live video feed would be broadcast to many down links around the world. This was the plan.

In order to get near the facility I had to once again pass through a group of armed guards who surrounded the JAMINTEL building. I tried to play it cool as I approached the building with my two ganja-smoking military chaperones.

"Hey brothers, do you really believe someone is going to blow everything up around here?" I joked. Nobody smiled except me.

"Listen whitey, they've already blown up some of our important buildings and shot and killed several people." I stopped smiling.

"Who got shot?"

"Mon, we don't know."

One of the new set of guards barked, "Come over here mon. Open your bag and clean out your pockets." Six guards looked through everything I had on me, which consisted of airline tickets, a passport, a wallet, some house keys, and a small pair of binoculars. The binoculars grabbed their attention.

"Mister, what the hell is this?"

They turned the binoculars over in their hands and passed them among themselves. I thought they were looking for wires or dynamite sticks or both. These young soldiers thought I was an American cowboy sent to blow up their prime minister or the president of the telephone company.

"Mon, what are you going to use this thing for?"

I explained that I needed the binoculars to determine whether I had a direct line of sight from the roof of the JAMINTEL building to any part of the stadium. That got me into the building.

I met with the executive in charge of JAMINTEL's operations and found him to be knowledgeable and very cooperative.

"Yes, we have an uplink that can handle C-band signals and reach INTELSAT's satellites. We have an agreement to provide all government services in Jamaica, but we have no way to connect to the stadium."

"Will you give me clearance to go up on the roof?" I asked.

"Surely, Mr. Schwartz. My engineers will go with you."

The two military chaperones were still glued to me.

The executive looked at me and then looked at the two guards that had stuck with me since we entered the building. He was suspicious that we were planning to destroy JAMINTEL, starting with the equipment on the roof and working our way down until we reached his office.

"Do you need them on the roof?"

The question set my chaperones on edge. They were beginning

to feel that they were not being treated with proper respect. My twin guard-dogs lowered their rifles from their shoulders.

The executive twisted his face into an unpleasant smile. "Sure, sure, Mr. Schwartz, it's OK. Just don't let anyone get too close to the edge of the roof. It's flat up there with no railing. I do not want to be responsible for any accidents," he said with an awkward laugh.

The roof was clean. I could see an edge of the stadium without the binoculars but there were a lot of other buildings in between. I had to get a clear line of sight to the side of the stadium that faced the JAMINTEL building. I had to figure a way to install the microwave equipment so we could send a clear signal from the stadium to JAMINTEL.

I studied the stadium through the binoculars but could not pinpoint a location to place the transmitting equipment. Any blockage would completely throw off the microwave signal. I needed to be absolutely sure that a microwave antenna installed on the highest part of the tower could receive the video program sent from a microwave antenna installed on the highest point in the stadium.

"OK guys, I've got to climb the tower. I have to get up there to get a clear shot at the stadium."

"Shot" was the wrong word to use. My two chaperones, now operating as my first line of defense, unloaded their rifles from their shoulders again.

"For Christ's sake, I meant an electronic shot, not a rifle shot," I said. The tension was driving me nuts. I had another concern as well. I was wearing a toupee to cover my balding head. Between the force of the wind and the sweat that was pouring off of me, I knew it was going to be a challenge to keep my hairpiece on after all this physical exertion.

"Which one of you guys wants to climb the tower with me?" I asked.

They looked at each other and then looked at me. Neither

of them moved. There was a large gap between each rung on the ladder and it takes a lot of strength to climb that distance. I observed that the ladder was covered with Caribbean dust as I looked it over from the bottom. I made one last ditch effort to secure my toupee and stepped onto the lowest rung.

When I had climbed the sixty feet above the roof of the JAMINTEL building I got a clear sight line across Kingston to the stadium. I was now positive that we could get the job done. Then it hit me that I was hanging sixty feet in the air, clutching a flimsy tower that may or may not have been built to support my weight should the wind kick up. To keep my mind occupied as I made a deliberate retreat, I focused on the fact that I was going to be a part of the heavyweight championship fight between "Smokin' Joe" Frazier and "Big George" Foreman.

I was confident that I could pull this off. I was ready to meet with Prime Minister Manley.

Back in the military Jeep, my young chaperones talked between themselves but included me in the conversation more frequently than they had before.

"Hey brother, you look a little wind blown. Why don you take a swag?" They passed me a marijuana cigarette. I inhaled. They dropped me, half-high on marijuana, in front of the stadium and waved an enthusiastic goodbye.

After climbing the tower in the heat, my shirt was dirty and soaked with perspiration, my toupee was no longer securely stuck to my sweaty head, and my glasses were smudged to the point I could hardly see. I had looked very sharp, in my suit jacket and tie, when I got off the plane; now, I was a mess.

When I arrived at the room where the meeting was, I reached for the door, but before I touched the handle it flew open and nearly smacked me in the chest. I was suddenly face-to-face with a tall man wearing a $600 Hickey Freeman gabardine suit, a fresh white shirt, and perfectly groomed grey hair. He was immaculate. He was also my competitor—the CEO of a rival television production company bidding on the same job I was.

"Hi!" I said with a big smile, "How did you do in there with your meeting?"

My competitor walked right past me without answering my question or acknowledging my existence. That shook me up. Then came the stinger. It all became clear to me in an instant. That sly son-of-a-bitch Alex had brought more than one company to pitch their services to the prime minister.

How am I going to handle this? I asked myself. I could not let this high-society, grey-haired sharpie throw me off my game. I took a deep breath and walked into the conference room. On the table was a six-inch alabaster sculpture, no doubt pre-Columbian. It was a gift given by the smart-assed sharpie to the prime minister. Damn it! He was playing the role of the gracious diplomat and charming his way into a lucrative government contract. It had never occurred to me to bring an expensive gift. OK Hank, just be yourself and be cool. If you can't win on form, you can usually win on substance.

I scanned the room. It was easy to pick out Prime Minister Manley. He was the man petting the alabaster sculpture. To his right sat John Hall, the man who would actually make the decision.

"Mr. Schwartz, thank you for coming down on such short notice."

"Thank you for having me, Mr. Prime Minister. And for giving me the opportunity to review the facilities ahead of time so that I could check out the condition of the stadium and give you an accurate assessment of the issues that need to be addressed," I said confidently as I made one last ill-fated attempt to straighten my hair piece.

John Hall looked me over and stated, "The weather seems to have gotten you a little down."

"Well, Mr. Hall, before this meeting I had to do a little research to find out whether we could connect your stadium to the outside world in order to broadcast a high quality, live television signal. My company cannot and will not undertake the services we are discussing unless we are sure we can meet your expectations."

Everyone looked up and scanned me up and down.

"I am pretty disheveled right now. But I had to investigate the logistics of the situation before I felt confident working out an agreement with your government. I needed to make sure we would be able to install a new microwave link from your stadium to the top of the tower over at JAMINTEL's building."

The word "microwave" did not seem to be well known to these representatives seated around the conference table. John Hall smiled and said, "And how did you determine that?"

"Well, you can only do that if it is possible to draw a straight line, with no obstructions in the way, between the stadium roof and the roof at JAMINTEL on the other side of Kingston. So, I climbed up the 60 foot tower on top of JAMINTEL. Now I am sure Video Techniques can do the job for you, up to the quality standards you expect."

Everyone laughed including Prime Minister Manley, who got up, came over to me, grabbed my shoulder in a friendly way and nodded to John Hall. "We can work out an arrangement. I assume you mean a microwave transmission between those two buildings."

Well, this was a pleasant surprise. I was finally dealing with someone who knew what the hell I was talking about.

"I guess it was a little tough climbing up there in the heat. We appreciate your efforts," the Prime Minister remarked with a smile. "I think your TV production and international distribution experience will be a great asset for our tourist business here." He looked over to John Hall. "John, I'll leave it up to you to work out a contract with Mr. Schwartz and his company."

The prime minister walked toward the door of the conference room, turned around, and graciously bowed his head in my direction with a grin on his face. "I hope you enjoy your stay in our country," he said as he closed the door. I began to relax. Every bone in my body was beginning to ache from the climb and I needed to get my hairpiece re-situated. I was positively elated.

I settled into my room at the hotel and gratefully sunk down into the Hilton's white porcelain tub, filled with warm healing waters.

CHAPTER 5

WE HAVE A DEAL

November 28, 1972

After the soothing bath and a Jack Daniels or two, I was confident that my climb to the top of the tower was a big step forward in my rise to the top of sports broadcasting.

The phone rang. It was John Hall asking for a draft of the contract with Video Techniques. We arranged to meet in the morning in the Hilton lobby to go over the terms together. I had to call one of my Angels and ask her to go back to the office to help me out because I had not brought a copy of our contract with me.

"Karen, I really need your help," I pleaded. "I know it is after five in New York, but you've got to go back to the office and fax me the professional services agreement. I didn't think we would be this close to a deal in such a short time. Normally it takes months to negotiate and get a contract signed with a national government."

Karen said, "Hank, you sound exhausted. What the hell happened?"

"It is hard to explain. This country is full of logistical challenges. The whole situation has worked me over… worse than I thought it would."

I explained to Karen that I had to receive the sample agreement A.S.A.P. because the Hilton only made their ancient fax machine available to guests between certain hours. I had already paid the hotel's night manager some US dollars to get a typewriter delivered to my room so I could fill in the blanks and create replacement pages in the document.

I spent the next two hours at the hotel bar waiting on the fax. I was totally alone, which allowed me to collect my thoughts. I made notes of all the points that had to be addressed and considered how to handle each term in the agreement. There was no Jack Daniels available so I drank the Jamaican rum. I was focused and alert, even after a crazy day and a few rum drinks that were actually beginning to grow on me.

John Hall picked me up at 10 a.m. and took me to his office to go over all the points that were important to him. We spent the whole day filling in the blanks in the contract. Video Techniques was appointed the producer of the televised event, the worldwide distributor, and money collector for all revenues received outside of Jamaica. In addition to the technical aspects, we also had to select and state in the contract who would be responsible for the public relations work. The firm selected would have to strike a balance between publicizing the fight and encouraging the growth of Jamaica's tourism by showcasing its resort areas.

Looking over the retyped agreement, Hall asked, "Who is this Murray Goodman and what is he supposed to do for Jamaica?"

"He is the best public relations guy I know. He can handle the pre-fight publicity and the schedule of the fighters," I said. "He is well liked by the WBA and WBC, the two organizations that will get this fight into all the sports publications, and he'll start the publicity well before the fight happens."

I then told Hall about Shelly Saltman, who was the second

PR firm designated in the agreement. He was more important to the Jamaican Tourist Agency.

"Saltman is out of a Hollywood firm that is extremely well connected to all levels of the media throughout the world. He was responsible for all the public relations for Andy Williams's most recent world tour."

John Hall and I completed a draft that needed to be reviewed by Paul Fitzritson, the attorney for the government. A small payola to the manager got Paul over to the Hilton. Paul and I resolved a few small points and Video Techniques signed the contract.

Paul delivered the contract to John Hall and by the time I woke up the next morning it had been signed and slipped under my hotel room door.

Alex and I had a drink to celebrate the deal when I told him the contract was signed. We toasted a long-lasting friendship and the payoff for our good working relationship.

"*Herschel* (Yiddish for Hank), we have to tell the attorney who represents your competitor that Video Techniques got the agreement finished and signed," he said with a little hesitation in his voice I did not fully understand. "You have to let him know that they are out of the picture. They think they have the contract and that this is their deal." I knew that Alex was referring to the slick gray-haired sharpie that was the head of the other firm he brought to Kingston to pitch the board. But I was not clear why it was my job to tell these guys they were out of the picture.

"Alex, how can they think they have any kind of a contract?" I asked. "They don't have a clue about the technical side. They thought that an expensive gift would bring them the deal."

CHAPTER 6
ONE IN THE HAND IS WORTH TWO IN THE BUSH

"Good morning Alex. I'm catching the ten o'clock back to New York. Do you want to have breakfast to go over the next steps on the deal?" I said into the phone, but I could tell immediately Alex was preoccupied with someone talking in the background. I heard the unidentified voice say, "You need to get Schwartz over here to bring me up to date on this alleged contract that was slipped under his door." It seemed that this other voice knew when and how I had received the signed contract.

"Schwartz, why don't you come down here and join us for breakfast. Let's go over the terms of the contract." Alex didn't call me Herschel or Schvartz as he had before.

I met Alex and his mystery guest downstairs. He was a young man, three or four years younger than I. He sat across the table from me and seemed to be steaming as much as his coffee.

"Listen Mr. Schwartz," he said, "I do not know who you are, but I represent the company that has the contract to do the television production for this fight and market all the programming.

We had this deal arranged before you were invited to Jamaica."

Bingo. This guy definitely represented my competitor who passed me in the hallway as I went in to meet Prime Minister Manley. I had no idea what had caused this confusion—or what Alex had arranged with these other guys.

"What's your name?" I asked the stranger.

"I am Cyril and I have negotiated an agreement with National Sports." He wasn't looking at me when he said this, instead directing his glare at Alex. I watched Alex fidgeting and shifting nervously in his chair. I could not understand how he had messed this up.

I listened to Cyril carefully and said, "Do you have a copy of your agreement with you? I would like to see it."

"Well, my client's chairman never got anything in writing, but he was here yesterday morning and was promised the contract."

I reached into my attaché case and took out the signed contract between Video Techniques and National Sports of Jamaica. I turned to the last page and held it up so Cyril could see the signatures. "This is the agreement that was executed last night between Video Techniques and the National Sports of Jamaica. Your client does not have anything." I folded the agreement and placed it back into my attaché case. As I did this I picked up my coffee to take a sip and looked closely at Cyril. He was fuming but I had him up against the ropes. He wasn't quite finished, however.

"If you have the contract, we are entitled to 50% of it," he blurted out in an agitated voice.

I lost my cool. With the coffee in my left hand, I reached out with my right and grabbed the attorney by his tie. No one in Jamaica ever wore a necktie, unless he was a high social player going to church on Sunday. It wasn't Sunday and Cyril was the only one in the hotel's dining room wearing a tie. I yanked him across the table. His coffee spilled on his slacks.

"You son of a bitch," I said as coolly as one can in this

situation, "Get out of here and go learn how to run your legal business."

I dropped my cup of coffee on the saucer so that it splashed more hot liquid on his pants. Ten count. Down by KO. He was not getting up.

I headed toward the door of the restaurant, pausing as I put my hand out to touch the handle, and looked over my shoulder. I said to Alex, "I'll see you in my office when you get back to New York." He mopped the sweat off his forehead with the hotel napkin.

I walked out of the hotel and waved to the first taxi on the line. It was my old friend Joshua.

"Where the hell have you been? Are you hoping to pick my pockets again? You got shit scared and drove off leaving me in the hands of dangerous young kids with guns who think they are soldiers. You bastard, give me back half of that ten dollars I gave you day before yesterday."

"Boss, you still alive?"

"Give me back five US green and, while you're at it, give me one of those weeds you got in your pocket."

On the way to the airport I wondered how the heck I was going to make all of this happen. The contract with National Sports of Jamaica was signed on November 28, 1972 and the fight was scheduled for January 22nd, 1973. There was much to do and we had only four weeks before Christmas to rebuild the television system and part of the stadium, and then produce and market the fight. The pressure was mounting and I just hoped there was enough time to pull it off.

A couple of puffs of some fresh ganja calmed me down and made the ride to the airport more enjoyable. It seemed like it had been a hell of a lot more than 72 hours since I had arrived in this country. I was exhausted, but I knew I had time to catch up on some sleep on the plane ride home.

CHAPTER 7
AN OK FROM THE UK

After four days out of the office, I sat down to tackle the pile of messages on my desk. Karen walked in a little late but I let it slide since she had bailed me out the day before yesterday when she faxed me the sample agreement.

"Hi Karen. Believe it or not we got an agreement with the government of Jamaica signed and executed within 24 hours. You really saved my ass with the fax. You're an angel. By the time I got the terms of the contract in place, though, I was bleary eyed."

Karen just looked at me and shook her head. "What did you sell them?"

"Just the truth, angel. I told the board and the prime minister the honest-to-goodness truth about their lousy communication systems and what it would take to reach the audience. When you tell the truth, everything else falls into place. Anything happen while I was away?"

"The phone has been ringing off the wall all morning," Karen said.

"That started as soon as the fight was announced by the press in London," I speculated.

None of my contacts in London believed that a major sports event could take place in Jamaica and I suppose, prior to my experience with my guard dogs and Prime Minister Manley, neither did I. I assumed the British interest in the island of Jamaica explained the sudden influx of calls from the UK. I felt sure that Jack Solomons and Jarvis Astaire, the two most prominent boxing promoters in London, were behind the calls. Already they were vying to carry the Foreman-Frazier championship fight live in London via closed-circuit connected to the theaters and arenas that traditionally broadcast sports events.

I picked up the phone and called Solomons.

"Hello Jack. Yes, we are going to be broadcasting out of Jamaica. We will be working with some new technology using satellite connections we are installing there. That way we'll be able to send you a beautiful, full color picture."

"I hear that you are good at this stuff, Hank," he responded. "I understand that the Jamaican government has the fighters committed and your company under contract to produce and distribute the bout worldwide."

"I can offer you the rights throughout the UK, but Jarvis has expressed an interest in doing this deal also. If you want to broadcast the event we need to come to terms and get something on paper right away."

"There's a rumor that Frazier will generate winnings with big odds because everyone over here thinks Frazier's fighting style will beat that clumsy Foreman. They are putting 300 English pounds against 100 pounds that Foreman will lose. Their money is on Frazier... They think he will retain the heavyweight title."

Solomons filled me in on the gambling system in the UK, which was quite different than the system in the States. "My money is on Frazier. Frazier can hit harder. Foreman will be destroyed by Frazier's left hooks," I concluded. "But Foreman is a big, nasty challenger. This fight will draw a great deal of attention."

"I also hear that Ali wants a shot at the title," Jack ventured toward the end of the conversation. His friendly tone gave me the impression that he was thinking about how he might work with Video Techniques in the future, regardless of who won in Jamaica.

"If I get this off and running and you distribute the Jamaica bout in London, I expect you to back me when I do the next heavyweight championship fight with Muhammad Ali," I told him.

I knew that I would need several million if Ali was to be the next challenger. I was trying to get a feel for whether the Ladbroke group—the money behind Solomons' operation—would front the cash I would need to lock up the next championship event.

"Hanky, you have my guarantee that I'll take on either of them—whoever wins—for the next bout as well," Solomons hollered.

I smiled on my side of the Atlantic. If I were able to lock down a contract with Ali, everybody in the boxing industry would want a piece of the next deal. Alex could assist me in getting Foreman under contract, which would be substantially less complicated if he was treated well during this current match. I knew that Foreman was difficult to work with. If he won I would have to find somebody who could speak his language and earn his trust if I was going to try to pull off this rematch myself.

"Hanky, either come over here so we can talk or send me a draft of the UK distribution contract by fax. Keep it assigned to me and I'll give you cash and a letter of credit in the same format you requested when we did the Ali-Mac Foster fight from Tokyo." Solomons lowered his voice when he was talking about the money.

"Alright Jack, relax. Give me a week and I'll see where we go with this."

I said good-bye and hung up with Solomons. I asked Karen who else had called while I was away.

"Jarvis Astaire says he wants you to come to London and sit down with him to discuss UK distribution of the fight," Karen said.

"Well, we have six or seven countries to sell other than the US, which is under our own TV distribution agreement. Someone's already working on that, right? Let's string both of these guys along for a while until we see how sales go in the US. Then, once I see how things shake out in the rest of the world, I'll decide if I want to work with Solomons or Jarvis in the UK."

I didn't want to offend Jarvis, so I called and asked him what his group would pay to have the exclusive UK rights for the fight. His offer was substantially lower than Solomons'. I told him that I would call him back about the contract within the next week or two.

If Solomons wanted to sign a contract with cash on the table it would be easier and less time consuming than trying to deal with Jarvis. Plus, Solomons had the backing of Ladbroke.

I was laying the infrastructure for the new business model I had envisioned on the return flight from Tokyo.

CHAPTER 8
THE GANG'S ALL HERE

I had four weeks to rebuild the stadium in Jamaica, sell the distribute rights, and generate media attention. I was required to provide both the manpower and the expertise to make it happen.

I started with PR because we had to raise awareness of the fight immediately. I dialed Saltman.

"Hi Shelly. How are you doing with Andy Williams?" I asked.

"Well, I bust my balls to get the publicity done before we arrive in the next city on the tour. It's a rat race but I'm seeing the world."

"Shelly, how about doing some PR work for Video Techniques? I want you to create some buzz for my company and the work we are doing on the upcoming Frazier-Foreman fight. I need some stories about the new technology we will be installing to broadcast from Jamaica. We plan to put on one hell of a show."

Shelly answered, "I think you should talk to the people at this new cable network called HBO. They might be interested in broadcasting the fight. HBO charges their subscribers to see the programming in their own living rooms."

"You know Shelly, that's a great idea. Do you have a contact there?" It sounded like a good opportunity for the US market.

Once I hired Shelly to do PR for my company, I had to raise the visibility of Foreman and Smokin' Joe in the sports media. Murray Goodman was one of the most highly respected PR sources in the US. He had golden connections with all the sports editors. My conversation with Murray ran for no more than three minutes and closed with a simple, "OK. Let's go!"

Next call was to Paul Fitzritson. He was expecting my call asking for his help setting up air transportation and hotel facilities in Kingston for my staff. I remained concerned about the civil unrest and military presence in Kingston. I wanted to be assured that everyone would be safe.

"Hank, I am going to book you in a small, but lovely hotel outside of Kingston on the slopes of the Blue Mountains. That should keep you away from any problems in Kingston."

About one week after New Year's, as the Watergate story flooded the international news media, I arrived in Kingston's Palisadoes Airport with my wife, Connie. Connie and I walked off the runway and went to greet Howard Cosell, the well-known sports commentator, and Leroy Nieman, the renowned sports artist, who had arrived on another flight from New York.

As Shelly came off the plane I motioned to a ribbon-decorated military captain, who seemed to be the top officer among the security force. "Captain, you see that guy over there." I pointed out Shelly to the Captain. "Gather his luggage and let him check through. He doesn't have to be frisked. He is my chief public relations and media guy."

There was a tall African-American man getting off the plane who I didn't know. He caught up with Howard Cosell and was chatting with Howard while they were politely frisked for weapons. Later, I went over to Cosell to ask him about the man. I wondered why he was arriving so far in advance of the fight.

"His name is Don King," Cosell said. "I heard about him through my sports contacts. He operated a numbers game in Cleveland and then went to prison in Ohio for killing somebody in the racket." Cosell gave me the background as we both watched Don greeting the other sports writers who had assembled at the airport.

"So why did he come here so early?" I asked.

"He's managing some black fighters out of Cleveland." Howard waved at him as he was having his passport stamped.

I wondered who else knew Don King. "Hey Shelly, do you know that tall black guy who was talking to Cosell?"

"I think he was just let out of the prison in Ohio. He may be looking for something to replace his numbers business in Cleveland." Shelly was worth what it cost to have him on my team. He seemed to know everyone.

The Palisadoes was a lot smaller than JFK and we had no problem getting through the security screening at the airport. Prior to our departure from JFK, I had made arrangements with National Sports Ltd. to get myself cleared through airport customs. When we arrived, John Hall made sure that my production staff and equipment stayed together and were quickly processed through Jamaica's Passport and Cargo Import Division. He also had made it easy for my staff to get the equipment off the plane and moved to a secure site.

Cosell, however, did not want to carry his suitcase through the customs area. "Hey boy, pick up those suitcases and bring them to that customs agent over there." In his familiar nasal voice, Cosell directed a small, white Jamaican in short pants. When the man smiled back, Cosell pointed to his suitcase.

The "boy," standing with what looked like a government group assigned by Prime Minister Manley to welcome us, responded with a "Yes mon." He picked up Cosell's suitcase and helped him through customs without having the suitcase opened. The "boy" then helped a taxicab driver lift the suitcase into the trunk of the cab. Howard, without looking at or thanking the "boy," gave him a dollar.

As I watched this scenario unfold I recognized Cosell's helper. I remembered he had been sitting around the conference table at the stadium when the deal was made. He was Jamaica's Minister of Business and Prime Minister Norman Manley's second right hand man, after John Hall.

The Minister of Business said a few words to the others in the group and they all stared at Cosell as he got into the taxi.

This was an unforgivable faux pas on Cosell's part. I locked this in my memory so that I could use it later, if I needed to.

CHAPTER 9
THE STONY HILL HOTEL

As we made our way outside of the airport building there were a lot of photographers from the *Gleaner*, the Jamaican newspaper, and the flash bulbs started popping. To keep from going blind, I turned my head to my left. Standing near me was Don King, smiling broadly and wearing what looked like some local junk jewelry around his neck. Don did not look in my direction and I decided not to introduce myself to him. When our eyes adjusted following the barrage of flashing bulbs, we were greeted by John Hall.

"Hi Hank. Your staff has been picked up and sent to the Hilton Hotel." Hall then turned to Connie. "So nice to meet you, Mrs. Schwartz."

"You can call me Connie," she said. They both smiled while Hall explained the details of our accommodations at the Stony Hill Hotel.

"I hope that Fitzritson has told you that I have arranged for you to stay at a great area up in the Blue Mountains outside of

Kingston so that you can have a quiet place to rest in the evening." Hall was trying to be as warm as possible to offset the military presence surrounding us.

Hall had our luggage gathered by real porters and, instead of calling a taxi, escorted us to what looked like an old 1940's limousine. A young military guard sat up front next to an older driver and Connie and I sat in the backseat with three suitcases piled next to us. A second military guard sat in the back facing us on a pull-down seat.

"Is that an old World War II M1 rifle under your feet?" I looked down under the guard's feet and knew the rifle could not shoot or hit anything.

"Yah mon," he said as he pushed the rifle a little forward with his feet so I could have a good look at the rusty bolt on the M1's top.

We drove for over an hour through the green landscape that replaced our view of the shabby side of Kingston. We found the Stony Hill Hotel built into the side of one of the foothills of the Blue Mountains. It was beautiful. Arbors of hibiscus and other exotic flowers covered the suite-sized bungalows that ran along the main walk.

Standing to one side of the entranceway to Stony Hill was an interesting looking character with a neatly trimmed beard. He was about 5'5" and wearing oversized Bermuda shorts covered with colorful flowers that matched the surrounding arbors. Bright patterned suspenders held up his shorts. This odd figure was standing in the middle of what seemed to be a flat circular plateau which had been painted with concentric white rings.

"Hello Mr. and Mrs. Schwartz. Welcome to Stony Hill," he said. Then the man rose on his toes, performed a pirouette, jumped into the air, and landed in the center of the circles.

"My God, Connie look at this guy," I whispered. "Here comes another crazy experience. I don't know how we are going to handle this one."

"Let's go over and talk to him," Connie whispered back. "Thank you for welcoming us to this lovely hotel," she said to the flamboyant stranger.

"I'm so glad the government made the arrangements for you and Mr. Cotail to stay with us." I was sure he was referring to Howard Cosell. "Are you folks from New York City?" he asked.

"Yes we're from New York City. Where are you from?" I asked. "You don't look like you are from Jamaica."

He giggled back at us and said, "Well, I'm from Brooklyn and I am Jewish also."

I tried to keep the dialogue friendly even though we were dead tired. "What is your name? What were you doing just then?"

As his smile started to fade, Connie kicked me in the shins. I had hurt his feelings. I had not appreciated his pirouette… he was no Nijinsky. He didn't look like Fred Astaire or Gene Kelley either. They were the only three dancers I knew about. At that moment, my mind was preoccupied with pulling off a boxing event in a troubled country.

"My name is Max and I was a ballet dancer before I came to Jamaica and got into the hotel business."

"Are you the owner?" Connie tried to make Max feel more comfortable.

"I am. I married a Jamaican woman who owned this mountain where she was building this hotel." As our conversation went on I saw a tall, handsome woman, out of the corner of my eye, wearing Jamaican-style clothing approaching us. She was twice the height and width of Max.

"Mr. and Mrs. Schwartz, this is Yolanda, my wife." Max looked up at her and blew her a kiss. Yolanda turned to us and seemed to be waiting for a reaction perhaps to the unlikely union of the short Jewish ballet dancer to a six foot one inch light brown Jamaican woman, who owned the Stony Hill Hotel.

"What is this? What are we standing on?" I asked.

Yolanda smiled and this time she floored me. "This is a landing pad for a helicopter." Her English was perfect. "The famous author Ian Fleming stayed at this hotel while he was working on several of his James Bond books," she said.

"He traveled by helicopter?" Connie asked.

"Not only Ian Fleming, but also our Queen of England and the British prime minister with several of his staff. We needed the helicopter pad to move them back and forth to the airport or to their offices in Kingston."

Connie and Yolanda continued the conversation as we walked up the main steps. Connie inquired about the sculptures that surrounded the patio displayed on a decorative railing.

"Yolanda, I am an artist and curator in New York. I'm intrigued by these primitive wooden sculptures. What do you know about the artist? They are quite remarkable."

"The artist is quite renowned… his name is Mallica 'Kapo' Reynolds. His intuitive art is an extension of his spiritual development here in Jamaica. He is also well known as a healer. People come from all over the world for his healing powers. I had a health problem and Kapo healed me by putting his hands on my body and summoning spiritual powers that flow from his mind. He has given most of the sculptures you are looking at to offer support to the spirits that lie within the Blue Mountains."

Yolanda seemed impressed with Connie. She told Connie that when Kapo came by in the morning she would tell him that an artist from New York City was visiting the hotel.

Max showed us to our bungalow suite. It turned out we were staying in the same suite that Ian Fleming and Queen Elizabeth had occupied. As he turned to leave I asked him, "Is Howard Cosell staying up here as well?"

"Oh Mr. Cotail? He's right across from you in the suite over there."

After we unpacked and settled in, Connie and I took a stroll around to check out the surroundings, which included a lovely pool area landscaped with flowers and palms.

"Hank, I told Yolanda that I was a painter and a curator but I didn't tell her that I was a student of Mind Dynamics. I am really looking forward to a conversation with Kapo about how spirituality, cultural rituals, and mysticism contribute to his art."

Although I did not understand too much about the art world, I knew that Connie was very interested in these issues as a result of her experience with Mind Dynamics. Everywhere we traveled Connie could always find something that added to her fascination with art and contributed to her skill as a painter.

CHAPTER 10
A LABOR STAND-OFF

While the Watergate scandal unfolded in the newspapers back home, there was also coverage of the political problems that dominated the headlines in Jamaica. Civil unrest was hurting tourism, especially in Kingston. The two political factions, the People's National Party and the Jamaica Labor Party, known as PNP and JLP respectively, instigated bloody conflicts that involved most of the country's citizens. The killings, written up in gory detail in Jamaica's newspaper, the *Gleaner*, caused great alarm among my crew.

Even John Hall seemed concerned about our safety. I had two soldiers traveling with me back and forth from Stony Hill to the stadium, and then to the Hilton in Kingston, where my production staff was housed. I had only a week and a half to set up the equipment and test communication between the stadium and the telephone company.

The plan was to assemble the TV equipment and install it in the new broadcast studio we had built inside the stadium. My

#1 cameraman and crew chief, Juan Bererra, would be circling the boxing ring during the fight using one of the new shoulder-mount TV cameras so that he could get previously impossible footage of the match. Juan was a Cuban I had encountered at one of the studios in New York City. We had worked together from the beginning of my career in television production. I met Juan in the lobby of the Hilton to make sure everything was moving along as quickly as possible. When I entered the lobby I noticed my whole staff was sitting around on the sofas and chairs and nobody was moving in the direction of the stadium.

"Juan, what's up? We need to get everybody over to the stadium to get the equipment unpacked."

"Hey Boss, our guys are a little uncomfortable about the stuff going on here out on the streets. Are we going to have any personal security? And who is going to be watching the equipment and making sure nobody touches it after we get everything set up?"

"What do you mean they're not comfortable? They have to be comfortable. The equipment came in on the cargo section of the plane and was checked in right away because we have to put up the lighting and the ring tomorrow." I scanned the hotel lobby where my team was watching Juan act as their spokesperson.

"Juan, we are surrounded by the Jamaican military. Nobody is going to mess with us—we stick out like a sore thumb. The local citizens wouldn't dare touch one of us."

"Hank, are you kidding? We are the only white guys in Kingston. The crew is afraid to go out of the hotel… they are afraid they will be jumped for money or for political reasons. The average citizen in Jamaica is not happy that this fight has been brought here and so much money is being spent on the production rather than helping the people."

"Forget that bullshit. This is not a racial issue. Frazier and Foreman ain't white. People are thinking about them as fighters; not about who is white and who is black. You are reading too much into this, Juan. You have nothing to worry about."

I pushed Juan into a car that was driven by an unarmed military private and had him take us to the stadium.

"This is where we have to set up the equipment, cameras, and the microwave link to connect to the JAMINTEL building." I showed Juan around the facility and explained the plan. "We have to get the ball rolling. We are already behind schedule. The government is investing a lot of money in this event in hopes of building up the tourism business." I hoped that the general population would understand that their government was trying to bring much-needed capital into the country's economy.

"The average Jamaican citizen doesn't understand why the government is spending money this way and they do not want this fight to happen here. The guys feel like they could be ambushed any second," Juan said.

"Listen Juan, I talked to the Minister of Tourism and they're going to give us military support to ensure our safety."

Our conversation was interrupted by the noise caused by a number of old army trucks rumbling into the middle of the stadium. Forty soldiers who looked like scared kids going to summer camp hit the ground. Juan looked as frightened as they did.

A platoon of very young soldiers had been assigned to me, along with some local contractors. The two groups, strung together, constituted our makeshift labor force. I could use them to make any changes in the stadium, on the field, or in the building itself. My plan was to use them to erect the boxing ring, install lighting, and construct the platforms we needed at several locations throughout the stadium for the TV cameras.

"Hank, what the hell are these soldiers here for? Are these kids our security?" Juan wasn't his normal happy self.

"They're here to help you and do whatever you want them to do. And yes, they are also here to protect you, our crew, and our equipment," I explained to Juan. "These soldiers are going to help you put up the ring, install the lighting, things like that."

"It looks to me like they are carrying rifles, not tools. They look scared as hell. Do they understand they are supposed to help us?" Juan was still not convinced.

"Juan, you know I will make sure that they all have some pocket tools, crescent wrenches, and that kind of thing… with your people skills you will make sure that they work well with our team."

"Holy shit. You are asking a lot! I don't think this is going to be easy." Juan was not a happy camper.

"Yeah, but it is not as bad as it seems. You can talk to them, give them reassurances, and make sure that they're not scared."

The rest of the staff had arrived at the stadium but everyone was still uneasy. They scanned the empty stadium seats feeling exposed and vulnerable while they were working in the middle of the field. In my imagination, I conjured up images of an old western film in which General Custer stands in the middle of a field fighting a huge number of charging Sioux. Custer is surrounded by his platoon of soldiers, each man standing back to back, trying to save their General. But as each soldier is killed, left with bloody arrows sticking out of their uniforms, only General Custer remains until the Sioux get him as well. I wondered why I wasn't scared when I looked at my staff surrounded by two platoons of soldiers standing with their old rifles slung on their shoulders in the center of the National Stadium.

"Juan, we need to find some deep blue paint so that we can paint the ring canvas and have it dry by tomorrow."

"Are you crazy? Where am I going to find blue paint? Why do you want it done that way?"

"For the optimum color image we need to show the feet of the boxers—moving, dancing, and shuffling around the ring—they will show up best against a deep blue canvas. When you get back to the Hilton, tell the manager that John Hall asked to have a blue canvas that matches the ocean off the beaches on the North Shore."

It took two days and one night to get the canvas painted blue, the ring assembled, and the lighting installed. But it was worth it. This technique would greatly enhance the quality of the broadcast image.

It was getting late and time to test all the systems and make sure they were working together.

John Hall stopped by to see how we were doing. "Hi Hank. What's that big metal pot you're putting up on top of the stadium?" John was a very distinguished gentleman and a Rhodes Scholar.

"It's called a microwave. It's not a pot. It's a big metal antenna, though, now that you mention it, I suppose it does look like one of those big Japanese pots. In any case, that's how we're gonna transmit the fight over to a similar dish on the tower at JAMINTEL."

Hall stroked his small white Vandyke. "We have never tried that in our country before. How do you know it's going to work?"

"I don't. That's why I'm going to test the whole system tonight. We'll send a picture from one of our cameras here over the micro link to JAMINTEL. Then it will be transmitted to the uplink to the satellite and finally back down to the studio in New York." I tried to explain how the system worked in the most non-technical terms I could think of.

Hall was silent, so I asked, "Does that sound do-able?"

He stroked his little beard again and said, "Whatever you say, as long as it generates the capital we're looking for."

We were two nights away from the fight. I hoped Frazier and Foreman were as ready as Video Techniques; if so, the show would be a smash hit.

CHAPTER 11
A TOUR OF THE BLUE MOUNTAINS

While the New York staff and I spent most of our days building the television communications system, Connie and a few of the other guests at Stony Hill had time to explore the country. At night, however, the two of us were escorted to a nightclub or restaurant in Kingston or Montego Bay. We had the same security guard from day one and he traveled with us in that old Hollywood-style limo.

Every time we got out of the limo there were crowds of locals standing around watching us as if we were famous film stars. I envisioned the two of us as Myrna Loy and William Powell in the fabulous old Thin Man movies. They were chauffeured around in the same type of limousine, solving crimes while drinking martinis in the back seat. Our driver had no uniform or cap on his sweaty head, but it was easy to overlook these details and imagine we were Nick and Nora Charles. Connie loved to watch old Hollywood films and I knew that she was hoping our driver would pull over any minute and serve us two ice cold martinis, in beautiful crystal glasses, as we lounged in the back seat of the limousine.

The fantasy rapidly dissolved when two young soldiers got into the car, one sitting up front with the driver and the other facing us on the fold-down seat.

One afternoon I decided that we should drive up into the country and act like tourists. "Let's take a ride and look over the Blue Mountains," I told our driver.

The limo had been parked in the sun for several hours and as we got in Connie said, "Hank, roll down the window so we can get some fresh air."

I tried to open the window but it was broken and opening it was no longer an option. I opened the door, just to let some of the hot air out, and saw a young fellow I knew named Bob Arum. Arum was a boxing promoter who had an interest in Frazier. I had arranged for National Sports to provide him with accommodations but I did not know that he and his wife, Barbara, were staying at the Stony Hill.

"Hi Arum! Connie and I are playing tourists for the rest of the afternoon. There's plenty of room, care to join us?"

Arum looked over the inside of the limo, "Where the hell are you gonna go in that piece of junk?" The driver, clearly offended, frowned at Arum.

Arum hesitated but Barbara jumped in and sat staring at the young soldier, who began to show signs of agitation. Apparently, he had not been ordered to provide security for more than two people.

To give us some relief from the heat, the driver pushed down the dirty windows with his hands as far as they could go. We were ready to begin our tour.

The landscape, which had appeared grey through the dirty windows, turned into a deep, jewel-like green as we cruised through the countryside. The air no longer smelled like Kingston's Trenchtown slum area, but was perfumed with the fragrance of hibiscus flowers. The lovely scenery cleared my head of any notion that we were there on business. It helped me forget about the stress of the production and the hustle and bustle of the city.

I was brought out of my dreamy state when the limo slowed down and the driver and the two soldiers started to talk among themselves in their native dialect.

"What's happening guys?" I asked.

Arum shoved his head out of the window and looked up ahead and stammered, "there are three guys blocking the road and waving the driver to stop."

The driver stopped the limo in the middle of the road and got out. He walked to the rear of the car, followed by our two security guards who held their M1's in their hands high above their heads. So much for protection. The local language went back and forth between the soldiers and the guys in the road. The only thing I could understand was the word, "mon." I was sure they were saying "Mon, what the hell are we going to do with these white people?" and "Mon, they're gonna kill us." It was quite clear they were scared as hell.

I opened the door and looked down the road. The three menacing figures were wearing hostile expressions, shabby clothing, and knotty hair strands that ran down past their shoulders. We didn't see eccentrics like these even on Halloween in New York City.

"Hey Connie, take a look at these characters. What's that cloud of smoke around them?"

Connie looked out of the window and started to fidget and giggle.

"Hank, they look to me like Rastafarians."

"What the hell are Rastafarians?"

Connie quickly filled me in that they were a religious sect that resided in Jamaica and they represented His Imperial Majesty, Haile Selassie, Emperor of Ethiopia, who was at that time a major African religious leader. She told us that Haile Selassie was known as the King of Kings of Ethiopia, conquering the Lion of Judah and developing the religious sect around Ethiopia. In Jamaica he was worshipped and adored by the Rastafarians.

"Get back in the car Hank. Are you crazy?" Barbara was looking at me, then out the window, and then back to Connie. She looked scared to death after she heard this religious bullshit.

"Alright I am going out to talk with them," I said in a calm voice.

"Don't you go out there, Hank. Why doesn't our security go and talk to them?" Arum asked in a panicked voice.

"Mon..." More talk between our security and the craggy old driver. I still did not know what they were saying.

"I'm going to tell the Rastafairies to get out of the middle of the road. This is Jamaica, not Ethiopia," I said. "They can't stand there forever, even if our driver and our alleged security force keep standing behind this old piece of junk waving their hands in the air."

I got out and walked towards them. "Hey brothers, what can I do for you?"

I was trying to act friendly and non-threatening. I hoped I could understand if they responded so I carefully listened to each word.

"What are you brothers smoking?"

All three faces turned to smiles and I quickly realized what the smoke was. I looked to the left and to the right. I could see that the road was cutting through fields of coffee plants. On closer inspection, I realized hashish had been planted between and under the leaves of the coffee plants in a small area shielded from the casual observer. Now I understood that these three shady characters had blocked the limo trying to sell us some ganja or hashish.

"What do they want?" Arum called from the relative safety of the limo.

"They want to sell me a shopping bag full of ganja," I hollered back.

Barbara stuck her head out of the window and we heard her high pitched voice. "That's great, Hank. Buy the stuff. We'll have fun."

I turned back to the three Haile Salaisie salesmen.

"My smiling brothers - is this enough to buy the whole shopping bag?" Before they answered, I shoved three bucks into the shirt pocket of the tallest man, grabbed the shopping bag out of his hand, and started walking backward, still facing my Rastafarian brothers. In this position I was not only worried about getting shot from the front, but also in the back by one of my own security force's ancient M1 rifle.

When there was enough space between me and the Rastafarians, I calmly turned around and continued to walk back to the limo, acting like this was just your everyday business transaction. I yelled back over my shoulder: "Now will you guys get off the road." They rapidly disappeared into the coffee plants.

Both soldiers scrambled for their seats as the driver got back in and started to drive the car, without me in it. Arum threw open the door and I jumped in while the car was moving. The driver floored it. On the worn limo tires we proceeded in our mad escape as fast as we could go – about 35 mph.

Our tour of the Blue Mountain was cut short. Our still-frightened driver dumped us off at the Stony Hill Hotel and he and the two security soldiers retreated as fast as they could.

Once we were back at the hotel, Barbara wasted no time in preparing the ganja for international travel. She pulled the cotton out of her tampons and filled the cardboard cylinders with ganja. This way, she thought, she could get it through customs at JFK so she could roll some "happy" cigarettes once she returned home.

Connie was very glad to be safe and back at Stony Hill. "Hank, let's put on our swim suits and sit around the pool with a couple of cold martinis and pretend we are Nick and Nora Charles. You played the part of the detective hero very persuasively this evening in the episode of The Blue Mountain Rastafarians."

I laughed as we walked out of our suite and headed toward the pool. Unfortunately, the day's excitement was not over. People were running past us on either side.

"Get a doctor! Get a doctor!" someone shouted.

We ran the rest of the way and upon reaching the commotion, found Bob Arum lying face up on the flagstones surrounding the pool. We all thought he was having a heart attack. He looked like a zombie with his eyes wide open, staring at the setting sun. Before someone tried to wrap him up like a mummy, I shouted, "For God's sake. It's Arum. Did he get murdered? Was he shot? Get a doctor!"

I noticed he was holding something in his right hand, perhaps to defend himself. On closer look, it turned out to be a rolled-up, smoldering, cigar-sized joint, which he had apparently been smoking. A local MD got there almost immediately. He worked on Arum with some herbs and had him inhale some oxygen to help him breathe.

Arum moaned and opened his eyes even wider and stared at me as if I was in another world. "That was some ganja you got for me," he said. He then finally closed his eyes. The hotel staff picked him up and carried him off to his bed.

Thankfully, Arum's life didn't end that day, but it was a close call and everyone breathed a sigh of relief when we learned he was fine. "Connie, I need a strong, cold drink to settle myself. Let's get those martinis in milk shake glasses."

CHAPTER 12

A NIGHT ON THE TOWN

John Hall called up to me where I was working on building one of the platforms intended to hold two TV cameras. "Now that you got that metal TV dish working, let's have a little drink tonight and celebrate," he said.

"If you're driving, let's go, but I want to stop by and pick up Connie so we can have a night on the town."

"We'll pick up Connie and then I'll pick up my friend. We will take our ladies to a place where we can drink a little and dance a lot."

I was completely comfortable with John Hall. More importantly, I was very pleased with the way the Jamaican government had responded to their part of the promotion agreement.

We arrived at Stony Hill and Connie joined us in the car.

"We've got to make one more stop now to pick up my girl friend." John smiled at Connie and we sped off into the suburban streets of Kingston.

John was singing Jamaican songs as he drove to the street

where his friend Helen lived. He slammed on the brakes, got out of the car, and stood under the streetlight in the middle of the road so that he could be seen clearly.

"Helen!" John hollered, looking up at the second floor of the adjacent apartment complex. No answer. John went over to the door and kicked it but Helen still didn't answer. He walked back to the center of the street, removed what I later found out was a German Luger PO8 pistol that was nested in his back holster. He fired three shots in the air. Still no answer.

I just figured it was John's way of getting his girl friend out of bed but Connie had a different reaction. "Hank, let's get the hell out of here, this guy's dangerous," she whispered to me with wide eyes.

I didn't like the gun, but we couldn't just leave. "He's part of the government, Connie, and my key contact on this project. And I don't have the car keys… what can I do?"

John fired the fourth shot directly at the streetlight, which popped and scattered glass onto the car and over the front stoop of the apartment building. Finally, Helen opened the second floor window and yelled down, "John, stop the shit with the gun. I'll be right down."

John put his Luger back into his holster and waited for Helen to come out. When she did, John greeted her with a kiss and she got into the back seat of the car with Connie while I sat up front with John. I was interested to see how Connie handled this relationship.

"Nice to meet you Connie. I'm sorry it took me so long but he didn't call to tell me we were going out tonight."

"Sometimes Hank doesn't call me ahead of time either," Connie replied and then reached over and tapped my shoulder. "But Hank doesn't carry a gun." Both women laughed.

"In Jamaica, you've got to carry a gun," Helen said. I moved the visor mirror to take a look at both women in the back seat. They appeared to be comfortable with each other. Connie was very good at building rapport with people and I felt sure she could handle this.

The evening was filled with drinks, dancing, and conversation. John and Helen explained the political problems in depth. Although we had some business conversation, we thoroughly enjoyed the music, the Jamaican culture, and the great local rum.

By the time we were ready to call it a night, John and Helen were both a little high on rum and ganja. John let me have the car keys and he and Helen got in the back seat of his car. I drove back up the mountain to our hotel hoping I could find a chauffeur there to drive Helen and John back to their respective homes.

John had dozed during the drive and he was very woozy. I tried to find my way back to Stony Hill, but I was not clear on the directions and so I kept asking him for help. He would fall asleep, wake up for a few minutes, and then pass out again. I didn't know whether he was fighting too many drinks or too many puffs. It was 3 a.m. by the time I found Stony Hill and there was no one around that I could tap to drive John and Helen.

"Jesus Christ, I think we should let them sleep it off for a few hours in our room." I wanted Connie to agree even if it didn't fit social conventions. I parked the car and started to wake John again. I knew it would be best if they stayed over until they sobered up.

John was far from being sober but I got him up and out of the car. He was singing again as I tried to steer him through the parking lot. After a few steps he stopped and looked around to see where he was. Then he hollered, "Who the hell does this Cosell guy think he is… where the hell is he staying?"

"He is a big celebrity sports commentator in the U.S. He is staying somewhere here in one of the bungalows." I was still holding John to help him walk forward without tripping into the surrounding garden and I started to worry about why he wanted to know where Cosell was. Cosell had been hired to announce the fight and give the blow-by-blow live commentary during the broadcast. His unique speaking style was recognized all over the world and both ABC and HBO felt his participation added to the excitement.

"I know that," he mumbled. "But where is he?" he asked as he removed his Luger for the second time that night.

"Holy shit, John, why are you pulling out your fucking gun again? Cosell is not involved in the Jamaican political turmoil."

"That son of a bitch ordered our head of business and tourism to carry his luggage. He has a big mouth," John hollered out again.

"That's why he is a great commentator." I tried to calm him down and led him and Helen into our suite.

"Bullshit. Where is he staying?" John asked, waving his gun at me.

"He's across the patio, past the other arbor. And he's asleep. It's late."

"Not anymore," John shouted. "Cosell. You have a big mouth."

Though I supported John so he could stand up, I made sure I was behind him. He aimed the Luger randomly but had enough coordination to pull the trigger. He squinted at the arbor of greenery in front of us and shot Bang! Bang! Bang! Bang! Each shot a punctuated expression of his feelings toward Cosell.

When I was convinced there were no bullets left, I took the gun out of his hand, put it back in his holster, and led him into our suite, while Connie and Helen cautiously followed. We decided they should stay with us until morning. We found some pillows and extra blankets and John and Helen settled down quietly on the floor next to our bed. Connie and I removed our shoes and laid down on top of the bed spread. I felt sure we would have a conversation about this in the morning.

We drifted off into a deep sleep. By the time Connie and I woke up, John and Helen had snuck out. I was thankful for the peaceful ending to our double date and relieved they had sobered up enough to safely find their way home.

Connie and I showered, changed, and walked to the patio where breakfast was being served. Cosell, and his wife, Edna, were sitting on the other side of the dining patio, appreciating the greenery and sipping their coffee. After a few minutes, Cosell came over to say good morning.

"Hank did you hear anything last night? Was there a commotion out here?" Cosell asked.

I glanced at Connie, "I heard a couple of bang bangs—thunder maybe. Or it might have been a tire blow out on the road that runs below the hotel. What did you hear, Howard?" I asked innocently as I nursed the last drops of my coffee.

"We were so tired when we went to sleep last night I honestly don't remember whether I heard anything or not," he mumbled. Then Howard went back to Edna and whispered something across the table.

I was sure that Cosell had heard each gunshot and every word. I suspected that he knew I had heard everything as well. He was going to leave it alone and I was glad that he didn't know we were out socially with the guy that caused the "Cosell disturbance."

CHAPTER 13
SHOT AT IN THE CHEVY

January 21, 1973

After our adventurous night out, it was time to settle in and put the phone lines to work. The microwave dish had been installed and we tested the communication equipment four days before the fight. HBO confirmed that our test signal had gone through to their studios in New York. Everything was in order; I just needed to make sure it remained that way.

The evening before the fight I got worried about security at the stadium. I wanted to take a ride over there and check in with the staff. My military escort had left and so I needed transportation.

"Max, can I borrow your car for a few hours tonight?"

Max started to frown. "Why do you need it?"

"I called John Hall on his mobile telephone. You know how that is right? I asked him for a military car and he said that at this time there was no car or driver available."

"Why do you want to go to the stadium tonight?" He was still frowning at me.

"To check the microwave dish and make sure no one moved it or screwed anything up." Max needed more convincing so I lied and told him that John had sent a message to the head of military to let me into the stadium. He gave me the keys to his old Chevy and I slipped out of Stony Hill while everyone else was eating dinner.

I drove by the Hilton where my staff was having dinner in the restaurant. They were in good spirits, drinking local beer and no longer concerned that they were exposed to local terrorists. The mood was relaxed and comfortable and I thought everyone was ready to put on a spectacular show.

From there, I drove Max's Chevy to the stadium and prepared myself for the obstacles that the military security was going to throw in my way. I found the stadium completely abandoned. I walked into the main entrance and looked right and left. There were only a few lights on and I was glad I knew my way around. There was an eerie silence in the usually bustling stadium. I carefully walked up the steps toward the ladder I used to reach the roof. I wanted to check the microwave dish.

As I put my foot on the first rung of the ladder I heard the distinctive "Click, click" of an old M1 rifle. It stopped me dead in my tracks. Through all my experience in Jamaica dealing with security and military personnel, armed political leaders, and Rastafarians, this was the first time that I had a loaded rifle pointed directly at me. I stepped down and slowly turned, holding my empty hands in front of me. The officer was pointing the rifle at my stomach. He held his position silently as he watched me climb the steps heading towards the stadium's transmission room.

"Brother put up your rifle," I said softly, showing my empty hands. "I'm the guy who was hired by your prime minister to broadcast the big boxing event here in this stadium. I have to check that piece of metal up there to make sure that the TV picture is working."

We stood there looking at each other for a full thirty seconds. I started to elaborate.

"I know what you said," he responded, "but someone should have told us before you came." I was relieved that he had some knowledge of what was going on.

"Come with me. You can climb up the ladder with me and watch everything I do. Let's go up together and take a look at my equipment to make sure it will be working perfectly tomorrow night."

He shifted the position of his rifle, smiled and said, "I'll wait for you to come down, the same way you climbed up."

I quickly turned around and climbed up to the roof where I used a direct phone line to call the communication engineer on duty at JAMINTEL. Our equipment was generating a color bar that satisfied the standard NTSC television signal, which would be broadcasted continually until the fight.

"How is the signal coming in? Clean and steady?" I asked, focusing on the work rather than the military watchdog waiting for me with a loaded M1.

"Mr. Schwartz, it is perfect and we will make sure that the signals reach the right levels for our uplink test later."

I came down from the roof with my hands in front of me as I approached the officer. "OK brother, walk me down and out to my car and lock this place up real tight."

"I am staying here. Those are my orders. You can get out of this stadium by yourself, the same way you came in." So much for the "brother" approach. At least I got out of the stadium in one piece.

I got into Max's Chevy and started to back out of the parking lot when suddenly, without a sound, the car's windshield shattered into slivers of glass that covered my hands and my shirt. Someone was shooting at me using a modern rifle. I didn't know where the shots were coming from and I did not want to hang around to find out. My instincts took over as I shifted the car into gear, revved the motor hard, and raced out of the lot as fast as the old Chevy would allow. I could barely see where I was headed now that the car had no windshield. Thank God there was no rain to worsen my visibility. That would have made my night really dangerous.

Once I got back to Stony Hill, Connie saw me walk in with blood dripping from my left hand.

"What happened? Are you all right? I told you not to go out without a military driver."

I didn't want to tell Connie about Max's car. I decided I would explain everything over breakfast, especially to Max. But how was I going to explain? I borrowed his junky Chevy and brought back a bigger mess. I would ask the government to fix his car right away.

"Honey, it is just a few little scratches. Clean out some of this glass and let's order a round of martinis. Then, I will fill you in." Connie looked me over and started to pick glass out of my shirt and clean the scratches on my left hand.

"Darling, you're nuts to go out this late without military support."

"I know, but I thought it would be easier to check everything out before the fight."

"Let's have that martini and take a late night swim in the pool."

We both calmed down as we sat around the pool and enjoyed the soft night breeze.

CHAPTER 14
"DOWN GOES FRAZIER!"

January 22, 1973

Fight night had finally come to Jamaica. National Stadium was covered in lights and the stands appeared full and filled with excitement. The blue canvas looked great, my crew was sharp and in position, and we had a heavyweight champion defending his title against an up and coming challenger.

Practically everyone in Jamaica knew Frazier, the 5 foot 11 inch, 214-pound heavyweight champ, whose relentless attack combined speedy left hooks with a perpetual forward motion, which kept him moving into any barrage of gloves that were thrown at him.

Foreman, on the other hand, was as strong as an ox and the human equivalent of a slow-moving tank. Dick Sadler, his manager, believed he was ready to meet Frazier and capture the heavyweight championship. The odds makers did not agree, leaving it 3 to 1 in favor of Frazier.

"Alright gang, look alive—I want everybody viewing this fight to feel like they are right here with us. Anything you can do to make it real… give me your best," I said to the crew in the studio and the guys on headsets out in the stadium.

Juan talked to me on the small microphone that was strapped to his shoulder-mounted camera and wired into our studio's audio system. I had situated him so he could capture shots of the crowd in the packed arena. "Hank, there are several school buses coming in the entranceway," he said. "They're going onto the field and they're surrounded by three Jeeps that seem to be loaded with soldiers. What the hell are they doing on the field?"

"Hang on, Juan. Let me see what's happening."

By the time I was outside the studio, the buses had stopped. The soldiers had jumped out of their Jeeps and now surrounded the three buses. The passengers stepped out of the buses and onto the grassy field. Among them were Prime Minister Manley and roughly 40 guests.

Cosell had arrived two hours earlier. He was scared as hell. He had no military personnel protecting him. He was a pain in the ass. He nervously tested and retested his headset and microphone. When he saw this group arriving in the buses with the military escort, he figured out that they were the VIPs being escorted to their front row seats. Cosell took up his commentator's position at the apron ring.

"Cosell, you've got to quit acting like you are a nervous wreck," I said through his headset, trying to calm him down. I was going to tease him by saying his hairpiece had shifted, hoping it might lighten the mood, but he wouldn't have found it humorous at the time. Once the VIP group was seated directly behind him, Cosell managed to pull it together and adopt his professional demeanor. I'm sure he decided he was part of their crowd and afforded the protection provided by the nearby senior military officers.

Mike, one of my cameramen, did a scan of the entire stadium to pick up the frenzy of the crowd.

"Has anyone seen Connie?" I asked the guys in the stadium.

Juan, who was now in the ring, called me on my headset. "Hank, Connie is sitting right next to where I am. She is beside a guy who looks like a general or something; his uniform is decorated with a shit load of ribbons."

"Mike, swing Camera #1 so I can get a look at Connie."

"She looks fine and has started a conversation with one of those military guys. Yeah, he is a general," Mike relayed back.

Because Juan was only a few feet away from her, I told him to walk over and tell her not to leave the stadium after the fight. I was still concerned about security and didn't want her leaving in the bus. No one could be certain what might happen after the fight ended and the stadium emptied back onto the streets.

Camera # 3 swung around and looked up the middle aisle as the fighters made their way to the ring. Frazier came first. Foreman wanted Frazier in the ring before he made his entrance. "He wants to keep himself as far as possible from Smokin' Joe's first left hook," I joked with the crew.

"Hank, do you know who that big, black guy is walking down the aisle with his arm around Smokin' Joe?" Mike asked.

"Yeah, that's Don King. Let's keep an eye on him so he doesn't screw up any shots of the fighters in or out of the ring."

When the first round bell rang, the camera crew was in position and prepared for a sixty-minute fight. Foreman and Frazier came out of their corners with two completely different styles. Foreman fought flat out, swinging wildly and rolling through the ring. Frazier danced and bobbed, but held back his left hook. Foreman, in the meantime, landed solid punches to Frazier's gut. Then, out of nowhere, Frazier went down and hit the canvas.

Cosell had started describing the fight in his typical even-tempered fashion but when Frazier went down in the first round, his voice completely broke. "Down goes Frazier!" he shouted into the microphone hysterically, causing the sound guy to have to make an immediate adjustment. Everyone, including Cosell, was stunned that Foreman had knocked down the champ.

"Down goes Frazier!" Howard shouted a second time when Frazier hit the canvas again. Foreman, with his greater reach, dropped Frazier a total of three times in the first round.

In the second round, Frazier was still moving heroically forward. He was met with a left and a right combo to his jaw that dropped him onto the canvas once again.

"Down goes Frazier!" Cosell shouted for the fourth time.

Frazier struggled to get back on his feet. Dazed after the mandatory eight count, he started throwing punches in the air around him. He stumbled into a right shot from Foreman that lifted him off the canvas and sent him to the floor yet again.

"Down goes Frazier!" Cosell shouted again, creating yet another refrain of those three simple words that echoed around the world. Each time a little louder and a little more incredulous.

Foreman looked over his shoulder at Frazier lying on the canvas as he walked confidently to his corner. "Stay down Joe. You had it," Foreman said, loud enough so that Frazier's cornermen could hear. But Frazier, with the iron will of a true champion, pulled himself up one more time.

When Foreman started to move in for the kill, referee Arthur Mercante saw Frazier having trouble keeping his balance and bleeding from his mouth. Mercante called the fight. It was over in 1:34 minutes of the second round.

Cosell jumped out of his chair and began his on-site extemporaneous reportage which had gained him celebrity status across the globe:

"The battle that drew over 36,000 to the National Stadium and had been billed to be a contest of two formidable opponents with the betting odds 3-1 in Frazier's favor, became a one-man show that ended with a knockout in one minute and thirty four seconds into the second round. George Foreman, the 6 foot 3 inch, 217 pound slugger from Marshall, Texas has become the heavyweight champion of the world." Cosell spewed the story into his microphone, wondering whether anything he said was being heard over the pandemonium in the ring.

Foreman, who had a difficult personality, had refused to be interviewed before the fight. In his moment of victory he actually said something nice for the broadcast. "I don't know how long I will be the heavyweight champion," he spoke quietly into the microphone. "We only borrow it for a short time."

"Hey Hank, did you see my wide shot on your TV monitor? Every time Frazier was hit by Foreman and went down, that guy Bob Arum who was sitting behind your wife, hit her in the head with a rolled up program," Mike laughed.

I replied, "He was frantic because it was fucking up the deals he thought he had lined up."

"They are walking out of the ring," Juan said, following the Foreman procession with his camera while adding, "Hey Hank, there is a guy over here who wants to talk to you. He says he is the promoter from London. He says he did the deal with Video Techniques to broadcast the fight in the UK."

The camera focused on the older balding man who had buttonholed Juan. The man was moving his lips at the camera in an effort to get a message to me. Juan shouted over the noisy crowd that he was Jack Solomons. Solomons had told me he would meet me in Jamaica. He was well dressed but harried. He was an older British gent who always had a cigar in his hand or his mouth and was generally considered one of the greatest boxing promoters in the history of the sport.

"Tell him that I'll see him over at the Hilton when we get done here," I said.

Now it was Mike's turn to get a message to me. "Hank, remember that big black guy I picked up when he walked down the aisle with his arm around Frazier like he was part of his corner?"

I looked over at the monitors and there was Don King, walking down the aisle with his arm around Foreman.

"I guess he is not attached to anyone. He seems to be playing both sides of the fence… getting both fighters to listen to him." The crowd started to break. "I see that the VIP group is heading back to the buses. Juan, get hold of Connie and tell her to wait for me."

There was no longer any military support around the stadium and there was an angry mob outside. I told the crew to gather down by the entrance and wait for me there. I rushed out of the TV studio and fought my way through the crowd that had lingered. I grabbed Connie and met the staff at the designated spot. We had arranged for cars to drive us back to the Hilton.

It was as crazy in the Hilton as it had been in the stadium. The fight had astonished the boxing world. No one expected Foreman to beat Frazier. The result was totally unexpected. No one thought it could possibly have turned out the way it did and the lobby was a frenzy of excitement.

Solomons emerged from the crowd. He was with Ted Francis, who was employed by Solomons as their technical man. He was there to make sure that my operating satellite system could be connected to various theaters and hotels in the UK.

"Hank, let's sit down and talk. We have a new champ and the best thing we can do is set up a fight between Foreman and Ali right away." We moved into the bar.

It was a lot easier to talk with Francis than with Solomons. I was sure that any TV broadcast sold to Solomons would work well on the technical side if Francis was a part of the picture.

"Come to London, Hank, and work with my people to see if we can get Foreman to fight Ali," Solomons repeated at least ten times. "Get cleared up over here and meet me back in London. Let's see what we can work out."

"Sure, sure Jack, as soon as I get my equipment and staff out of Jamaica I'll come over to London and sit down with you." I didn't know what we could do because any future deal relied on our ability to get Foreman to sign an agreement with Video Techniques.

"But first I've got to get back to my office in New York and make sure that everybody has paid for the delivery of this fight, including you, Jack."

"I sent you a letter of credit two weeks ago that is set to clear as soon as the fight is over and the bank is open."

"I'm not worried about you, Jack. It's the rest of the world. I have to get my Angels working, so give me a couple of weeks."

"Hank, you're waiting too long. I want to get Foreman under contract right away."

"I got the picture. I'll let you know when I'm coming to London."

I was glad to shake off Solomons. I still had a lot of work to do before contemplating the next fight.

My crew, Connie, and I had a great private party with the Jamaican government officials. Even Prime Minister Manley came to congratulate us.

I found out that the gate proceeds were decent but somewhat lower than expected. Thank goodness Video Techniques' contract was for a fixed amount plus a percentage of the revenue collected by National Sports outside of Jamaica.

I took a long sip of a Jack Daniels and looked back on our progress. Everyone on the crew knew, without a doubt, that the fight in Jamaica was a realization of the goals we had set after Tokyo. That production ended up being an important stepping-stone that taught us how to handle the challenges we faced in Jamaica. It had shown us how to build the communications infrastructure and caused us to perfect how we used the satellite technology. We accomplished all this even though we were literally dodging bullets. Just as Tokyo taught us valuable lessons, so did this fight in Jamaica.

It was time to innovate Video Techniques' business model once again. I was very clear that we needed to focus our efforts on getting contracts signed with the top fighters. We needed to be the promoter. No more middlemen! Work directly with the fighters. I got it!

PART 3

FOREMAN-ROMAN IN JAPAN

CHAPTER 1
WHO THE HELL IS DON KING?

February 1973

My first day back at the office in New York, the phones were ringing off the wall.

"There's another phone call for you from this guy that says he works with Don King," said Helen, one of the Angels. "Who the hell is Don King?"

"He's some big shot from Cleveland. Haha! As if there *are* big shots in Cleveland. Hahaha! Who's the guy on the phone?" I asked.

"He says his name's Elbaum and he's got a suggestion for you," Karen sniggered.

Now that Video Techniques was gaining traction and attracting the attention of the boxing world, people were coming out of the woodwork with suggestions as to how they could help and, of course, get a piece of the action.

"All right, put him on the phone so I can dust him off."

"Hi Hank, Don Elbaum. I saw the fight that you did out of Jamaica and it was terrific. Great quality. We had it on pay-per-view in six theaters here in Cleveland. That was the first time they paid the extra money to have a championship fight on the big screen and it sure worked out great."

So far, I liked what this guy was saying.

"The word on the street is that you are interested in signing some of the top fighters for future events. I am sure you realize that you need someone who can speak the language of these fighters if you are going to take over their promotion. Let's face it Hank, you are a Jewish engineer with Polytech credentials… There is no way you are gonna connect with these fighters and get them to sign a contract with you." I saw the pitch coming.

"Yeah, but I'm learning how to think—and talk—like the promoter," I replied in my defense.

"Hank, you got no chance in hell to do it by yourself. Have you ever used the word "motherfucker' in a business transaction in your life? The only way you will get these top fighters to listen to you is by speaking their language and dealing with them in the way they are accustomed."

I didn't need *this motherfucker* to preach any bullshit to me about the realities of the street. He kept talking until I had to shut him down.

"Get to the point, Elbaum. I got a lot going on here today. Why are you calling me and how did you get my name?" I was getting pissed and did not need this shit.

"Did you hear about the fundraiser that Don King did with Muhammad Ali for the Cleveland Children's Hospital?"

I told him I hadn't. "Tell me more," I said, beginning to pay a little more attention when I heard Ali's name.

"King and I worked a couple of small fights together in the last few months," Elbaum said. "When King got out of prison he started managing some of the black fighters here. Now he's looking to build a fight promotion business for himself."

"What was he in jail for?"

"He killed a guy in the numbers business, some slip and cash collector. King did a couple years for manslaughter." This was information that I had not heard before and it didn't exactly paint Don King in a positive light.

"How did you get involved with him?"

Elbaum said that King had called him in Buffalo when he was putting together the team for the children's hospital event and asked him to come back to Cleveland that night. King was with a friend of Elbaum's and said he was not leaving until Elbaum showed up. So Elbaum drove all night and worked a deal with King by dawn the next morning to manage the boxing aspects of the children's hospital fundraiser.

"Listen Hank, I think it would be a good idea if I told King to call you and see whether you two guys can work together."

By the end of the conversation I wasn't convinced I needed Don King in order to negotiate with the fighters, most of whom were admittedly from the streets of African American neighborhoods. But hey, I grew up in Brooklyn. So what am I, chopped liver?

"All right Elbaum, let me think about it. Give me your number and I'll call you back after I have sorted this out."

After the conversation, I called up a friend of mine who was an attorney and asked him to get me any information he could on King. It turned out that King's first profession was as a numbers racketeer in Cleveland. In December of 1954, King killed a man trying to rob one of his gambling joints. Prosecutors determined that King was defending himself and declared the death a "justifiable homicide." A few years later King brutally kicked a man to death. The man owed King about 600 bucks. Although convicted for second-degree murder, the trial judge reduced the conviction from murder to manslaughter and King served just under four years. King's ability to influence the legal system, even then, was legendary.

Once he was released from prison, King decided to shift his focus to boxing. His first order of business was getting Ali to do an exhibition fight at the children's hospital event. There was no denying King's ability to get things done.

Two hours later, Helen greeted me at the door after I grabbed a lousy hot dog for lunch from the vendor on the corner near my office. "Hank, we've had more telephone calls coming in while you were out. This one guy has called you a half a dozen times, even though we've told him you were traveling."

"Did he leave a telephone number?" I asked.

"Yes. His name is Don King." She said as she handed me the message.

"I know who that is." I growled back, thinking of my conversation with Elbaum. "Next time he calls, I'll take the call and see if I can get rid of him."

Before the day ended, Helen buzzed me. "He's on the phone again."

"All right, connect him and let's see what's bugging him."

"Hi-ya, brother." The voice boomed with a deep southern drawl. This did not fit with everything else I knew about Don King.

"King, I'm no brother. Why are you calling me?"

"Man, you've got a good company and you are doing good things with televised sports. But you got nobody that can talk to a nigger fighter the way I can. How do you hope to take your business to the next level without a partner who can deliver the fighter for your grand promotional scheme?"

"Don, first of all who told you to call me and why?"

"Elbaum told me that you wanted to start signing up fighters for championship fights or undercard bouts. You just don't have the ability to talk t…"

"You refer to niggers again and I'll hang up on you." King was bothering the hell out of me. I did not like his attitude.

"Excuse me. I was just making a point about black American fighters and how they do business. It ain't like what you think."

I had called my friend Gene Kilroy, who traveled with

Muhammad Ali and worked with him in his training camp. Kilroy had filled me in on Don King. Kilroy gave me the low down on the children's hospital event and revealed that Ali did not actually do an exhibition in the ring, despite all the hype, although he did make an appearance.

"Brother, I want to join your team. I have the ability to make a deal with George Foreman and I can talk to Muhammad Ali on levels that you can't. Nothing personal, man." Don yelled into the phone without any southern accent. He switched from the southern charm to plain, intelligent business talk.

Whoever I talked to about King, one thing they all agreed on was that he was well-read. He had had plenty of time to read the classics when he was in the Ohio prison. I decided that perhaps we should meet and discuss the issues he was raising face-to-face.

"You got enough money to take a plane from Cleveland to New York?" I asked.

"Man, I can travel anywhere in the world on my own money."

I didn't know what to make of that, but I invited him to come and meet with me at my office on West 55th in Manhattan.

CHAPTER 2
BENIHANA'S BENTLEY AND BLONDES

I had set aside an entire week to clean up all the work I had lingering on my desk when I got back to New York from Jamaica. I had to make sure that National Sports received the revenue that was due them from the Foreman-Frazier fight.

We had successfully sold the championship fight throughout the world and made the deal for the first sports event carried on the new HBO cable channel. I had to contact the TV stations, cable networks, and theaters that had broadcast the event, live or delayed. I was busy working the phone collecting the dough from the networks that were slow to pay.

"Hank, someone from a Japanese restaurant chain called to set up a dinner meeting with you. I think his name is Rocky Aioki, or something like that," Karen called out. "He wants to talk to you about producing a boxing championship in Tokyo."

I was always on the lookout for sponsorship for future events. I told Karen to make a date with this Rocky guy for next Wednesday.

"He will pick you up in front of our office and take you to the Benihana restaurant," Karen filled me in.

He showed up in a gleaming black Bentley driven by a handsome chauffeur. I got in and was greeted by two gorgeous Swedish models in shimmering low-cut mini-dresses sitting next to Rocky in the back seat. I said hello to Rocky as the blondes kissed me and said *"Hej,"* which I hoped meant nothing more than "hello." Rocky and I exchanged the more traditional handshake. When we arrived at the restaurant, the models slithered out of the Bentley and I saw that both were over six feet tall. Rocky was a lot shorter than I was and I laughed as I wondered why he would go out with two such tall blondes. This was going to be an interesting night.

"Hank, Nippon Educational Television has suggested that Benihana and some of our associates sponsor a heavyweight championship fight in Tokyo in September," Rocky told me.

"Any particular reason why they want to bring an American heavyweight fight to Japan?" I smiled and thought it was a funny line and a friendly opening in view of what had happened between our countries just thirty years ago during World War II.

Rocky did not smile at all. "It is important that you can distribute the broadcast to other Asian countries."

"Which fighters are you interested in?" I speculated the backers were talking about having Foreman, the new heavyweight champion, fight a Japanese challenger.

I was having a hell of a time getting the sushi we had ordered into my mouth using the chopsticks.

"Someone named Valdez called my organization and suggested we try to arrange something with the Latin heavyweight fighter Joe "King" Roman. Valdez indicated that Roman would fight Foreman anywhere in the world." I had not been in touch with Alex since the Jamaican fight and did not know that his group was still acting as the matchmaker for Foreman.

"How the hell does Valdez think he can get that deal done?" I asked as I dropped another piece of raw fish in my lap. I knew that dealing with Foreman was not easy. Foreman's manager, Dick Sadler, was difficult to work with and didn't make the negotiation process any easier.

Rocky saw my worried face and said, "Valdez indicated he had negotiated the agreement with the same business group that has managed Foreman for years."

Alex knew that Video Techniques was in a position to bring everything together if the fight was going to be broadcast from Japan with sponsorship from Benihana and NETV.

"It has to be a pretty large purse and a lower tax bite if it's going to work for Foreman." I made it clear that the Japanese promoter would have to put up meaningful US dollars to get this fight up and running.

I turned my attention to the chopsticks to see if I could get a better grip on the technique. One of the blondes, who had been observing my struggle, leaned over and put her arm around my neck. She leaned in and started feeding me sushi from her lips. The other blond had taken the same approach with Rocky. I decided to give up the use of chopsticks—forever. Needless to say I was distracted. Rocky continued the business conversation.

"I would like to be the ringside announcer for the fight." He said somewhat abruptly. My eyes darted across the table as a piece of tuna slid into my mouth. "You can manage the production and distribution. We will, of course, pay you a fair fee," he said.

I smiled. The beauty feeding me thought I was cheered up by her feeding technique—which was true. "Eel would be lovely, darling." But I also liked the sound of "fair fee."

"OK, I am sure we can reach an agreement on the fee, but the promoter will also be expected to pay all the travel and entertainment expenses up front for my audio guy, my lighting expert, and the rest of my staff, in addition to myself. We need to arrive in Tokyo well before the date of the fight in order to get everything in place so that the television picture is as good as it can be," I countered.

"Anything you want, Hank. We will make sure that everything goes smoothly. When we're done with the fight, I invite you to spend some time in Japan and travel down to Kyoto on one of our super-fast trains."

"Go easy on the wasabi, sweetheart, it makes my nose run."

CHAPTER 3
A BROMANCE BEGINS

The day after the meeting with Rocky, King arrived at my office without an appointment. My Angels were shocked to see this six-foot two African-American man walk into my office. He brought with him four small floral bouquets—a gift for each of the Angels.

I brought King into my office and closed the door. I still had not quite figured this guy out and was not sure how to handle him. But, as he did at the end of our last phone conversation, he scrapped the southern drawl and spoke with considerable eloquence.

King gave me a long and clearly thought out lecture as he paced around my office, moving with grace and style. He ended with a rousing climax. I wondered where the hell the street talk was. How could he use this type of oratory with fighters like Foreman and Ali and get them to sign a contract with Video Techniques?

"Will you please sit the fuck down? Where the hell did you

get all these flowery words you're throwing at me?" I interrupted in exasperation.

"Hank, would you believe I acquired my vocabulary in prison? I read everything I could get my hands on. I had enough time to read *Mein Kampf* and Schopenhauer and loads of classical texts about politics, and philosophy and government. I also read some business books about great companies run by top corporate leaders."

"Well, I guess that's fine with me, but how does that work when you are talking to the fighters?"

King's eyes rolled up to the ceiling as his southern drawl came back. "You are my man, my brother, and I'm sure we can get some key niggers workin' in our cotton fields or on our TV events." He instantly reverted to the character of his alter ego. The quick change from the scholarly discourse to the cadence of streets of Harlem… or Cleveland… caused me to realize that King could be a valuable resource to Video Techniques.

I asked King to fill me in on his background. He arrived at the Ohio prison a street-smart numbers racketeer who had dared to fight the system and the white bosses who controlled the economic infrastructure of the American black ghetto. He was a street hustler without any formal education serving time for manslaughter, not a philosopher or historian. His prison life had its share of live-in cockroaches looking for little morsels of food perpetuating their million-year fight for survival. But King's cell was different from the others. His cell was filled with books. King's cell was full of hard-cover textbooks, well-read and dog-eared—Nietsche, Shakespeare, and *The Rise and Fall of the Third Reich*.

I was amazed that anybody serving time in prison could come out this smart and self-educated. The other thing King did while in prison was to learn a lot about boxing. He had listened to the Ali-Frazier fight that was broadcast from Madison Square Garden on the radio in his cell.

"What if I made you an offer to join forces with me as a vice president in my company?"

"My man that's the way to go," King smiled. "But I still want to keep Don King Productions alive, even though I will give 100% of my time to Video Techniques." He grinned at me this time.

"Have you talked to George Foreman at all?" I asked.

"He's hard to reach," Don replied. Then, after a beat of silence, "But I reached him."

"Who do you think we should match him with for his first title defense?"

Our conversation progressed smoothly. King seemed focused and honest. I thought that we could work together well and that he definitely had the ability to get the top fighters under contract. With King able to deliver the fighters, Video Techniques could function as the promoter for the entire event rather than serving only as a contractor to someone else providing the TV production, marketing, and distribution. This was a much better business position, but there was much more at stake.

"Listen Don, a big Japanese television station working with the owners of the Benihana restaurant chain are about to sign George Foreman to fight the Puerto Rican heavyweight Jose 'King' Roman. They are planning to hold the fight in Tokyo sometime in September at their major arena. I'm sure Foreman thinks this will be an easy first test of his hold on the title. Jose "King" Roman is about the same size as Joe Frazier—smaller than Foreman." I filled in the details and gave Don the lay of the land.

"Yeah. But are black fighters really marketable in Japan?" Don asked.

"We did the Ali-Mac Foster bout in Tokyo last year. Both fighters were big black guys and neither of them champions. We were still able to distribute the fight to some key networks around the world and make a little money. The big issue for us with that fight was the condition of the broadcast technology in place and the thick-headed anti-American network executives who thought they understood the production and broadcast of live television."

King agreed to come with me to Tokyo. "You know, if Foreman retains his title and you want him to fight Ali, I could talk to him after the match in Tokyo." King outlined his strategy and explained how he would approach Foreman and his manager.

"What if we invited Ali to come with us?"

Having both fighters at the title defense should give us a leg up on the contract negotiations. I watched King's eyes to see how he reacted to our conversation and we both chuckled.

"Can you get Ali to Tokyo if we pay his ticket?" I asked.

"When are we leaving, man?"

"Why don't we think this over, Don. I'm willing to teach you the broadcasting formula, if you will teach me how to deal with the fighters."

King laughed out loud as he shook my hand and said, "You can teach me what you know about satellites and distribution, but you will never learn how to talk to these black fighters."

I said goodbye and walked King out of the office. I needed time to decide whether or not Video Techniques really needed a long-term relationship with Don King. I would use this trip to test his ability to deliver. Could he get Ali to come along for the ride?

It would also allow me to determine if he could work with Foreman.

CHAPTER 4
A MATTER OF THE MIND

August–September 1973

Jose "King" Roman trained in the ballroom of New York City's Wellington Hotel for several weeks prior to his departure for the fight in Japan. The staff set up a large video monitor in his training area for him to watch the tape of Foreman beating Frazier over and over again. I wanted Roman to learn Foreman's ring technique. We wanted a good battle for the Japanese audience.

Watching Foreman beat the shit out of Smokin' Joe was not good psychologically for Roman. He made no bones about the fact that he did not want to go to Tokyo and kept backtracking in rounds with his sparring partners. Anyone in the press who came to watch Roman work out in the ring knew right away that Jose "King" Roman was scared to death.

A rumor was circulating that Roman's ranking had been tinkered with and he had been pushed up from the number ten slot into the first or second position as a title contender. Nobody understood why he had agreed to fight Foreman.

Video Techniques had entered into a final agreement with

NETV and the Japanese promoters. We were spending our time and energy marketing the Foreman-Roman fight to key networks around the world. I was increasingly concerned that Roman would back out at the last minute. We would be in a very difficult position if the fight did not come off. We would lose our stature as a fight promoter and jeopardize our reputation as a television production company.

Early in 1970, my wife Connie had begun to study with Bob Cummings and his "brain training" organization to support her painting and other artistic endeavors. His program, called Mind Dynamics, focused on mind control and self improvement. As I learned more about Cummings' approach, I shared with Connie the problem we were having with Roman. Connie agreed with me that Mind Dynamics could help Roman because it enhanced the mind of anyone that learned how to use it.

"Do you think you could work with Roman and see if you could help him get past his fear of meeting Foreman in the ring?" I had to do something to get this guy on the plane to Tokyo and into his corner.

"Well, I need to bring my teacher with me and work with Roman for about a week. If we don't totally eliminate his fear we might at least be able to bring it to a lower level. We don't want him to run away from Foreman when the bell rings." Connie thought they could simplify the learning process, but we both knew there was a possibility that it might not work at all.

"OK. See if you can get your teacher to work with you and I'll get you at least one session with Roman."

Roman agreed to a session with Connie and her teacher. When the three of us arrived at the Wellington, he was talking with Al Braverman, his manager, about going home and walking away from the fight. Al was desperately trying to get him into fight condition. During the next week, Connie used every element of Mind Dynamics that she knew and got Roman into an almost self-hypnotic state. Roman envisioned himself with a huge fist that would emerge like a sledge-hammer to knock Foreman out. Jose 'King' Roman finally felt cocky enough to face Foreman.

"I did everything I could," Connie told me after her last session with Roman. "He seems better, but we'll have to wait for the fight to see if he gets in the ring."

When Connie and I got to Tokyo, Roman was already there and looked aggressive and focused at the televised weigh-in. Don King was also at the weigh-in talking to Foreman, who was surly and uncooperative with the press.

In these last few days leading up to the fight, there was rarely a moment when King wasn't at Foreman's side. Don King was nearly as broad and as tall as Foreman. When these two giant African-American men walked the streets together, the little Japanese kids were terrified and ran for cover as the two hulking men strolled through the city. As I watched how Don King handled himself, I gained confidence that it would be a good move to make him a vice president of Video Techniques.

My side of the operation was running smoothly. Mindful of Japanese protocol, I held a number of meetings with NETV management to express in clear and simple terms what had happened the year before when I tried to get the rival Japanese TV station to improve the video production of Ali-Mac Foster fight. This time the Nippon Educational TV executives listened to my advice. They agreed to increase the lighting over the ring, relocate the cameras, and utilize some new technology in their mobile studio. Whenever they tried to ignore me, I would ceremoniously bow and say "This championship fight will not take place in Japan if the television production is not perfect." All of my suggestions were eventually put into place.

We still had anxiety over whether Roman would meet Foreman face-to-face. Foreman's technique had always been to stare down his opponents with menace in his eyes. His persona was built on intimidation and he carried the act with him to press conferences, in the dressing room, and in the ring. I had heard that Foreman's trainer, Archie Moore, told him to "hate down your opponents." This attitude helped Foreman with his self-confidence and it gave him more power in his punch.

The night of the fight I waited impatiently, praying two fighters would climb through the ropes and step into their corners.

Roman made his way down the aisle first. He got into the ring and danced from corner to corner waiting for Foreman to arrive. We all breathed a sigh of relief when we saw him moving easily in the ring looking relaxed and loose, like a plausible contender.

Rocky Aioki was the ringside announcer as agreed. He gave his blow-by-blow of the fight in a mix of English and Japanese that caused everyone in the mobile studio to break out in hysterical laughter. But those of us who did not speak Japanese did not know what the hell he said or why it was funny.

Don King and I had invited Ali to Tokyo to give him a platform from which he could taunt Foreman. Our goal was to lure Foreman into negotiations for a major championship event with Muhammad Ali. We felt sure that Ali would sign a contract to fight Foreman if it could happen in the very near future and with a large purse. But nobody in the boxing industry believed the Foreman would take that fight. It would be too big a risk defending his title against the dancing, fancy-talking, scene-stealing Ali. If we were going to get a major championship heavyweight fight, Ali would have to goad Foreman into it. We positioned Ali ringside near Foreman's corner so Foreman could easily hear Ali's insulting chatter.

Foreman lumbered slowly down the aisle, flanked by his corner men and a throng of Japanese reporters. Ali stood up and let 'er rip. Nothing could block the sound of the words he yelled at Foreman. "When are you gonna play with me? I dance like a butterfly but I'm gonna sting you like a bee." Foreman climbed into the ring acting as if he hated Japan, the ring, Roman, Ali, and everybody in the arena.

The referee called the two combatants together to go over the rules and regulations. Roman looked up at the taller Foreman and met him eye to eye. Just before they returned to their respective corners, Roman growled at Foreman with the deep, threatening, guttural sound of a bear about to attack. I was proud of the work Connie had done using Mind Dynamics, and gave her a wink of love and appreciation.

Unfortunately, the bear's growl escaping from Roman's chest turned Foreman into a raging bull. Within 45 seconds of the first bell Foreman landed massive blows on Roman's chin, behind his ear, into his ribs, and finally on the top of his head. Foreman had become vicious, hitting Roman again as he fell to the ground. It was over in two minutes.

Roman ended up on the canvas lying between Foreman's legs with Foreman glowering down at him. Even when the referee came over and raised his arm as the winner and still heavyweight champion, Foreman didn't crack a smile.

I felt the blood drain out of my entire body as I considered how this outcome would affect distribution sales. The fight lasted less than one round and even though Foreman's power was mesmerizing, the event would not be an easy sell to the stations. At least when Foreman knocked down Smokin' Joe six times, Frazier had provided some drama by getting up each time. The Foreman-Frazier fight had been broadcast live for nearly two rounds. It was a significant fight because the title had switched to the challenger. This Foreman-Roman bout would most likely be a money loser for everyone except Foreman.

There was a dinner that night to honor the returning heavyweight champ. Foreman and his business associate, Leroy Jackson, sat on a dais facing the other guests. The two talked among themselves, never acknowledging anyone else in the room.

Ali, who had made his presence known at the fight, was

noticeably absent from the dinner. He, along with everyone else in his entourage, felt disheartened. Roman was no more than a punching bag for the powerful Foreman.

Foreman wanted easy fights that would last one or two rounds and allow him to retain his title while earning him large sums of money. Even with Don King added to my team, I had a big challenge ahead of me in getting Foreman to accept Ali as his next opponent. After the latest display by the defending champ, we might even have difficulty getting Ali to fight Foreman.

CHAPTER 5
WATERMELON AT THE VICTORY BANQUET

September 1, 1973

At the dinner, Foreman and his associate Leroy Jackson asked to be served watermelon. I have never understood the exact reason for the watermelon but I thought they were sharing some inside joke at the expense of the members of the Japanese media that filled the tables in the ballroom. Maybe after winning his big purse in Japan, Foreman wanted to make a statement about his roots—using the watermelon as a symbol of the oppression of African-Americans throughout the modern history of the United States.

"For God's sake. They're eating that watermelon without any utensils, as if they're on a farm," I said to Shelly, the PR man. After another few minutes went by I spoke to Shelly again, "Shel, they're spitting the seeds at the waiters. Go over and see if you can stop them before the Japanese media have a field day with this." I was terribly embarrassed.

"I doubt I can stop them," Shelly said, "but I'll go see what I can do." Foreman and his sidekick laughed between themselves as they shot seeds across the ballroom and tried to hit targets that were sometimes outrageously inappropriate—light fixtures, other people's plates, body parts…

"Foreman refuses to stop," Shelly said when he came back. "I asked them to stop making a scene but for whatever reason he wants to continue." I was furious at the disrespectful display.

"You know we're supposed to leave tomorrow to go to Kyoto on the speed train with Muhammad Ali. Maybe we can leave Foreman here in Tokyo."

I watched Foreman the rest of the night as his behavior became more annoying. "Shelly, let's make a point to leave Foreman and Leroy here. I don't like the way they are acting."

Shelly was also watching Foreman. "You know the trip was set up primarily because the Japanese people love Ali so much and want him to understand their culture. They probably won't even miss the champ. It's Ali they want to honor."

CHAPTER 6
TOURING KYOTO WITH MUHAMMAD ALI

The next morning we assembled, without Foreman, and were brought to a beautiful new bullet train. We left at 10 a.m. on the button and arrived in Kyoto in less than an hour, passing through rice fields with lovely mountains in the distance at 180 mph. Once in Kyoto, we were taken to what looked like an American diner.

"This looks like we're back in New York," Connie whispered.

We were graciously led to the diner's counter. The diner reminded me of old Hollywood films set in the 1930's. We were the actors, sitting somewhere in Brooklyn or the Bronx, waiting for a nickel cup of coffee, which was all we had during those Depression years.

We watched a group of hyperactive cooks and waiters grill and serve us what were called Kobe steaks. Kobe beef, which comes from the Wagyu cattle raised in traditional settings under very rigid domestic regimes, was not known or available at the time in the United States. It was delicious—very tender. I had never seen a steak that looked or tasted anything like it. There definitely weren't any cattle in the United States that were treated the way these animals were. Our cowboys out west didn't feed their herd with special vegetables and would never massage their cattle's behinds the way the Japanese ranchers did. Unfortunately, I had to deal with chopsticks again as I attempted to get the delicious steak to my mouth. Before I could finish, several cars arrived to pick us up and take us to the next stop on our cultural tour. Rocky had told me we were going to visit a geisha house and some of the shrines in Kyoto. He also said we would be meeting a Japanese actor who wanted Ali to visit him on his film set.

We were shuttled over to the Japanese film location to meet the distinguished Japanese actor who was outfitted in a Chinese general's uniform and surrounded by what appeared to be a World War I battlefield. It looked as if the action were taking place in Germany, except for the fact that all the actors were Asian. The actor we were meeting turned out also to be the director of the film. Our interpreter spoke rapidly with the actor and then translated, explaining that the scene they were shooting was based on a historic battle between Japan and China. Japan would emerge triumphant.

The actor invited us into a studio conference room where he ceremoniously gave Ali a gorgeous robe in honor of his visit to Japan. The robe was lavishly embroidered with gold and silver threads that depicted Ali's name across the back. We were all moved by the respectful manner in which the actor presented the gift to Ali.

Our host then brought us to a geisha house where he had his resident geisha. She was a beautiful woman who did not wear the traditional white face makeup because she belonged to the actor, perhaps for her lifetime.

None of us had ever been to a geisha house before. Ali sat across the table from Connie and me and entertained the group by performing magic tricks accompanied by "Ohs" and "Ahs" from the geisha girls. Then it was their turn to entertain. The geisha played Japanese musical instruments and performed a ritual dance using beautifully colored fans.

When the geisha finished, they immediately flocked around Connie. "What are they doing to me?" Connie whispered in my ear. I didn't know but it looked like they were undressing her. Most geisha do not speak English and have never seen a Caucasian woman in the flesh.

Connie whispered again, "They're taking off my eyelashes, looking at my breasts, examining my hair and makeup. This is creepy."

"Don't fight it, just go with it," I said. "They're just trying to learn what American women look like under their clothing and how they make themselves up."

"This is one night I will never forget, Hank."

"At least nobody is spitting seeds at us and Ali is having a wonderful time."

Connie put herself back together and it was time to leave the geisha house. As we got back into the limousines I observed that the sky was clouding over and the wind was howling ferociously. It was the beginning of a typhoon.

We checked into the hotel minutes before the typhoon hit with full force. Shelly said, "I'm staying in the more modern section of the hotel. Rocky put you and Connie in a suite in the original section, which is furnished with Japanese artifacts and decorative items that date back several centuries. He knew Connie appreciated fine art and would enjoy it."

Shelly and the rest of the group, which included King and Ali, checked into their modern rooms. I didn't know where Rocky Aioki went but I felt sure that, as a member of a prominent family in Japan, he had a residence nearby.

There were futons on the floor, in lieu of beds, and a hot tub in the middle of the room filled with bubbling hot water. The pouring rain and the howling wind rattled everything and lightning seemed to strike just outside our windows.

"Come on honey, let's get into the tub and relax. It will be fine even if they turn off the electricity and we lose the lights." Connie lit the candles that were placed around the room and we got undressed and slipped into the hot tub. It was a surprise to discover that the tub was less than three feet across but four feet deep. There was a little stool under water in the tub that you stepped on to get in and out. Connie took the stool out of the water and as she reached to place it on the floor it tumbled out of reach.

When the water had cooled almost to room temperature and we were ready to get out, I realized we couldn't get out of the tub without the stool. While the storm raged around us and the wind continued to howl, we laughed 'til we cried trying to climb out of the tub. As Connie continued to giggle, I pushed her up and out and hoped she could stop laughing long enough to drop the stool back in the water so that I could escape.

We cuddled in one of the downy futons, even though I was sure that Japanese protocol did not allow for mischief to be carried out in this part of the hotel.

The next morning the entire group had a simple Japanese-style breakfast and Shelly leaned over to me and said, "I guess Don King is afraid of lightning, especially when it is hitting so close by. He was so scared last night that I couldn't get him out of the lobby to go to his room."

It was time to end our brief Japanese vacation and get back to New York so we could concentrate on the marketing of the Foreman-Roman fight. The fight had been mediocre at best, and I had to come up with an angle so we could sell it as an exciting defense of the heavyweight title.

PART 4

FOREMAN-NORTON IN VENEZUELA

CHAPTER 1
A NEW VICE PRESIDENT

I settled back into my offices in New York where my four Angels were busy at work on the sales of the delayed broadcast of the Foreman-Roman fight. It was a tough sell after the networks saw the live broadcast of the KO in the first round. I had enticed Barry Burnstein to join Video Techniques to become one of our marketing experts. Barry was well connected with a number of the larger theater networks in the United States. My staff was able to secure deals in each country capable of receiving the program signal from one of INTELSAT's satellite networks. Distribution agreements went out by fax or by certified mail.

Don King and I hadn't had too much time to talk in Kyoto so I decided to give him a call one morning to catch up. I had observed that he had Foreman's ear during the days leading up to the fight and he had been instrumental in bringing Ali with us to Tokyo. I was eager to hear if he had made progress advancing these relationships. The Angels made sure that a phone call from Don King reached my desk right away.

"Hank, did you get back from Tokyo OK?" King asked. He returned to Cleveland several days after Connie and I flew back to New York.

"Oh yes, back a couple of days now… any developments I should know about?" I asked.

"Man, I see now how we can work together. I am clear on the possibilities. You and I both know what we do well… and together we can make magic: me with the fighters, and you with the TV production and on the technical side. The sky's the limit, man."

King seemed ready to become a part of the Video Techniques team. I knew that my time was best spent working on the technical and communication side of Video Techniques developing more exciting marketing approaches for sports events. I knew that my company could not grow the way I wanted it to unless we began to sign contracts with champion fighters, leveraging our strong track record with pay-per-view, the networks, and international distribution. Video Techniques had the capability to use the latest technology connecting into the developing satellite and microwave networks. I was confident we could deliver the best possible sporting events worldwide, but I needed King's skills to pull it off. He could deliver the fighters.

"Alright Don, come to New York and let's sit down and work something out between us… then we can tackle what we have to do to get Foreman to defend his title against Ali."

"You got it, man! I'll see you in a couple of days at your office," King said, laughing.

This time when he arrived, the Angels were prepared for the loud-talking, larger than life character that was Don King. He sat down and filled me in on what was going on with our heavyweights, from his perspective. We agreed that signing Ali was the key factor to ensure that Video Techniques remained part of the next championship fight. I offered him the vice president position with the understanding that his primary responsibility would be to sign the fighters. He accepted.

"Alright Don, go out there and contact Foreman and Ali directly," I told him. "Or reach them through their business managers or their trainers. Get in touch with them any way you can and get them under agreement with us."

As I thought later about the approach we were taking, it occurred to me that it might be better to pursue an indirect rather than a direct path to Foreman. I had attended the Ali-Norton fight earlier in the year and watched Ken Norton break Ali's jaw in the second round. Ali had gotten up off the canvas and fought the rest of the ten rounds in a lot of pain. Norton kept hitting Ali on the broken side of his jaw throughout the rest of the fight. Ali lost the fight on a narrow points decision.

I called King and suggested the possibility of signing Norton as the next opponent for Foreman and we began to brainstorm.

"Ali has a super big ego. He had a second non-championship fight with Norton last September and Ali won that by decision. Norton is pretty high in the rankings…" Don said as he considered the alternative strategy.

"Maybe you could also approach George Foreman, if you think that he still hates Ali after the way Ali taunted him in Japan." I knew Don would respond to that angle.

"My man, my man, that's the way to go. Maybe we can get Foreman to fight Norton first. Then I can get Foreman to sign an agreement to fight Ali if he beats Norton." We were a couple steps ahead of ourselves, but it sounded like the best course of action.

"Yeah, if we can get Foreman locked in for two contracts and he beats Norton, we got a big winner on all fronts," I concluded.

"Hank, you know Foreman got crazy when Ali entered into a new fight contract with Frazier. Shit, that caused a lot of animosity between the Foreman camp and Ali's group."

After Ali won the fight with Norton in September, he

immediately signed on for another non-championship fight with Smokin' Joe Frazier. That fight was scheduled for January 1974. If Ali beat Frazier, by KO or decision, we could most likely get Ali to agree to fight Foreman so that he had a chance to regain the heavyweight championship title.

CHAPTER 2
FORMING TELEMEDIA DE PANAMA

"Karen, who did you say was on the phone?"

"I don't know who this one is but he's calling from Venezuela. Maybe he wants to buy the Foreman-Roman fight. Pick it up and see what he wants," Karen said, implying that it might be an important call.

"Hola, Señor Schwartz. I am Aldomero Romero and I have been assigned by the President of Venezuela to operate the promotion of events to be conducted in our new sports arena in Caracas."

I was having difficulty understanding what Romero was saying because of his thick accent. I paused before answering any of his questions so I could be sure I fully understood what the hell he was talking about.

"We have built a new coliseum in Caracas and I represent El Poliedro De Caracas and Instituto Nacional De Hipódromos. I am calling you to arrange a championship fight with Señor Foreman."

I started to wonder if perhaps this man was somehow involved in the entertainment industry but I didn't know who on my staff would have made contact with anyone in Venezuela.

"I have been speaking with your associate Sr. Valdez," Romero stated.

"*Sí,*" I answered as the conversation began to make sense.

"Venezuela will like if you could arrange for George Foreman to have his next championship fight here at our new arena." I figured that Alex Valdez was talking to his friends in South America about Foreman's second title defense. Hopefully Alex could convince people that the next fight would be a lot better than the first one.

After he gave me a few more details about who he represented and what they were looking to do I said, "Let me get back to you in a day or two."

I got King on the phone and told him that people in Caracas were interested in sponsoring the next fight. "Don, where are you with Foreman? Give me some direction as to what our options are."

"George is currently having a lot of problems because he is going through a divorce and involved in a lawsuit with his former management company—everyone involved has a piece of him. He also has alimony problems with his last wife down in Texas. George doesn't want to have anything to do with a contract in the United States."

"Well, maybe we can get him to fight in another country like we did in Jamaica," I said.

"Yeah, but he has gotta be paid outside of the US to keep the money out of the reach of these legal proceedings."

The solution suddenly presented itself to me. "I am working on a project with some guys in the government in Costa Rica…"

"What does that have to do with anything?"

"Just listen. I am setting up a new company with them in

Panama. The shareholders want to keep their money out of Costa Rica. My man," I said, borrowing an expression from King, "Maybe we can set up a company in Panama that will also solve George's problems. The Costa Ricans gave me the name of an attorney in Panama that I will use to handle all the legal stuff." I paused to see if Don was following the logic.

"I can do the whole promotional deal off shore… in Brazil or with this Romero guy I am talking to in Venezuela. That way Foreman's money can be funneled through our Panamanian company. George can draw down the money he has earned where and when he wants to." I explained a few more of the logistics to Don.

"Why don't you get back to George and tell him Video Techniques represents a promoter out of Panama and we will put together a championship fight somewhere outside of the United States. See if that enables you to put a deal together with him."

King called the office before noon the next day. He laughed so loud that he nearly broke my phone. I took this as a good sign.

"My man, my man. I just talked to George and we discussed a championship fight with Ken Norton." Our plan seemed to be falling in place.

"Look out, Don. Stay close to him and keep on top of it. I happen to know there are other people talking to him—Jerry Perenchio, Jarvis Astaire, and Solomons are all trying to talk Foreman into taking a fight against Ali. You really need to stay on top of this so he does not slip out of our hands."

"If you form the Panamanian company, I can get Foreman to sign. But he won't sign until we show him Norton's signature first. He thinks Norton is scared to fight him."

"Is the deal really subject to getting Norton's signature on the contract first?" I hoped that King wasn't feeding me a line of bullshit.

"Go to Panama and form the company," he said without hesitation. I had Karen get my attorney in Panama on the phone and we set up a meeting.

Getting to Panama was easy because there were a lot of flights from Miami to the Tocumen International Airport in Panama City. My attorney met me at the airport and drove me through the narrow streets about 20 miles east to Panama City's older section. The streets were filled with military personnel. I asked Ernesto (this was the only one of his many names I could remember) about the soldiers in the streets.

"In 1968, the National Guard, led by Omar Torrijos, overthrew the government and Torrijos emerged as the leader of the new military junta. He is working very hard to repatriate the Canal. His troops watch the ships, the cargo, and everyone else passing through—very closely."

The lawyer and I sat and talked in a small bar in the El Panama Hotel, where I was staying. I ordered a Jack Daniels, which I desperately needed after the bumpy ride through the city.

"Ernesto, I need to have a new company set up that is a legitimate Panamanian operation. It needs to be formed right away. I want to call it Telemedia de Panama."

Ernesto smiled. "I could form a new company for you today but the shares cannot be issued to anybody except a Panamanian citizen. We can name you the president, my associate Julia Rivera as the secretary, and myself as the treasurer."

This started to worry me. "How am I going to do business if I am not a shareholder in the company but only its President?"

"Ah, you can act as the authorized agent of the company in any country other than Panama."

I thought through the legal scenario. "So if I was entering into a contract in Venezuela, I would be able to execute the agreement as the legal agent?"

"Absolutely! Now we just need the capital to form the

company in the amount of one thousand US dollars."

"OK. Get it done." I counted out a thousand dollars in one hundred dollar bills on the bar's counter. Ernesto gathered the money, stuffed it into his jacket pocket, and said, "I will be back with the filed documents in a few hours." We shook hands and he left.

I finished my Jack Daniels and checked into my room. Before 8 p.m. a lieutenant arrived at my door, saluted, and handed me a large official envelope from Notaria Segunda del Circuito addressed to Telemedia de Panama. It was stamped with the logo of Oficina de Registro Público of the Republic of Panama. My brief trip to Panama was a success.

Before leaving for the airport, I called King. "Greetings from Telemedia de Panama and its agent, Henry A. Schwartz. We're in business. Get things going with George Foreman right away."

CHAPTER 3
SIGNING NORTON

I talked to Romero, down in Caracas, to make sure his group was still interested in sponsoring the next heavyweight championship fight. He said they needed to know how much it would cost before making a formal commitment. I begged the question because I didn't yet know the amount that was needed to put the deal together with the champ and the contender. I was pretty certain, however, that there was money somewhere in the government channels. After all, they had come up with the funds to build the new arena.

King was working on Foreman and had gotten him to agree to work with us as long as the fight would happen outside the United States. Foreman had said he wanted some money up front for on-going training and related expenses, with the remaining balance to be issued as a letter of credit to be paid off-shore within 24 hours of the completion of the fight. The cash due the fighters would be deposited into a major bank which would issue the letters of credit payable when evidence, such as the

New York Times, was produced that showed the fight had taken place. Further conversations with Romero gave me confidence that I could get his group to arrange the letters of credit.

"You have to get Norton to meet with you," King said, "and you will have to pony up some cash to get him to sign the contract with Telemedia. But offer a lot less than what George is asking for."

King still hadn't told me the dollar amount needed to get Foreman's signature on the last page of the contract.

"Give it to me straight, Don, what does Foreman want up front?"

Usually King never stopped talking, but this time there was silence.

"For Christ's sake, how much does Foreman want?"

I needed to know the number so I could get back to Romero with a cost estimate. Finally King answered me: "George wants $500,000 against 40% of the revenue." King's voice was harsh and quiet.

That was a lot more than Foreman was paid for the one round fiasco in Tokyo. I hoped Romero's group had that kind of cash available and that they seriously wanted the next Foreman fight in Caracas.

"I think I can get George to take $50,000 in cash up front… after we get Norton to sign," King added.

I was still scrambling to collect the revenue due from the Foreman-Roman fight. "Don, it's going to be almost impossible for me to advance that much cash to Telemedia."

"I can get the cash to cover Foreman from one of my contacts in Cleveland. I'll send a messenger over with an attaché case filled with $50,000 cash. But it will have to be paid back with interest from the fight."

I chose not to ask any further questions because I really didn't want to know where the cash was going to come from.

"If I can get Norton to take less cash up front and a smaller letter of credit and then get both letters of credit backed by the government group in Caracas, then I think we can get this to work." I knew roughly how much Video Techniques had coming in from marketing the Foreman-Roman fight. I thought that I could advance the cash to Telemedia to get Norton to sign the agreement, and then we could get the funds to cover the letters of credit from the group in Caracas.

"Hank, you've got to get Norton and his manager to sign. Then we can bring the agreement out to Foreman in Oakland to get his signature." King finished our conversation and I knew he was reading the deal the same way I was.

I was increasingly concerned. Were we going to be able to pull this off? If the contracts were entered into between the fighters and Telemedia de Panama, everything could still fall apart if the big money backing the letters of credit was not deposited almost immediately. The letters of credit then had to be delivered to the fighters within a few days of their commitment.

I spent the next few days looking for Norton. Through my contacts in Los Angeles, I located Arthur Rivkin, who was Norton's business manager. When Norton wasn't training, he worked as an actor and was trying to make it in Hollywood films. Rivkin represented him in both pursuits.

Rivkin did a little due diligence on Video Techniques and decided he liked the Foreman-Norton scenario. He volunteered that, unlike Roman, Norton looked strong and wasn't afraid to face the reigning champ in the ring, especially after what he had done to Ali's jaw just a few months earlier.

"Have you drawn up a contract?" Rivkin was back on the phone with me.

"I can get that done within a few hours," I answered. As long as my Angels were on top of things, I could stay one step ahead of the rest of the industry.

"Foreman won't sign his agreement for the fight without first having Ken's signature on the document." I explained to Rivkin, omitting the fact that the whole deal was going to blow up if I did not produce Norton's signature first. I wanted Rivkin to think it was a mere technicality.

"I need you to make sure Ken does not talk to any media guys about the match until we get both contracts signed," I emphasized and Rivkin agreed.

"Can you fly out tomorrow? Bring a form contract with you and bring whoever has the authority to sign on behalf of Telemedia de Panama as the promoter. I think we are close to an agreement on the terms."

I got on a flight to Los Angeles early the next morning. Helen, one of my Angels, had set up the meeting in a conference room at the airport. As soon as I exited the plane I strolled into the business center where the room had been reserved. Rivkin and Norton were already there, along with several other advisors on their team.

The agreement I brought with me still had some blanks in it stating the amount of up front cash to be given to Norton when he signed, and the amount for the letter of credit and the due date.

"Who represents Telemedia de Panama?" Rivkin asked.

"I am the legal agent and I sign for Telemedia," I answered.

"Is Video Techniques operating an off-shore company and you guys own it?"

"It doesn't make any difference as long as the event happens and the money is paid on time," I dodged the question.

It didn't take more than two hours to fill in the blanks and sign the agreement. A secretary at the business center retyped the document. It was signed by the "Boxer's Group," who would receive the cash and would get the letters of credit in the minimum amount of $200,000 to be applied against 20% of the net revenue.

"If we are going to sign the agreement now, we also want the license to sell the fight broadcast to theaters in San Diego. We will share the proceeds with your company," Rivkin added toward the end of our talk.

"You got it! I will send you the license once I get back to New York," I said as I took $20,000 out of my attaché case and put it into Rivkin's hands. Nobody wanted to count it.

I was out of the conference room by 6 p.m. LA time and caught a red eye back to New York.

CHAPTER 4
A BRIEFCASE FOR FOREMAN

I brought King up to speed regarding the Norton negotiations and we shifted our focus to Foreman.

"OK Don. So far, so good. I've drafted an agreement for George for $500,000 paid by a letter of credit and $50,000 in cash up front for training and other expenses," I said. "Don, you know George and Leroy will want that $50,000 cash delivered immediately—as soon as he signs the agreement with Telemedia. You promised me that if Video Techniques provided the cash for Norton, you would arrange for a messenger to deliver the $50,000 for Foreman. Your messenger hasn't showed up yet. Is that going to happen as promised?"

There was a silence on the other end of the phone. Then King reverted to his ethnic speak. "I have to be in New York in a couple of days. I'll get the cash from this real estate guy in Cleveland and bring it with me… but we gonna have to give him a piece of the deal so he can get his money back… with some meaningful interest." Again, I didn't want any details about where the money was coming from.

While King worked on the money, I had to secure a meeting with Foreman. I was not able to reach him directly, but got his manager, Dick Sadler, on the phone. I was still not clear who made the decisions in the Foreman camp.

"Dick, we need to arrange a meeting with George right away so we can get a fight agreement in place." The situation was much more urgent than I could let on.

Dick seemed comfortable with me. "I'll set up a meeting in San Francisco, where you can meet with George and Leroy, but it has to be tomorrow."

I had to race across the country again to keep this deal alive. "Helen, get me a ticket to San Fran ASAP and a room at the Fairmont Hotel."

I got King on the phone and told him he had to get his end of the bargain pulled together because I needed the cash in my pocket—actually in my briefcase—right away.

"I'm leaving for San Francisco to meet George and Leroy tomorrow morning. Where is this case with the cash?"

"Which airline are you flying on?" Don asked.

"It's American Airlines from LaGuardia." I told him when the plane was scheduled to take off early the next morning.

"My man, trust me. I'll get a messenger to you or I will meet you there myself and get the money into your hands before you board the plane. Just don't let anyone know what is in that case. It will look like a regular business briefcase," King chuckled.

I had a vision of myself in a spy movie passing a case full of cash to a beautiful French girl just before I board a plane.

I got to the airport at 9 a.m. and the departure area was almost empty. I sat down getting increasingly agitated because the flight was about to board and I still had no case. I noticed a big guy walking into the gate area whose hair was knotted in strands that came down to his shoulders. He scanned the waiting area and spotted me. He walked toward me. I had a flash back to the anti-government tensions we experienced in Jamaica before the Foreman-Frazier fight.

My first instinct was that the large man was an assassin hired to bump me off because I had worked with the Jamaican government. As he walked toward me he kept looking at an object in his left hand while his right hand held onto a large briefcase. When he got in front of me he held up what turned out to be a photo of me that was taken by the Jamaican newspaper, the *Gleaner*. The odds were even money—either this Rastafarian was a hit man and I was going to be rubbed out at LaGuardia or he was King's contact with the money.

Getting closer to me, he held the photo close to my face and flashed a grin with two teeth missing in the front. He held out the briefcase.

"Hey mon. I was told to deliver this to Hank Schwartz."

"That's me," I said. I was a little disoriented as he handed me the briefcase.

"OK mon, sign this here," he whispered as he turned over the photograph and asked me to print my name with the words "That's me" above my signature. I reached out and grabbed the briefcase with one hand and signed the photo with the other. The man pocketed the photo and I quickly walked away. He watched me go through the gate and board the plane.

I carefully slipped the briefcase under my seat and wondered why the United Parcel Service didn't use this simple receipt approach for their guaranteed deliveries.

I kept my foot on the briefcase while we were in the air, but never opened it. When we landed in San Francisco, I took a taxi to the Fairmont Hotel. I checked in, carried the briefcase to my room, and double locked the door. I sat down on the bed and opened it. It was full of one hundred dollar bills. I counted $50,000 then neatly stacked them back.

I started looking for Foreman but could not reach him or Leroy, so I called Dick Sadler again.

"What the hell am I doing here if I can't sit down with George?" I asked Sadler.

"Go down to the bar and I will be over in an hour. I'll see if we can find George." Dick always talked in circles but this roundabout statement sent me down to the bar. Of course, I was still carrying the briefcase. I ordered a Jack… and then another, and eventually Dick joined me as he said he would.

"George and Leroy are at the football game you're watching on that TV set over the bar. Leroy told me before they left that they would contact you later."

While Dick and I sat at the bar waiting for Leroy and Foreman, he explained some of the details of the lawsuit that was hanging over Foreman. The suit had been transferred from Texas to California and was moving rapidly toward a trial. "We're in a squeeze right now, Hank," Dick seemed to be in the mood to spill his guts. I ordered another round.

As Dick continued to talk it became obvious that there was some kind of split in the Foreman camp, Leroy being on one side and Dick on the other. I learned that after the Roman fight in Japan, Dick's role had been reduced and he had been removed from the position of business manager. Leroy was now the manager and Dick only the trainer. It also became clear that several other people were trying to negotiate a contract with Foreman for his next title defense. I was not sure why Dick was telling me all of this.

It was another hour before Leroy Jackson walked into the bar. "Leroy, where the hell is George?" I asked, beginning to lose my patience.

"We are anxious to get the Norton fight all sewed up… we don't want any issues with George's grasp on the heavyweight crown," Dick said as Leroy sat down.

"That's right Hank. But if we do this deal, I need to know what's in it for me?" Leroy said.

I was getting tired of all these players trying to advance their own position at my expense. "We can talk about that, Leroy, as soon as I get George's signature on this contract."

Dick also seemed to be getting restless. "Leroy, it's getting late and I don't know if George is going to show up or not."

"Hank, relax. He's coming when the football game is over." The three of us sat in the bar for another hour and a half waiting for Foreman to return from the game.

"Well Hank, if I was you I would leave and go home," Dick said seemingly trying to raise the stakes. "You are not going to be able to tie this heavyweight champ down to a contract no matter what," he continued. He made it clear that he no longer had the power to negotiate on behalf of Foreman.

Here I was, the legal representative for Telemedia de Panama sitting with $50,000 cash in a briefcase on my lap, a copy of the contract signed by Norton on December 11, and a contract that needed to be signed, but no George Foreman.

Leroy excused himself to make a phone call and came back to the bar. "I'm having a party at my house this evening and George will be there. Why don't you join us Hank, at my house."

"Listen you get on the telephone and tell George that if he doesn't sit down and complete the deal right now, I'm going to leave on the next plane." This was over the top.

"Let me take a look at the contract," Leroy said. He reviewed it, suggesting a word change here and there. Dick kept mumbling under his breath. He was losing patience also. Finally Dick said he was going home and left.

"Come with me, Hank, I'll drive you up to my house to the party. I'm sure George will be there." Leroy handed the contract back to me with a few minor changes written in the margins.

I was now getting the circular talk from Leroy instead of Dick. I figured going to the party was the only way I would get to see Foreman, so I went along. We didn't talk too much during the 30 mile drive. I was getting totally pissed off. When we arrived at Leroy's house, there was a party in full tilt with a lot of men drinking heavily. Not the kind of guys I would ever want to meet again.

"Leroy, where's George?" I went from being pissed to completely steamed.

"He just called and told me he'll see you first thing tomorrow morning." That was the last straw!

I exploded. "Give me a phone book. I'm calling a cab to take me back to the hotel." I grabbed Leroy's phone that hung on the wall. "Operator! Give me—"

Leroy grabbed the phone and disconnected the call. "Hank. Don't get sore." Leroy was trying to be friendly. The volume of the party was cranking up.

"I'm sick of your bullshit, Leroy. You're wasting my time while I am flying back and forth coast to coast. If George wants to see me, he better show up tomorrow morning at the hotel."

"All right, all right Hank. Stay calm. Here are the keys to my car. Drive it back to the Fairmont, park it in the garage, and leave the ticket and the keys with one of the guys in the lobby. I'll have one of my friends drive me back out there in the morning." Leroy handed me the keys to his car.

I got behind the wheel of his dilapidated car and started back down the highway to San Francisco. I kept looking in the mirror to see if anyone was following me to knock me off for the $50,000 in the briefcase. Leroy's car was running low on gas so I chugged into a gas station. I asked the station attendant for only three gallons because I didn't want to be there long enough for someone to come up behind me. At this point I wasn't as much aggravated as I was scared.

I paid for the gas and jumped back into the car. I floored it, which wasn't more than 65 mph. I finally got back to the hotel, took an empty elevator to the room, and double locked the door again. I was furious, nervous, and scared, all at the same time. It did not look like this deal was going to happen and I had fronted $20,000 to Norton. Gone, I thought!

The next morning at 10 a.m. my phone rang. I had finally fallen asleep around 6 after tossing and turning the whole night. It was George Foreman.

"Is this Hank? Come on down and I will take you out for breakfast," he said.

Outside I spotted Foreman sitting in a fancy sports car. He said, "Good morning, Hank. I got a favorite breakfast joint that has great pancakes on Sunday mornings."

I was a little worried about where we were headed. But I got into the car and we drove to a place around the corner from the Fairmont. It was a short ride but I had enough time to ask some questions.

"George, what the hell is going on? King and I set up the off-shore company so that you could be paid outside of the US. Aren't you looking for a big pay day right about now?"

I told Foreman everything that had happened the previous day and his face brightened.

"Do you still have the $50,000?"

"Yeah, but you won't get it until you sign the contract that Leroy and I went over yesterday. He made a change here and there that I initialed." Even though George was relaxed and friendly, I wanted him to know that I was still pissed as hell because he had stood me up about six times the day before. As we were eating the lousy pancakes, Foreman read through the contract over and over.

"Come with me, Hank. I'm going to the Oakland airport to catch a plane to Los Angeles this morning to appear on 'Hollywood Squares,'" he told me as we got on the freeway in the direction of the Oakland Airport.

"George, I'm not going anywhere with you. I'm going to turn around and go back to New York since this deal is not going to happen. You can forget the whole thing with Norton," I yelled at him I was so irritated. After a few minutes, with a cooler head I continued, "If you remain the heavyweight champ, maybe later on we can try to work something out with Ali. We'll see if he can give you a run for your money and take away the championship." I did not want to close off communication just because I did not like the sloppy way this guy handled the business end of things.

We got out of the sports car after he parked in a short-term parking spot at the airport.

"Leroy's meeting me here and buying the tickets. He can get you one as well Hank so you can come down to L.A. with me."

"Not a chance, George," I said.

"I've got to take a piss. Let's go into the men's room." Foreman kept walking and I followed him into the men's bathroom.

From the urinal: "Did Leroy see the fight papers?"

"Yeah, he did. I told you…he looked over your contract and the one signed by Norton."

"What do I get?"

"You get $50,000 in cash up front and a letter of credit for not less than $500,000 against 40% of the net revenue after Telemedia deducts $750,000 for expenses." I went through the provisions of the agreement standing over the porcelain in the men's bathroom. I was pissed. Ha ha.

"Did Leroy go over these terms with you?"

"Yeah. Leroy went over the whole agreement and made some small changes that we both initialed," I reiterated for the third time.

"Am I gonna be paid outside the United States?"

"Yeah it is an off-shore company called Telemedia de Panama—you can see that here in the contract."

"Open up the case and let me count the money."

"Wash your hands first."

I handed the open case to Foreman and walked over to place my back against the entrance door so that no one could walk in while he counted the money.

"Everything there?" I asked.

"Yeah. It's all here," George said.

I handed him the contract folded open to the last page and gave him my Mont Blanc.

"Sign the fuckin' contract," I said, trying the tough street talk approach that I was learning from King. I probably should have said "motherfucking contract." Foreman signed it and handed it back to me. I left a copy on top of the cash, closed the briefcase, and handed it to him.

Foreman then grinned and added, "If Telemedia de Panama produces the fight and Norton shows up, I'll give you the rights to promote all my upcoming fights."

I grabbed a piece of toilet paper trying to get this down for him to sign. He waved it off but assured me "my word is my bond." I put the signed contract and the unsigned toilet paper inside my jacket pocket and we walked out of the men's room. Leroy was heading toward us with the tickets. I walked past him without a word.

CHAPTER 5

BRINGING THE FIGHT TO CARACAS

I called King to update him about my progress in San Francisco. "Foreman signed the agreement. We have both fighters under contract. My man, it looks like I'm picking up the skills of working with these guys. I got George and Leroy on track."

"My man, the money talked for you," King shot back.

"OK, we've spent $20,000 of Video Techniques capital. We owe some thug in Cleveland $50,000. We have no one lined up to underwrite the letters of credit and no place to have the fight. Other than that, we're in great shape. What's next?" I asked.

"Before I tell Ali the Foreman-Norton fight is on, I think we need to lock in the where and when and line up the dough for the letters of credit."

"I have already talked to several foreign governments through their ambassadors at the United Nations here in New York to gauge their interest. It takes too long to get an answer that way. They move too slowly. We have to move fast or we will blow the deal. Let's go back to Alex Valdez. He will meet me in Caracas if we want to get the Venezuelan government to sponsor the fight in the new El Poliedro de Caracas Arena."

"Why do you want to work with Valdez? Why don't you bring me along with you?" King asked, sounding frustrated.

"Don, I don't speak Spanish and neither do you. Valdez can influence the government group. I'll call you from Caracas and let you know how we make out."

I spent a lot of time during the next week on the phone with Venezuela. I decided it was time to sit down across the table from Romero. Alex flew in from Peru and was at the airport when I arrived. "*¿Cómo está?*" Alex smiled at me and extended his hand.

"Hello my friend, long time, no see." We shook. "I'm glad you're on board Alex, I don't have too much time to find a location for the fight. These contracts cost a lot up front and I have to get these other details pulled together as soon as we can." I was no longer smiling. Alex could sense the tension I was feeling about getting the rest of the deal put together.

As we walked through customs, a slew of military personnel were looking at everyone coming out of the immigration checkpoints. Why is it that everywhere I do business, armed soldiers are monitoring the borders?

"Would you like me to help you with your luggage and get it checked through quickly using the Latino approach?" Alex asked.

"I didn't bring any luggage with me except some shaving stuff." Alex looked surprised.

We hailed a taxi and headed into the city. The low mountains that surround Caracas were visible in the distance. The deep rutted dirt roads ended in precipitous drops and were bordered by row after row of small shacks made mostly of red clay blocks. Some of them were topped with thin metal sheets that served as roofs and some were painted white in an effort to keep it cool inside. The shacks ran one after the other all along the drive to

Caracas. A few ran up the side of the mountain. Over two million Venezuelans lived in these shacks.

As we approached Caracas we could see El Poliedro in the distance. It looked new and expensive, made from blocks of stone and topped with a bright white dome. We made our way through the heavy traffic and reached the government building where we were meeting Romero. I was pleased to see that the building did not have a military barrier around it. When we reached the conference room Romero was waiting for us.

"Ah, Señor Schwartz. I am glad you were able to come and meet with me. Our ambassador made all the arrangements as you requested." The Angels had contacted the Venezuelan UN Ambassador's offices to enable a smooth entrance and exit out of the country. Romero's English was much easier to understand in person than over the telephone.

"Before we get down to business my driver will take us to El Poliedro so that you can see the new building. You will see how well it will work for the championship fight."

It was very hot in the small car that took us to the arena. Romero explained to Alex in Spanish that a new air conditioning system was being installed in El Poliedro de Caracas. Once we entered the building we could not continue our conversation over the steady din of the power saws and welding apparatus. It was even hotter inside the arena than out on the street.

"We are working very hard so that in a few days, El Poliedro will be inaugurated as South America's first world heavyweight championship site." His statement indicated that he was in a position to make a deal for Venezuela. We still needed to sit down and work out an agreement.

"Have you prepared an agreement for my attorney to review?" Romero asked when we left the El Poliedro. This was the second time I had inspected a newly-built, unairconditioned stadium and then, drenched with sweat, walked into a conference room to negotiate with the government. Romero served us a refreshing local tea.

"Here is a draft of the agreement specifying the terms we agreed to over the phone. There are some blanks to be filled in, provided that your group is in a position to produce the money." I spoke a little too fast. "Alex, please translate so we don't have any confusion over the provisions concerning funding and services." Alex looked through the document and read aloud in Spanish. Romero nodded each time Alex asked him if he understood.

I turned to Alex. "Be sure to repeat each line of what I'm about to say in Spanish. We must get this signed and the required funds made available as soon as possible."

Speaking slowly, watching Alex translate, I made a list of the key points: "In order to make the championship fight happen here, Video Techniques will produce the event and broadcast live from the arena. We will provide all the television equipment and the personnel to install the ring, the lighting, and the blue canvas. You will provide everything else. We will expect help from your building crew to install the new microwave system in order to reach the satellite uplink. All these additional services must be provided at your government's expense. You will also be responsible for the airline tickets, hotel rooms, and meals for George Foreman and Ken Norton, their trainers and managers, and for the members of my staff." I took a breath.

"We need your communications minister to cooperate with us and coordinate the installation of a complete telephone and telex system operating for the world press. All of this has to be ready, tested, and operational three days before the weigh-in." I looked at Alex as I spoke.

Alex said, "I am sure that all the points you are making are being fully understood by Romero."

"*Venga conmigo,*" Romero said. Alex leaned over to me and said, "We're going back to his office to complete the deal."

It took six hours to finalize the terms and execute several copies of the agreement. We had to get the approval of the lawyer for the Venezuelan government.

"All set, Alex?" He nodded. We drove back to the airport and waited there through the night. I grabbed the first flight back to New York at daybreak.

It was less than thirty days since I had signed the contracts with Foreman and Norton. We were able to get the money and the production happening in accordance with the terms specified.

The letter of credit, funded by El Poliedro, showed up in Video Techniques' bank account within five days after I returned to New York, just like it was supposed to. A big sigh of relief. It was time for a press party to announce the heavyweight championship fight between Foreman and Norton scheduled to take place at the new arena in Caracas, Venezuela.

CHAPTER 6
ALI-FOREMAN: WE CAN DO THIS!

February 1974

"Our VP is waiting in your office. I let him stay there. He arrived yesterday. He said he had no one else to visit here in New York," Karen said as I walked in one morning.

King was sitting at my desk. "My man, can you speak Spanish yet?" he asked.

"Fluently," I joked. "Enough to get the deal done."

"When are we going to hold this fight?" King asked. He wanted to see if there was any change in his plans.

"It is scheduled for March 26."

"Now is the time to line up Ali and get Foreman to sign on for the next title challenge." Don said as he rolled his eyes up to heaven, which indicated to me that his plan was becoming a reality. "Maybe we should contact Herbert Muhammad now." He was thinking out loud trying to envision the groundwork that was needed.

"Don, if you're able to speak with Herbert, try to get a sense of their level of interest."

"Even if Foreman beats the shit out of Norton, it's going to be tough to get George to agree to the next bout with Ali."

"I'm not so sure about that. A championship fight with Ali would pay him more than five times what he is going to earn against Norton," I replied as I watched Don's eyes roll around.

"Who could you talk to—right now—about financing Ali's attempt to take the title from Foreman... how could you get the money on the table right now?" King asked me.

"There are a couple of people who would like to lock up this fight." I told Don that Jack Solomons had repeatedly expressed interest in the Ali-Foreman championship bout.

"Has Solomons told you how much he has got behind him?" King asked.

"He has called me several times and wants to set up a meeting with Leroy Jackson. He told me that he has $7.5 million to be divided between the two fighters. But we would have to show up for the meeting with both agreements signed." I had been traveling back and forth between New York and London to market the license rights for the broadcast of the upcoming championship.

King jumped up and paced around my office. "I'll talk to Herbert about getting a commitment from Ali and you talk to Solomons and see what we can put together." King was eager to move the Ali-Foreman event forward even though we were still a month before the Foreman-Norton fight in Caracas.

I had no trouble reaching Solomons in his London office the next morning but he did not seem interested in the UK rights to broadcast the Foreman-Norton fight. I started shopping the fight to other promoters and wound up in negotiations with a guy named Richard Saul. Saul told me he had the money available and wanted to pay $140,000 for the UK broadcast rights.

I decided to give Solomons one more shot before I made the deal with Saul. King was back in my office listening to my side of the phone conversation.

"Jack, I have had several meetings with Richard Saul and

his company. I am coming to London again soon to close the deal on the distribution. I know you initially didn't seem interested in the exclusive rights, but I wanted to give you a chance to match any offer that was on the table. You made money on the Foreman-Frazier fight, why aren't you interested in this fight with Norton?"

"I have the money committed for the Ali-Foreman title fight, you schmuck. Don't you understand? I told you this before," Jack hollered back and I held the phone up so King could hear it as well.

"One more time, Jack. How much have I got to work with? What is the amount to be divided between Foreman and Ali?"

"Get over here to my office as soon as you can. I have a film company that will put up anything we need. But don't come without the executed fight contracts in your hand!"

I put the phone down and looked at King.

"Hey man, we can do this," he said, almost as if he truly believed it for the first time.

"I have to set up a press conference to promote the story about Foreman's second title defense. Once we get this story in the newspapers, I am sure Ali will want to sign an agreement to be Foreman's next challenger, if he wins. Or if Norton beats Foreman, Ali will fight Norton." King and I were in complete agreement as to how to reach Ali.

"That should get to Foreman's ego. And Ali's ego… hell, he thinks he can destroy Foreman." King was ready to advance Video Techniques' position as a boxing promoter.

I called the Angels into my office before King left. "Work with Shelly Saltman to set up a press event at the Plaza Hotel so we can announce Foreman's second title defense against the handsome film actor and ex-Marine, Ken Norton… you get the pitch, girls?"

As King walked out of the office he said, "As soon as this is out in the papers, I will call Ali and Herbert and tell them that we are ready to go with the agreement for Ali to fight whoever wins in Caracas."

The fight was scheduled for March 26, 1974 and we had to secure global distribution before the event happened to insure we would turn a profit. International media visibility was a key factor in securing the license agreements. A world-class press party triggers worldwide news placement.

The ballroom at the Plaza was filled with newspaper sports writers, TV announcers, and sports radio personnel. Our PR consultants, Murray and Bobby Goodman, were taking care of the sports writers while Shelly kept the top executives of the major television networks happy.

"Murray, what do you think? Will Foreman knock out Norton in the first or the second round?" a radio commentator asked.

Everyone in ear shot of that question laughed. An executive from HBO to whom we had sold the live rights from Jamaica grimaced and added, "That Foreman championship fight from Tokyo lasted less than one round! Not good for television."

HBO was worried about taking on another Foreman event, not knowing how it would affect the revenue earned by their new pay-per-view division. They were hoping the fight would go at least a few rounds.

Part of our job at the press conference was to make sure the sports writers left the Plaza knowing plenty about Norton's boxing background. I hoped the sports writers knew enough about Norton to believe he could hold his own against Foreman. His tall, six foot three inch frame made for a powerful punch despite his unconventional boxing style. Most of the writers had covered Norton's stunning twelve round upset by decision against Ali, on March 31st, 1973. After that loss, Ali had fought Norton again the following September and won by decision. By the time everyone left the press party, they had a complete picture of Foreman's and Norton's ring record. People left exchanging their predictions of the outcome of the fight.

Shelly called me aside. "See that fellow over there, says his name is Richard Saul. He came in from London early this morning to attend the press conference." Shelly pointed to a man standing by himself across the room. I told Shelly that I knew who he was and that I had spent some time with him in London trying to sell the distribution license for the UK.

Setting my champagne glass down on the nearest white table cloth. I rubbed my hands together, blew in my fist, and walked across the room. I extended my hand. "Richard, where have you been?"

"Hank, we haven't finished our deal yet," Saul responded, "We want to obtain an exclusive license in the UK to show the Foreman-Norton fight on closed-circuit TV in theaters in London.

"Tell me a little bit about your company," I asked.

"We are similar to Video Techniques and would like to discuss future events we are planning to show through the new closed-circuit broadcast network in all major theaters in the UK. Then we want to do a joint venture with Video Techniques to license the Foreman-Norton fight."

"Did you bring the $140,000 letter of credit with you as we agreed over the phone?"

"It will be sent to you as soon as I return to London. I have to look at the fighter's signed contracts before we can commit the money," Saul said.

I walked Saul over to my office which was only a few blocks away. He sat with me at my desk and read over the signed pages of the Foreman and the Norton agreements.

"You know, Richard, I have an offer pending from Jack Solomons and Mickey Duff. If you can't send the letter of credit immediately, you will have to tell your investors the fight will go to somebody else." I was watching Saul's hands holding the two agreements. They started to twitch.

"Don't worry, Hank. The funds will be in your bank within the next couple of days." I sent him off with a farewell pat on his large shoulders.

CHAPTER 7
A WALK IN THE PARKING LOT

February 14, 1974

Our press conference yielded three full days of global news coverage about the Foreman-Norton fight.

King wasn't at the press party, presumably because he was busy following up on the talks with Foreman and Ali. We had spent only a few hours together after I returned from Venezuela and I wanted to make sure he had seen the press stories.

"OK Don, who are you going to call now that the news is out?"

"I think I should get a hold of George and talk to him first," Don offered.

"Yeah. Jack Solomons, Jarvis Astaire, Jack Kent Cooke, Bob Arum, and I think Perenchio are all trying to get Foreman and Ali under agreement to fight. You need to turn up the heat."

"Tell George we have offers through Telemedia, offshore, for three or four million on his contract. That's a lot of money above what we're paying him to fight Norton. Since we've lived up to all the terms on this deal, maybe he will commit to the Ali fight now for the three or four million." I was anxious to hear what Don thought he could do.

"What about Ali? Did Herbert indicate what it would take to get him on board?" I asked.

"Hank, Herbert told me that if you want Ali to sign now, you should mail him the contract covering a total of $5 million with some cash up front and the rest paid with letters of credit like you are using for these other fights."

"Maybe we can get both of them to sign an agreement with Telemedia. That would give us a few days to raise the cash they want up front." I was trying to figure out how we could move in quickly and seal the deal before somebody like Jack Kent Cooke made his offer with millions and millions of Canadian money.

Two days later, King called me late at night eager to share some progress. "Foreman will sign before Ali signs provided we give him $200,000 up front."

"Let's work it this way. Tell Foreman that his contract with Telemedia will pay $5 million for a championship fight with Ali. That it will be $200,000 more than we have agreed to pay to Ali."

"What do we say to Ali and Herbert?" King asked.

"We tell Ali the same thing, that we are paying him $200,000 more than we are paying Foreman!"

"OK, OK, my man, send the agreement to Herbert and I will tell him that Telemedia will pay the up front money shortly after Ali signs the contract."

"Call Herbert and tell him we will send the agreement by express mail." I hoped that we could get Ali to sign the agreement right away before we would be pushed out by one of the other groups trying to do the same deal.

At 11:00 that evening Don called me from California. "Foreman said he will work with us, but I really have to talk him through the terms first. He's training now for the Norton fight and I have to talk to him face-to-face to draft an agreement similar to the one you drew up for the Norton fight."

"Where do you want me to meet you and Foreman?" I asked King.

"He's training at a motel in Dublin, California."

"Where the hell is that?"

"You gotta get out here tomorrow afternoon. I will meet you at the motel where Foreman is staying. Bring the contract with you," King said.

I hoped this wasn't going to be a repeat of the last round of negotiations with Foreman—no-show after no-show. But, what the hell. It was worth a shot to see if we could get Foreman to sign on for what would be one of the highest-profile heavyweight championships ever.

"Karen, get me on a plane to Oakland and rent a car." Timing was very critical and I hoped that Dublin was at least within a hundred miles of the airport.

I found the motel with some difficulty and settled down at the bar to wait for Foreman to go over the new agreement.

King walked in. "My man Hank, you got here alright? I have to pick up George and see if he'll go over this with us."

"It's been a long trip. Here's the agreement. Get George to sign it as soon as you can. It says that we're going to pay him two separate payments of $100,000 well before the fight. I left the timing blank. That should make him happy. And if we get Ali to sign we will have to produce an additional $200,000 up front cash for him. That's a total of $400,000. I have no idea where this money is going to come from."

"You gotta get Solomons and his backers at Ladbroke to fund the letter of credit and the cash, if I get the contract signed." King looked worried.

"Go pick him up, Don, and let's see what happens." I was exhausted.

King took off and I went back to my Jack Daniels in the small motel bar. This could be just a waste of time. Maybe I should focus my attention on the production and distribution of the fight in Caracas.

An hour and a half went by with no further word from King. "Have you seen a big black guy around?" I asked the front desk manager. "His name is Don King."

The manager didn't look up from his paper work. "He came in a little while ago and asked me for a couple of pieces of paper." I figured the manager was just blowing me off.

"You got any idea where he is now?" I tried to be cordial but I really wanted to hit the bell ten times to get him to look at me.

"Two big black guys are walking around and around in the parking lot." This time he looked up from his books.

"Are you being cute?" I was getting sore.

"No sir. Just look out the front door and you can see them walking around the parking lot. One has his arm around the other. They've been doing that for at least fifteen minutes. Maybe his car doesn't work."

Maybe the manager wasn't being cute after all.

I stuck my head out the door and saw King strolling in circles with his arm around Foreman, exactly the way it was when he walked up the aisle of the National Sports Arena in Jamaica. I went to the bar and ordered my fourth Jack Daniels.

King found me later still at the bar. "I'm driving Foreman back to his training camp," he said as he handed me three blank pieces of paper, one signed a third of the way down the page, one signed in the middle, and one signed way down at the bottom, all by George Foreman.

"Foreman spoke with his attorney. This is the address and telephone number of the law firm." He handed me a scribbled note. "Foreman told his attorney to make whatever changes that are necessary in the agreement and type a new copy of the document making the last paragraph line up with one of the signatures on these blank pages."

I was stunned. "Does that mean George has signed the

contract?" It was unusual that someone would enter into a multi-million dollar agreement signing blank sheets of paper that later become the last page of the contract. King had convinced Foreman that signing the contract at this time would make him a lot of money.

The next day, I had a meeting with Foreman's lawyer in San Francisco. It was good to see Dick Sadler there acting on Foreman's behalf in the negotiations. We worked out a few details and then Telemedia de Panama and Dick Sadler executed the contract. It ended at the bottom of the last page next to one of Foreman's signatures, dated February 14th, 1974.

A second agreement, similar to the one we just signed with Foreman, was sent to Herbert Muhammad in Chicago for Ali to sign. I called Herbert and told him Foreman and Dick Sadler had signed the contract for the fight. We were on track for the next defense of the heavyweight title.

"Where are you going to stay tonight?" Sadler asked me. It was getting late and I had not made a hotel reservation.

"I didn't know it was going to take us so long to get this wrapped up."

"Come home with me, Hank, and stay at my house. We'll hang out there and wait to hear from Herbert. You know that the agreement only holds together if Ali signs agreeing to fight George." Dick seemed very tired.

"You know if Foreman loses to Norton, then the contract disappears and any cash we have given to George has to be returned to Telemedia," I said, trying to keep him uneasy and worrying about whether or not they would receive the money.

We looked at each other knowing that the deal was not really done. I sat down at the piano in Dick's living room and started to pick out some old tunes with my left hand while holding a Jack Daniels in my right. Dick took his sax off the stand and filled in the melody.

Take my lips
I want to lose them

Take my arms
I'll never use them

Your goodbye left me with eyes that cry
How can I go—

Somewhere in the middle of "All of Me" we heard the phone ring. Herbert and Ali had signed the agreement.

CHAPTER 8
A STAY OF EXECUTION

In my office, following a morning flight from San Francisco, I rang back Jack Solomons as soon as it was 9:00 a.m. in London.

"Hi there Jack, I'm home from a quick flight to the west coast and I have two fight contracts in my hand: one signed by Muhammad Ali and the other signed by George Foreman. Of course, it only holds together if George wins his fight with Norton."

"How the hell were you able to do that? Everyone in the boxing business has been trying to get that deal done." He sounded surprised.

"Never mind the details. I'll fill you in later. Get on the plane and come over here so we can arrange for the transfer of about ten million bucks including some cash we need right away," I told Solomons.

Jack remained surprisingly quiet. He was not quiet very often. Normally he yelled in the phone similar to Don King.

"Jaaaaack? You told me the last time we met in your office

that you had a commitment from Ladbroke's for $7.5 million. If that is in place, then we have to get the rest of the cash right away." I started to worry. Normally, Solomons would have bolted out of his office and jumped on a plane while we were still talking. Something wasn't right.

"Jack, you and Arum, and a lot of other people tried to get Ali to sign an agreement to fight Foreman for the title. You couldn't get it done. The bottom line is none of you could get them to meet in the ring. Don King and I have the fight under contract." I finished my pitch to Solomons to make sure he and his moneymen were available to meet my terms.

Solomons started to yell into the phone again. "Bring the contracts and get over here. Let's sit down and work this out." I felt better. He was back to his usual self.

"Jack, I need to know the funds are available right now." I hollered back.

"We have the dough. Come over here with the contracts and we will pull this together."

"OK Jack, but if we can't get this done in less than two days, Telemedia cannot keep the fight contracts in place and Video Techniques will lose the ancillary rights." I cringed at the thought of having to fly to London again. I was dead tired from traveling and I did not want to get back on a plane.

"We'll let you know where I am staying. I'll be on the next flight available." I hung up with Solomons.

"Karen, get me a round trip to London on the earliest flight possible in order to get there by sunrise. And get a room for one night in one of the hotels where I usually stay." As I gave her these instructions, she handed me a list of the telephone calls that had come in while I was on the other side of the country.

As she walked out of my office, Karen looked over her shoulder. "Hank, you're nuts."

On the overnight flight I was able to doze. I settled into the Grosvenor Hotel and was ready for my meeting with

Solomons.

I called Solomons at 10:00. "Jack, when are we meeting?"

"How about this afternoon and I'll bring the money guys who are in the film industry," Solomons said in a calm voice.

"Who are these guys? You know I can't play with this deal too long."

"Stop worrying. Ladbroke could only go for $7.5 million but these movie producers can go for the whole $10 million and some cash."

Solomons set the meeting time at 4:00, which I thought was pushing the limit in order to get the deal done in time. I was increasingly worried whether I would be able to arrange the cash and keep the contracts alive. Then there was the issue of the letters of credit, both of which would have to be delivered to the fighters after the Foreman-Norton fight, if Foreman won and retained the title.

That reminded me of the unfinished Richard Saul deal. I called Saul. "Richard, you were supposed to send out a letter of credit for $140,000 for the UK rights. Where is it?" I asked.

"It will go out in a couple of days," he said.

"Richard, I'm in London. I'm at the Grosvenor Hotel. Why don't you come over and we'll have lunch?"

"Why are you here?" He seemed jittery.

"I didn't come to see you. You know we did an agreement with Jack Solomons's organization for the Foreman-Frazier fight. He's talking to me about a championship bout with Muhammad Ali," I briefly explained.

"Hank, you know I want that fight as well. Why didn't you offer it to me?"

"Why don't you produce the letter of credit for $140,000. Then we'll talk about doing some bigger things? If Solomons doesn't come through, I will talk to you about the Ali fight."

"If I can see you tomorrow, we will talk more about that."

It was 4:20 when Solomons arrived with two neatly dressed

men who looked like twins in their identical suits and shirts, clearly the uniform of the London banker. One was a representative from Ladbroke and the other from the film company. A third short, sloppy guy who looked like he was right off Miami Beach accompanied them. His name was Marx and he was never introduced to me. Solomons remained quiet while everyone read the contracts with Telemedia de Panama. I explained that we had the right to sell the ancillary rights in the UK, as well as seek the investment group to provide the $10 million plus cash that was needed for Telemedia to move forward under the agreement with both fighters.

"How many theaters do we have in the UK?" the film company guy asked. I thought it was odd that he did not know how many theaters there were in the UK.

"What would you charge for theater admission to see this championship fight on this so-called closed circuit… whatever that is?" the other suit asked.

"How much revenue would be generated?" the mysterious Marx asked.

"Who is going to provide the $10 million?" which was the most important question from my perspective. "Who will act as the funding group and become part of the enterprise with Telemedia?"

It became obvious that Solomons had not provided these men any of the information I had faxed over two days prior. I looked at Solomons, but he wouldn't look directly at me. Despite our previous working relationship, he wasn't giving me assurances or responding to the questions I was asking. An hour and a half later, after I presented all the information I had available, Solomons and his cronies left.

For hours the next day I tried to reach Solomons and finally got him on the telephone. "For Christ's sake Solomons, we were supposed to close a $10 million deal. Who the hell were those guys?" I asked, even though I knew the answer before it came.

Solomons spoke quietly; he was hardly talking at all. "I'm sorry Hank. Ladbroke pulled out and I was looking for another group that could put up 7 to 10 million dollars. I thought that these guys could do it."

"So a commitment with you and Ladbroke is not really a commitment. It's just a bullshit conversation that wastes time and puts our agreements with Ali and Foreman in serious jeopardy," I spewed back at him.

Solomons whispered, "I'm sorry, Hank."

I hung up and sat there on the bed looking at the phone for a long time. I picked it up again and gave my vice president a call.

"Don, this is Hank. I just got my answer from Solomons."

"Hey man, so we're in business, right?" Don chuckled.

"No, we're screwed." I wasn't chuckling. "Jack did not have a real commitment from Ladbroke. It was all bullshit."

"Oh man, you've got to find a way out of this. I talked our way into these contracts. We have to pay them a couple of hundred thousand dollars each in the next few days, otherwise the contracts will go up in smoke. I'll never get Ali or Foreman to sign anything ever again if this deal goes down. I'll lose all my credibility." Don sounded devastated.

"I'll come up with a way to get around this, Don. I have no choice but to think of something."

I decided to take a walk to clear my head. It was pouring rain outside and the streets were fairly empty except for a few umbrellas here and there. I had a big, big problem. The future of my company was on the line.

I didn't know my way around the London streets. I was in such despair that I just wanted to disappear so that no one could find me. I wanted to escape. I didn't need anyone screaming at me that I was full of shit for claiming I had the Ali-Foreman deal done. I had no idea how I was going to pull this off.

I turned down a block I had not been on before. I was

completely soaked and started to wonder in which direction to walk to get back to the hotel. As I passed a beautiful brownstone building, the light caught a brass plaque on the wall; the kind you don't find on brownstones in the United States. It read Hemdale Films.

The words on the plaque rang a bell in my head and pulled me out of my dreary state. The name of the film company, Hemdale, was one I had encountered before. The head of Hemdale, a man named John Daly, had talked to me less than a year ago about figuring out a way to show their films as pay-per-view in small hotels in the UK.

"Shit," I suddenly recalled, "This guy John Daly told me that his father was a boxer."

It was late in the afternoon and beginning to get dark. The rain had not let up. To myself I thought, "What if I ring Daly's bell? Maybe the office is still open and he's still there. At the very least someone could tell me the way back to the Grosvenor Hotel."

I sloshed up to the big door, turned the knob, and walked in. The building had been built as an expensive society residence years before and later turned into an office. It had a gorgeous broad staircase leading up to the second floor.

"Can I help you sir? You look rather damp. Is it still raining outside?" asked the pretty receptionist with a bit of a giggle.

"Is John Daly in?" I asked.

She knew he was in but she didn't want to say yes until she knew who I was.

"I'll see if he's in. What is your name, sir?" she asked.

"Tell John my name is Hank Schwartz. He knows me and I am sure he wouldn't mind spending five minutes with me."

She dialed her phone and in a few moments John Daly looked down over the stair railing before disappearing again. I didn't know if I should take off my soaked rain gear and start drying off my glasses or get ready to leave. There was complete silence at the receptionist's station for at least two more minutes.

The receptionist finally got a ring and smiled over to me. "Go right upstairs, Mr. Schwartz. You can leave your wet things down here."

I smiled back. "I don't know if he's going to want to spend more than five minutes with me, so I might as well remain wet." I walked up the beautiful staircase.

"Come in, Hank. It took me a moment to remember that I knew you and that we had a conversation a little over a year ago." He extended his hand.

"Yes, we did. It's called pay-per-view today in the US and you should continue to work on that, John. But that's not the reason I dropped in." I took Daly's hand and we stood locked in our handshake for a moment as he tried to figure out why I had come off the street, soaking wet.

"John, give me five minutes and I'll tell you why I dropped in." I sat down in the chair he offered. "First off, I remember that your father was a boxer, and a good one as I recall."

Daly's face lit up. "So, are you here about boxing? Something about my father?" he asked.

"I'm here to see if you're interested in investing in the upcoming George Foreman-Muhammad Ali championship fight."

Daly popped out of his seat and immediately reached for my dripping wet rain slicker and pulled it off my shoulders. Finally —the reaction I was looking for! I felt better already.

"Absolutely, Hemdale would be interested in making an investment in that event, if it's really going to happen. Do you have it under contract? Or are you just looking for a dry place to get out of the rain?" He joked.

"I have a commitment from Jack Solomons and Ladbroke for five million dollars for each fighter," I lied, "but I remembered that you were always interested in the entertainment business and especially sports."

"That's a lot of money, Hank. Let me take a look at those

contracts."

"We need some cash up-front to meet the terms of the agreements and letters of credit to pay the fighters after they fight for the championship."

"Well, Hemdale would certainly be interested in putting up some of that money in order to be involved. Let me take a look at the agreements."

"If you're really interested, why don't you get me a cab to take me back to the Grosvenor, wait for me here, and I'll come back with the agreements for you to look at."

"That'll be fine. Do you mind if I ask my attorney to join us? Assuming we can meet before they turn off the electricity?" I learned that sections of London lost the electrical service at a particular time each night due to an energy distribution problem. But Daly seemed interested so even if it meant only getting the up-front cash to hold the agreements together, I didn't mind working in the dark.

"No problem, John. Get me a cab and I'll come back with the agreements."

It was dark when I returned. Hemdale's attorney and a co-director had joined John in his office. We sat around a conference table reading the agreements by candlelight. I found myself answering a barrage of questions.

My mind was still in overdrive and I conjured up a vision of the French gendarmes in the 1700's signing execution orders by candlelight. "Off with his head," pronounced an imaginary authority in the flickering light.

"Why is Telemedia de Panama the promoter on the contracts with the fighters?"

I explained the legal problems that Foreman was having.

"Where are you planning to hold the championship bout?"

"We haven't selected a site yet. It could be in the United States. It could be in the United Kingdom or even in the Coliseum in Rome." I was reaching for anything.

Daly's eyes lit up when I mentioned the Coliseum. I didn't know whether the Italian government would even let us set up a ring in the middle of the Coliseum and do the television uplink from there. But I had always thought it was a very romantic idea to hold an event in the middle of the ruins that were once the site of the battles between the Roman gladiators.

"Don't you think that the ruins of the Coliseum would be a terrific historical setting for two great, modern gladiators? And using technology that was only invented last year?" They were amused by the thought but I was just trying to hold their interest. Daly still looked charged up about the idea.

During the intervening period, Daly had been stepping in and out of the conference room and I wasn't sure what to make of that. But after he came and went for the third time he said, "Hank, let's draw up a simple agreement between Telemedia and Hemdale that my attorney will draft so that Hemdale has a piece of the pie. I just talked to my partners in the US and we're in a position to fund the letters of credit after they see the agreements and buy into the deal."

"John, when you read the Ali agreement, you will see that we need some up-front cash. We have to pay each fighter $100,000 in cash for their training and other expenses and we have a very small window of time to do this and keep the agreements valid. The reason that I didn't complete a deal with Solomons is because he couldn't come up with the cash." I wasn't going to tell him that Solomons was full of shit.

"You said you are going to New York tomorrow morning? I will see you there in a week so that we can meet with my associates who are ready, willing, and able to issue the letters of credit," Daly told me as his attorney drafted a simple letter of intent.

"John, I need the cash now. You read the agreements… the first cash payments have to be made within a few days. They signed the agreements February 14th. I am up against the wall."

"If Telemedia will sign the contract with Hemdale tonight,

then when you get back to New York in the morning, you can go to the office on Park Avenue and see my US president there. I will tell him to draw the checks for you on the spot."

A stay of execution… possibly?

"John, you can see that I signed as the legal agent for Telemedia de Panama on both of the fighter agreements, so I can sign the contract between Telemedia and Hemdale," I said, trying to hold back the outburst of relief as I put my signature on the letter of intent.

CHAPTER 9
THE FINANCING FAILS

The next morning, still early in Cleveland, I woke up King. "Hello Don. I'm back in New York."

"Hey Hank, you got the cash payments for Foreman and Ali covered right? What the hell happened with Jack Solomons?" King asked, half asleep.

"Solomons is full of shit! I had to make the deal with someone else—a film company called Hemdale. At least they can get the cash to Telemedia quickly and we can pay Foreman and Ali tomorrow." That really gave King a jolt.

"Man, I got to deliver the motherfuckin' cash *today?*" King reverted back to his ethnic speak.

"You're gonna have to use your powers of persuasion, Don. Explain to them that everything is under control, we just need a few more days before we can send the first $100,000. There is no way they could get a comparable agreement in place overnight with $5 million cash upfront for each of them. Get them to give us a couple of more days." I tried to put a positive spin on what he had to do.

I knew Ali did not want this deal to go bad because it was his best shot at a comeback for the title. Foreman couldn't jump into another deal because Dick Sadler and Leroy Jackson took forever to get anything done. I was confident we could buy another day.

"I have a letter of intent with a public company approved by its chief executive," I continued. "I'll fax you a copy if you want to look it over. This afternoon we will make arrangements with Hemdale's New York office for the wire transfer. We'll pay Foreman and Ali in the morning."

"OK, it looks like we got the cash covered. What about the letters of credit for the ten million?"

"John Daly, the head of Hemdale, called his US partners while I was in the meeting with him in London. These guys are the owners of United Artists Theaters, Loews, and RKO and I think they distribute Hemdale Films in the US. Daly is close to their top executives and told me that they were ready to fund the letters of credit." If I could get the first $200,000 wired out from Hemdale today, then everything would be on schedule and I could keep the deal together.

"Man, go get the money," King drawled again.

"John Daly is flying over from London and I'm meeting with him and his partners here in New York on Sunday. Talk to Foreman and Ali and assure them that everything is proceeding according to plan."

King called me the next day and told me he had gotten Foreman and Herbert Muhammad to agree to a slight delay on the wire of the $100,000. My meeting at the Hemdale office on Park Avenue went well and Daly authorized the wire transfers. I still had to get the second $200,000 and the letters of credit taken care of within the next twenty days; no later than March 15th.

Despite my faith in Daly, I was concerned prior to the

meeting. Boxing fans would be willing to pay a big-ticket price to see the live broadcast delivered directly to theaters, but the distributors might not clear enough of a profit over and above the $10 million out of pay-per-view revenues from their theater network. They would not put up ten million bucks unless they could make back twenty million on their investment.

They knew their business better than I. It was a good sign that the executives were flying into New York on a Sunday when they could be playing golf.

On the morning of the meeting, there was virtually no traffic on Park Avenue. I arrived at the Hemdale office and had to bang on the glass front doors until a maintenance worker let me into the building. The executives from the theater networks had been meeting for an hour prior to my appointed arrival time, making decisions among themselves.

I distributed copies of the contracts with the fighters, the agreement between Hemdale and Telemedia, and other supporting documents. I listened to the executives' carefully crafted terms describing the duties they had decided to undertake and how they intended to slice up all the revenue and earnings that would be due to Telemedia and Video Techniques. They didn't seem to understand that Hemdale and Telemedia had already entered into an agreement which specified who would do what and how revenues were to be allocated. They wanted to renegotiate all the terms. Hemdale had brought the film executives into the deal only to discuss the $10 million plus the cash investment. The film executives wanted to eliminate Telemedia de Panama and Video Techniques from the entire transaction.

"Gentlemen, Video Techniques has a contract to produce, televise, and distribute the Ali-Foreman fight worldwide. We have no intention of turning over those rights to you and ending up with zilch. You understand?" I assumed they knew what zilch meant.

Even after I said that, Daly and the theater executives

continued to talk among themselves as if Hemdale had all the rights and I was completely out of the picture. Since they didn't respond to any of my questions or statements and ignored everything I said, I got up, collected the documents, and walked out of the conference room without saying another word.

As I approached the elevator, Daly came running down the hallway. "Where are you going, Hank?" he shouted after me.

"John, I'm getting the hell out of here. I'm going back to my office. These theater network executives are trying to craft a deal that will screw both Hemdale and Video Techniques. They think they have the money for the letters of credit and they can rewrite the terms we agreed to in London. You should have offered them my business plan so they could see that they would get their investment back plus a fair percentage of the earnings. Instead, they came up with a deal that is totally unacceptable. They want 100% of everything above the $10 million. That is no way to do business and you should know that too." I furiously pushed the elevator "down" button.

"Hold on, Hank. We got $200,000 in this deal already and a commitment to put up some more money whether Foreman beats Norton or not," Daly said as he held the elevator door open.

"Let me talk to another group that is aware of our need for the $10 million to fund the letters of credit. Let's see if I can find a guardian angel on this deal."

I reached over and lifted his hand off the elevator door, allowing the doors to close. "Forget about the theater networks," I said. "It will never work, not even for your company, John."

When I landed in the lobby, I found the maintenance guy and got him to let me out the front door. I took a walk down Park Avenue. My only choice was to start working to secure the letters of credit. I had fewer than fifteen days to get it worked out and not lose the $200,000 Hemdale had put up, even though Daly deserved a poke in his ass.

CHAPTER 10
ACHTUNG! A TRIP TO PARIS

I had no choice but to go back to my UK contacts—Solomons, Jarvis Astaire, and Jerry Perenchio. I had to make calls across the Atlantic even if it was Sunday. I was not able to reach anyone. I finally went home very discouraged.

My private phone at home rang late that night. "My name is Fred Weymar," the voice said in a deep, guttural German accent. One of Alex Valdez's European friends had given Weymar all my numbers.

"Herr Schvatz, I can arrange for your Panamanian company the full $10 million, maybe in Deutsch Marks or Swiss francs, as well as the cash you need up front for the championship fight. Do you want to meet with me and see if we can work something out?"

"When can we meet and how fast can you put a deal together?" I only had a few weeks left according to the terms of the agreements and I wasn't looking for any more empty promises as the hands on the clock ticked toward failure.

"Herr Henky," Weymar said trying to be friendly, "I know that you need to fund the letters of credit. I am a business advisor for a country that used to be occupied by Belgium."

"What country is that?" I asked.

"It used to be called the Belgian Congo and it is now named the Republic of Zaire. It has a leader who is a big man with a lot of money. His money is everywhere in the world but mostly in Switzerland." Weymar was speaking my language and I was anxious to continue the conversation.

"Why is this leader interested in putting up the money for a fight to take place in this country—what is it called? Zaire?"

"The head of Zaire is Mobutu Sese Seko and he wants the world to consider him a major leader and an icon for all of Africa."

"OK, how does that connect to boxing?" I responded.

"Mobutu wants to stage this championship fight as the world's most important sporting event and he wants it to happen in the stadium in his capital, Kinshasa." As Weymar hit on all the important points on his side, I began to reconsider staging the fight in the ruins of the Coliseum in Rome. That now seemed totally nuts. But this new idea—holding the fight in a stadium in a little known country in Africa, run by a dictator nobody ever heard of—also seemed totally nuts.

"Herr Henky, I want you to send to my office in Bermuda a breakdown of the money that you need, how it will be used, and when it is supposed to be transferred to your company."

I knew I couldn't go forward with the theater network that Hemdale brought to me and I thought it might be even worse to get the letters of credit out of an African country, but at this point I didn't have any options. It was worth a try.

"OK Fred, I will send you the information tonight but you've got to call me back right away."

By this time it was very late. Within the hour there was another call from Weymar. "OK Herr Henky, I've got this approved. Come to Paris. Joining us will be a couple of interested parties, Raymond Nicolet and Mandunga Bula Nyati."

I wasn't completely convinced yet that this deal had promise and I needed more information. "If I come to Paris, what will we be able to accomplish? And who is Nicolet and the other guy with the strange name?" I asked.

"Nicolet represents a Swiss company called Risnalia Investment, which is owned by Mobutu. Most of Mobutu's money flows into that company. Bula lives in Belgium and is the representative for our President, Mobutu Sese Seko. Bula is the foreign minister of Zaire and he speaks six languages. These men are ready to sign a contract with you." Weymar sounded positive.

I agreed to meet with Weymar in Paris. I waited until early the next morning to call King. I wanted to bring him with me on the trip to help at the negotiating table.

"Don, it's taking me a little longer to get the financing in place but we have an appointment set up in Paris with representatives from an African country called Zaire. That's the only funding group on the front burner, so we've got to make this work."

"Man, you'll get it done. You'll get it done. But you've only got three weeks before Foreman fights Norton in Caracas…"

It took less than a week to set up the meeting in Paris. The timing was becoming critical. I had to get back to Caracas to set up the television equipment and here I was on a plane to Paris. I was in yet another city on a whirlwind itinerary that was taking me to the corners of the earth. I was within inches of pulling off one of the most amazing fights in the history of boxing.

Fred Weymar had arranged for me to stay at the Lancaster Hotel where the meetings were going to be held. The Lancaster is a small hotel located on the Rue de Berri, about five blocks below the Arc de Triomphe. The hotel is not an imposing structure and is a rather old building buried among larger, more modern architecture which spills over from the Champs Elysée. When I looked at it from the outside, it seemed to be a delightful piece of the Old World nestled within the hustle and bustle of modern Paris.

As I walked through the canopied entrance, I entered a small yet beautifully appointed lobby. I felt like I might see Audrey Hepburn draped on one of the art deco chaise lounges in a little black dress and an enormous hat, a single diamond accenting her long cigarette holder.

Weymar, a big man over six feet tall and wearing heavily-rimmed glasses, was there instead waiting to greet me.

"Hello, Fred. So glad to meet you. Thanks for arranging my stay in this charming hotel."

Weymar gave me a European-style hug, stepped back, and looked around. "I selected the Lancaster because of its old-fashioned charm, fine food, and most importantly, it's one of the few hotels in Paris that has an international telex machine so we can communicate with the rest of the world," Weymar explained. "I've been in contact with Monte Carlo, Munich, and Zaire to set up the basic framework of the deal we are about to put together. Let me take you upstairs to the suite reserved for you."

I walked into a spacious sitting room which contained a white and gold filigreed baby grand piano. The bedroom was huge and lavishly decorated with three of its walls covered in mirrors making the room look even larger.

"Hank, we are going to have our meeting in the front room of your suite. You're going to meet an interesting cast of characters."

CHAPTER 11
A BRAWL AT BARCLAYS

Weymar was an impressive businessman who made a wicked vodka martini. He could effortlessly transition between speaking English and German, and he was also competent in French. He seemed to be highly respected for his business judgment by the other individuals who joined us. When the cast had assembled, we entered into serious negotiations.

It took two days for my staff to get the low down on Weymar and send the details to me through the international telex at the hotel. We learned that he was actually born in Garden City, Long Island. He had been a member of the US Nazi Party, served in the US Army in Korea, married a German girl when he was stationed in Germany, and renounced his US citizenship to become a German citizen.

We also dug up information on his professional background. Weymar had been involved in some high-stakes financial transactions and was a part of one of the leading European stock brokerage firms before becoming a business adviser to various foreign corporations. I pieced the rest of the story together while watching him during the negotiations. He drank a lot of vodka and tackled every problem by strutting around the room and shouting in German *scheissen* which I knew meant "shit."

Mandunga Bula Nyati, whom everyone called Bula, was also an amazing linguist. He was fluent in German, French, and Russian, as well as English and two of the languages native to Zaire: Lingala and Swahili. He was also a big guy, standing eye-to-eye with Don King.

As we started to talk about the Ali-Foreman championship fight, it became obvious that Bula was committed to bringing the fight to Kinshasa. Bula gave us some background on the capital. He told us it was formerly called Leopoldville, when it was part of the Congo, and that there was a history of frequent name changes as foreign governments moved in and out of control.

I learned that Bula had belonged to a political party that was in opposition to Mobutu when the dictator seized power. Mobutu, however, was clever enough to grant amnesty to his political foes. Because of this wild card move, and because of Bula's talents and knowledge of the world outside of Zaire, Bula was appointed emissary for the Zaire government for special international projects. But, because his loyalty was suspect, he was not allowed to reside within the country he represented. Bula, therefore, lived in Belgium for the most part. He was in total support of bringing the championship fight to Kinshasa, and went so far as to suggest that it would be important to the history of his nation as it struggled to define itself. As we continued the conversation, Bula arrogantly dismissed capitalism and made it clear that he did not like businessmen from the United States.

"Don, keep your ego in check with Bula," I whispered. "Try to get him to be a little more business-like and focused on getting this deal done through Weymar."

I had asked John Daly to join us in Paris since Hemdale had already put up a significant amount of cash and was in a position to provide the additional funding we needed to market the ancillary rights.

At the conclusion of the negotiations, Telemedia assigned its promotional rights in the fight to Mobutu's Swiss company Risnalia Investment. Risnalia was to issue three letters of credit the day the contracts were signed. Two letters of credit for $4.8 million each were made out to Foreman and Ali to be paid immediately following the event. The third letter of credit, in the amount for $150,000, was drawn as an advance to Video Techniques to cover its production expenses. To make everything work correctly with the offshore company, I had to carry the letters of credit back to the United States and deliver them to the fighters.

King and I met Bula at the Paris branch of Barclays Bank to pick up the letters of credit. We sat across the desk from the bank's manager, a delicate little white man who did not seem to be enthusiastic about dealing with customers who were both black and from somewhere other than France.

Bula was there to receive the letters of credit and hand them over to me when we all signed on the dotted line.

"Our Bank of Kinshasa has sent to Barclays Bank sufficient support documents for your bank to issue the letters of credit. What is the obstacle? Why have we not completed this transaction?" Bula asked after we had been kept waiting for hours, his anger growing every time he inquired. The manager refused to deliver the letters of credit to Bula. Bula looked as if he was going to execute the Barclays manager who kept smiling and saying "no" to whatever Bula said in any language.

"Don't tell me what to do," the manager snorted at Bula. "This is not your bank. You cannot tell me how to conduct business with my customers."

As the hours went by, the stand-off wound into a volatile silence.

Near the end of the afternoon, the manager turned to King and said, "You understand that this is not your bank. You cannot tell us that we're supposed to issue any letters of credit today, for whatever reason. I don't have to explain anything to you."

Bula was becoming increasingly heated and the tension in the room was accelerating. I turned to him and said, "Bula, if these letters of credit are not issued today and we go home empty handed, then the contracts that we are ready to sign with Risnalia will be void—the whole deal will blow up."

This was probably the wrong thing to say at the time. It added fuel to the fire. Bula exploded and started cursing in every language he knew. He jumped out of his chair kicking it backwards. He reached across the manager's desk and grabbed him by the throat. He jerked the little Frenchman to within striking distance and the two of them fell to the floor in hand-to-hand combat. They fought like they were going for the championship title. I could not help but observe the bank manager had a powerful left jab, but this was no way for a client to be treated.

"What the fuck is going on?" King looked at me and yelled as Bula and the manager rolled around on the floor.

"Let's get them apart before Bula kills this guy," I hollered back.

We ran around the desk and pulled Bula off of the little Frenchman to stop him from strangling the Barclays manager before we got the letters of credit. I tried to calm everyone down.

"Bula, take it easy. We can find another way around this."

King was desperately trying to restrain Bula while I helped the manager to his feet. His nose was bleeding but that didn't deter him from screaming racial slurs. "You niggers get out of this bank." Now *I* was ready to punch the guy.

I grabbed King and he grabbed Bula and we got the hell out of there before anyone could call security. I was afraid we were all going to get arrested.

Once Bula calmed down he told me, "Go back to New York with the signed contracts and I assure you that Barclays Bank in Manhattan will get those letters of credit to your office within a day."

I looked at King, who rolled his eyes up to heaven, as he always did when he was at a loss for words. We were both stunned from the incident. As we left Bula and walked back to the hotel King asked, "What the hell just happened?"

"Doesn't look too good, Don. After all we have been through… to get this far and have it all blow up."

"Hey man, I've gotten to know this guy Bula a little. I think he's the kind of guy that if he tells you it's going to happen, it'll happen."

"But I don't know why it didn't happen here. Maybe the Bank of Kinshasa didn't send them the right documents or the proper authorization…"

"I think if Bula tells us it's going to happen, it'll happen." King repeated this again and again as we walked through the streets of Paris.

"You think he would've killed the manager if we hadn't pulled them apart?" I looked at King.

"Forget about it, man," Don mumbled.

I decided I better execute the contracts and get out of Paris before Bula transferred his anger to me or Telemedia.

When I got back to New York the following morning, Barclays Bank on Park Avenue had left a message with one of the Angels that the letters of credit had been issued and were waiting to be picked up.

I called Bula, who was back in Belgium, to tell him that the letters of credit had arrived. He was no longer angry. He calmly explained that the executive of the Barclays in Kinshasa had not sent the supporting documents to the Barclays in Paris because he had been in a hotel room with his girlfriend in the middle of the working day. His replacement had sent the required documentation following the arrest of the former bank executive, under the direction of Mobutu. He would rot in jail somewhere outside of Kinshasa.

CHAPTER 12
GEORGE IN A FUNK

March 1974

After so many false starts and broken promises, I had finally put together the Ali-Foreman championship. Unfortunately, there was no time to waste celebrating this impossible accomplishment. Once we got the letters of credit and sent them by overnight delivery to Foreman and Ali, it was time to leave for Caracas and get back to work on the Foreman-Norton fight. It was going to be difficult to bring the crew together, fly my equipment into Venezuela, and set everything up in the short time we had to get it all done.

I arrived at the airport in Caracas with the production team two weeks before the fight and shifted gears back to television. "Take me directly to the El Poliedro arena," I told the taxi driver in the best Spanish I could manage.

The drive into Caracas was an eye-opening contrast to the fashionable streets of Paris. Looking out the grimy windows of the taxi I saw thousands of makeshift shacks built against the mountains. These living conditions revealed the unrelenting poverty in this country. After working the business side of my brain in the comforts of the fancy suite in Paris, it was back to reality. I tried to think exclusively about the production at the newly built arena. Not being as fully prepared as I would have liked to have been, I began to make a list of all of the potential problems.

"Wait here for me while I do a quick run through the stadium," I instructed the taxi driver. I had only visited El Poliedro once during my last trip.

El Poliedro was still under construction and there didn't appear to be much progress since my last visit. The sound of the construction workers yelling over the whining of the power saws echoed through the space. The bathrooms were still boarded up, which was unfortunate because I really had to take a piss. I assessed the condition of the facilities and realized we had to get the situation under control. I couldn't find a location designed to handle the installation and wiring for the TV equipment and no platforms had been built for the TV cameras to be mounted on. This driver, unlike my friend in Jamaica, followed my instructions and waited for me outside. He dropped me off at the Hilton Hotel where I tracked down Juan Berrara, the cameramen I had used in Jamaica.

"Juan, there is no broadcast equipment to lease here in Caracas that is up to our quality standards. Most of this country's TV studios are ancient. To deliver a television broadcast on par with what we did in Jamaica we're going to need to find some state-of-the-art equipment and bring it here. Any ideas?"

"Maybe you could lease one of those mobile units from the US. If you could arrange to fly it here, I think we have enough time to get it all hooked up," Juan said. This was a very expensive approach, but it appeared to be our only option.

I started calling the Air Force bases in the United States that used air transport planes to move large vehicles internationally. On the tenth call I got the 152nd Air National Guard Base located near Reno, Nevada.

I was told that Captain Sawyer was the head transportation officer and that he could help me out. "Let me talk to Captain Sawyer, please."

"Hello Captain, I need to move a 40 foot mobile television production studio from Florida to Caracas, Venezuela. Perhaps you can advise me how to do that," I stated, while Juan sat beside me with his eyebrows raised.

Captain Sawyer answered, "You can check out one of the local shipping companies and get it on one of their regular ships that runs from Miami to the port nearest to you. From there they can load it onto a truck and transport it by road."

"That won't work because we need this TV studio in Caracas right away. Doesn't the Air Force deliver large vehicles to our foreign bases by plane? I'm trying to figure out how our country moves military equipment quickly and which type of aircraft is used for the job."

"We use a plane to move equipment for the Marines. That is usually done on a Hercules C-103A. You can slide a full trailer into its cargo hold but you have to take it off the wheels so it will fit."

"Who would I talk to, to arrange this?" We were getting somewhere!

After forty-eight hours of communication with the firm that owned the Hercules and a group that rented a mobile studio, we had a plan in place for the Hercules to fly directly from Miami to the Caracas airport. Along with the mobile studio they were shipping a new lighting grid that would be hung over the boxing ring for "hot" lighting which would give us a better picture.

I redirected my energy to building a television studio in one of the rooms in the stadium that had not been completed. The government had given me access to some local workers so we used them to set up the ring's blue canvas, build and install platforms for the cameras, and to get an electrical generator set up for energy back-up.

The Hercules landed with surprising grace for an aircraft of such magnitude. The Venezuelan Customs Division met the plane to look over the cargo as it was unloaded. The cargo door of the Hercules slowly cranked open revealing the 40-foot trailer with a completely operational television production studio built inside it. Juan helped me keep the government staff working together as they slowly moved the mobile studio out of the belly of the beast. They had to remount it onto the truck wheel frame, which had arrived separately on a standard flight. The whole operation looked like a mother whale giving birth to a calf.

After the mobile studio was driven to the stadium, we had everything in place within eight hours.

Now that the technical aspects of the fight were covered, I focused on the fighters. Back at the hotel I ran into Bill Caplan, a public relations consultant brought to Caracas by Foreman's crew.

"Bill, when are we going to have a press conference with the media guys?" I asked.

Bill assured me, "Everyone, including the fighters, should be here within the next two days. Once we make sure that Foreman is comfortable in the hotel we'll figure out a time for the press conference." Foreman didn't have the most charming disposition and sometimes didn't want to talk with reporters. "We better make sure he's settled before we schedule," Kaplan continued.

Our contract with the Venezuelan government specified that fifty hotel rooms and meal accommodations be provided to the fighters, their managers, and their training staff for up to one week before the fight. Foreman and Norton, along with their respective entourages, arrived on time and settled into their hotel rooms at the Hilton. The journalists were beginning to arrive.

Foreman and Norton were both training at a facility within the stadium at alternate times. Foreman looked listless even though I knew he had been training in California before leaving for Caracas. Dick Sadler, who knew me well by this time, came to me to voice Foreman's complaint that the media were chasing him for a story.

"The bottom line, Schwartz," Dick said confidentially, "George is not going to be happy staying at the Hilton. There are too many newspaper guys around. He's got these personal problems and he wants to be left alone. You gotta get him into another place where he won't be bothered. He came here in good shape and I want him to stay relaxed."

"OK Dick, I'll see what I can do. We've got a press conference coming up and I want George to put on a good show." I had to do something to ease the distractions so he could focus on the fight.

The Venezuelan government was cooperative and agreed to move Foreman to a smaller hotel called the Avila. Trees concealed the entrance to the Hotel Avila, which was situated on a shady street in a quiet neighborhood at the foot of the Avila Mountain. It was the perfect hideaway for Foreman, since the only people around him there were the group that traveled with him. The relocation did not do much good, however. Foreman was still moody and uncooperative with almost everyone. He refused to talk to anybody. He had Leroy Jackson deal with the people who were trying to speak with him. Leroy kept telling the press, "He's still resting."

It was my job to trouble-shoot the technical and the non-technical issues that came up. I had to get Foreman out of his funk. His sparring partners were all killing time hanging out in the lobby. I found Foreman sitting next to the hotel's swimming pool staring down at the ground. A couple of journalists with local connections had found his hideout and were looking for a comment. Foreman's huge presence made everything at the hotel feel small.

"George," I said directly to him, "You've got to snap out of this and give these press guys something to write about." He didn't respond.

Finally, Foreman looked up and answered some questions from a local reporter who was hovering around the pool hoping for an exclusive. Foreman added a couple of remarks about why he was a great champion, why he was fighting Norton, and how easy the fight with Roman had been. The air smelled great with the aroma of flowers and there was a macaw squawking between the few quiet words that Foreman spoke.

It took two more days for Foreman to finally come around. He made time for a small number of media guys who found the Avila now that the word was out and sat around the hotel lobby with him and the sparring partners. He told them how he had grown up in Houston, one of seven children, all supported by his mother, who had been a cook. He talked about her strong influence on him and that he was still close with her. He discussed the vandalism, robbery, and purse snatching he was involved in as a kid. He said that although he was a total failure growing up, he always had faith that he would become something. In his mind this happened when he knocked out Smokin' Joe Frazier and became the champ.

"I want respect. I'm George Foreman," he concluded.

"How do you feel about boxing and being the champion?" one of the Miami writers hollered out with the macaw still squawking in the background.

"I'm in boxing because I found that's my job but there's a lot more important things in life than the next bout or beating another man."

Foreman wasn't really giving the newspapermen much to work with. They started drifting off after they realized they were not going to get anything out of Foreman that was useful. After a while no one was even listening to George.

Everyone eventually cleared out of the lobby and the piano player in the bar finished his last set. Dick Sadler sat down and took over the keyboard. He was happy and smiling. He played "On the Sunny Side of the Street."

Grab your coat, and get your hat
Leave your worries on the doorstep
Life can be so sweet...

Norton, in direct contrast to Foreman, didn't give the newspapermen any problems at all. He was a good-looking guy and moved with a certain charismatic cockiness. He wore his shirts open and sported flashy medallions around his neck, bracelets on his wrists, and huge rings on several fingers. He had a great muscular build and the machismo swagger of a film actor. Norton became the darling of the boxing press.

Norton also sparred energetically. Locals could pay the equivalent of 50 cents and enter the El Poliedro arena to watch the fighters train. Norton put on a great show and during one of his sessions, his trainer grabbed the microphone that our technicians had just wired into the audio system and broadcast a blow-by-blow report on Norton's shadow boxing in the training ring.

When Foreman showed up to train he slathered his face with a protective coat of Vaseline and the boxing he did with his sparring partners was ungraceful and couldn't compare with Norton's fluid motion. Foreman would sometimes shove his partners around in the ring like a schoolyard bully. One day Dick ran up the stairs, when Foreman sat down between rounds, to tell him not to put so much heft behind his punches or he was going to hurt one of his own sparring partners. It was not nearly as good a show for the spectators as a Norton training.

When it was time for a post-training press conference with Foreman, the newspapermen entered a small room in which Foreman was lying on a table set up in the middle of the room. He lay motionless with his eyes closed, offering no greeting to anyone. A reporter asked, "George, you're about to defend your championship title. How do you feel physically and emotionally?" The writer held his tape recorder close to Foreman's mouth waiting for the answer.

"I've been training now a couple of months so I don't have to feel anything," Foreman mumbled. That was all he had to say at the press conference. This is not what a promoter is looking for in his fighters.

"Don, you think we could call Herbert Muhammad to get him and Ali to come to Caracas before the fight goes on?" I asked King, who had been pretty quiet since he arrived in South America.

"Hey man, that's a good idea. I'll get him on the phone and see what I can do," he answered.

Ali arrived at the Hilton two nights before the fight. A noisy crowd gathered around him as he moved slowly through the lobby and a young, local girl jumped on his back and hung on as he made his way to the elevators. Ali spent the next day in the Hilton lobby with the sportswriters. He was talking to everyone, clowning around, signing autographs, and posing for photos with his arms around anybody, as if they had known each other for years. He made sure to bad mouth Foreman every time a journalist interviewed him about the match that was likely to follow.

Foreman continued his surly behavior with the press.

The general press party in celebration of the fight was held in the Champagne Room on the fifteenth floor of the Hilton. King arrived at the party theatrically dressed and I grabbed him before he walked into the Champagne Room.

"For Christ's sake, Don. This is not a press party for you. It's about the Foreman-Norton fight and where Video Techniques will go with the Ali-Foreman championship fight if Foreman wins this one. Please don't wear all that jewelry and talk so loud about how you got the fighters to sign." I was trying to get him to stop pitching Don King and focus on sending the Foreman-Norton fight from the corners of the ring to the corners of the earth.

"OK OK, man. I'll tone it down." The vice president of Video Techniques looked disappointed.

"We should announce the Ali-Foreman fight now so that the world knows about Telemedia de Panama and Video Techniques and who we are in the boxing world," I suggested.

Before King and I could strategize how to announce the upcoming title fight, Ali strolled into the room. He was accompanied by Gene Kilroy, who was introduced as Ali's business manager, and Angelo Dundee, Ali's trainer. This trio came into the Champagne Room and announced that Foreman had signed the contract to fight Ali on September 30th in Kinshasa, Zaire for the heavyweight championship title. We got upstaged at our own press conference.

After King saw this, he elbowed his way through the crowd and maneuvered to Ali's left. I hoped he would introduce himself as the vice president of Video Techniques.

"That's because George Foreman is going to keep the championship when he beats Ken Norton," King bellowed over the noise of the crowd.

We could not have made a better move with the media. Bringing Ali to Caracas to watch Foreman fight and then to release the story of the Ali-Foreman follow-up fight was a public relations dream come true.

For more photos, visit **http://www.cornersofthering.com/gallery.html**

CHAPTER 13
KNEED AN EXCUSE

March 26, 1974

We continued to have trouble with Foreman. The last two days before the fight, Foreman and Dick Sadler had several meetings with the local boxing commission. They wanted to select their own referee or have one provided by the WBC or WBA. The Foreman organization did not want to fight under the referee provided by the local boxing commissioner. We were blindsided because the referee issue had not been brought up during the negotiation of the contracts.

At 10 a.m. on March 26th, the morning of the fight, I was sitting outside the commissioner's office with a half dozen sportswriters waiting to learn who was going to referee. The door flew open and Foreman limped out like he had a problem with his left knee.

I could not believe what I saw. I grabbed hold of Dick Sadler by his shoulders. "What the hell happened?" I asked.

"He hurt his knee in the ring with one of his sparring partners," Dick said while looking me straight in the eyes. "He can't fight today."

As soon as the press heard that statement, they ran out of the room to get in contact with their editors to tell the world the championship fight was canceled. It felt like a grenade was dropped in the middle of the room.

I grabbed Dick by his shirt and pulled him closer to me. "You can't do this," I yelled at him nose to nose.

He looked weary and fretful and said, "If we get a WBC referee, maybe George's knee will heal in time."

"Are you crazy? Why didn't you straighten this out ahead of time… before George had his injury?" I was still yelling in his face.

"Man, you know I got no control over Foreman's brain or his body."

I stopped yelling and started speaking in a whisper. "How about the strings on his purse, Dick? You got any control over that? He's got to return the money that was advanced—in cash—immediately, like tomorrow!" I screamed. "Are you clear on that Dick? DO YOU HEAR WHAT I'M SAYING, DICK?" Spit was flying.

"I know, I know," Dick said.

"Either get a doctor to tape up Foreman's knee or go back inside and let the commission know that they're about to lose a lot of fuckin' money. Go Dick, one or the other." I pushed him away from me.

"I'll try Foreman again. Then I'll go back in and see if I can get the commission to appoint the *right* referee." He went back to the Hilton where an impromptu meeting for the media was being held.

The room was full of skeptical writers waiting for the full story. Dick took the microphone.

"Foreman hurt his knee and the commission's doctor is going to check it and maybe—"

He was interrupted by a shout from Angelo Dundee, "Is

the fight on or off?" Dundee shouted. Ali's camp knew that if Foreman didn't fight Norton, the multi-million deal they had for the next fight would go out the window.

"That decision will be made by the commission doctor today." Dick was like a politician with the microphone, never answering the question.

"You shmuck, this is the day of the fight," another member of the crowd yelled.

"Tell us yes or no!" screamed another.

"The commission doctor is in charge of that problem. It's out of my hands. It's just a sprain anyway."

"Quit jerkin' us 'round. Get a referee," Dundee shouted again.

"What is the recommendation of Foreman's own doctor?" This time it was my own voice yelling the question.

Doctor Hacker, who was part of Foreman's group, stepped up to the microphone, "My recommendation is to wait and see."

The press conference broke into chaos.

"Hold it! Hold it!" Dundee shouted. "Let's give a hand to Dick Sadler for being a super salesman."

"He's a super shmuck salesman," flew in from the crowd.

Dick struck the table and hollered, "God damn it. Everybody in this room knows that a fighter can't fight if his leg is messed up."

Everyone poured out of the conference room, running to get hold of their teleprinters or telephones to report the breaking news to the rest of the world.

I walked over to Dick, who was left standing alone, sweating and mumbling to an empty room. I did not grab him by his shirt this time. I simply said, "Dick, it's just past noon. Go back to the commissioner and make a deal on the referee… or I'm going to shove your fucking saxophone up your fucking ass."

CHAPTER 14

NORTON GOES DOWN IN 2

I decided to sit outside the office with all the sports writers while the commissioner met with Foreman's handlers. I had more money in the game than anybody else in the room. I prayed that the fight would happen according to schedule. The Venezuelan government was paying Video Techniques with a letter of credit. If Foreman did not fight, my company stood to lose all the money we had invested in bringing this championship fight into the new arena. The financial consequence to me was make or break.

It was unsettling when I didn't see the commissioner enter the office for the meeting. The only people in the meeting with the fighters and the managers were two high-ranking military officers and Jerry Izenberg, an influential sports reporter from the United States. I sat on a wooden bench with my heart racing.

It was 3 p.m. The fight was only a few hours away. Dick Sadler and George Foreman left the meeting room. Izenberg exited the commissioner's office next. I grabbed him as he walked by.

"Jerry, what the hell happened? Is the fight going to go on?

I've got to know now."

"Hank, you won't believe it. One of those men wearing the military uniform claimed to have been appointed by the Venezuelan *Presidente* as the new boxing commissioner. He was fully equipped with side arms when he sat down between the two camps. Everybody argued for a half hour trying to agree upon the selection of a referee who would protect both fighters under local rules. They forced Foreman to admit that his knee problem had disappeared.

"So? Did they reach a decision?"

"Oh yeah, they did. But only when the colonel took his revolver out of the holster, laid it on the table in front of him, and said, and I quote, 'I am the boxing commissioner. I select the referee and if everyone wants to leave this room in any way other than in a casket, you will accept the referee that I select.'"

"What?"

"Hank, that's the truth."

"Unbelievable. And did the colonel decide on a referee?"

"Yeah, Jimmy Rondeau. He just has to be approved by Raymond Velazquez and the fight is on." Velazquez was affiliated with the World Boxing Commission. Personally, I didn't care which referee was going to be in the ring as long as the fight happened on the agreed upon date and time originally scheduled so that I could be paid under the terms of my letter of credit.

"Foreman wasn't limping at all when he walked out of the meeting," I said to Jerry. "See ya ringside."

Jimmy Rondeau brought the two fighters together in the middle of the ring. I picked up a close view in one of the cameras of Foreman's ferocious face as he glared at Norton during the referee's instructions. I hoped that the ex-Marine would be able to stay away from Foreman's bull-like charge at least for a few rounds. Foreman had huge power with both hands and a hateful stare that scared the hell out of anybody he faced in the ring. When Smokin' Joe Frazier had gone down in two rounds, Foreman acquired mythic status. He was perceived as absolutely indestructible, even if he had a bad knee.

Bong! The fight began.

"Alright keep camera #2 and #3 on Norton. Camera #1, give me a wide shot of how this is going to start." I gave instructions to the crew while watching the images on seven monitors.

Foreman came out of his corner pushing forward in his usual style and Norton danced backwards to stay away from Foreman's brutal swings. During the next three minutes Norton took a lot of hits, particularly the devastating left jab.

"Camera #1, keep the shot on Norton's face while he sits in his corner and bring in the boom so we can hear what his trainer is telling him to do."

Bong! Round two. Early in the round Norton got pummeled with four murderous right-hand punches.

"Hank, Foreman just landed a big uppercut," Juan yelled through the headset.

"Camera #1, hold tight on Norton." Another brutal uppercut lifted him off his feet and then sent him down.

"Holy shit! We're not going to get a twelve round television program," I shouted to the crew.

"Norton got up on the count of five," Juan shouted back.

"Camera #2, focus on his face," I said, hoping that Norton would shake it off.

Foreman hit him again with another uppercut, knocking Norton across the ring against the ropes. "Norton is tangled in the ropes," Juan almost whispered.

Foreman rushed the stunned Norton and immediately caught him with yet another uppercut. Norton landed flat on his back with his head thumping against the canvas. He got up but he didn't look good.

Foreman hit him with a left and a right and Norton went down again. He could no longer stand up. Norton turned from

Foreman stumbling into the arms of his trainer who had run up the steps signaling Rondeau to stop the fight. This championship bout lasted less than two rounds.

"Camera #3, go in close and take a look at Foreman standing in the corner where Norton went down." I was looking for some type of emotional expression from Foreman.

"*Cabrón*, that *puta* is still glaring at him. Foreman is one hell of a hard-hitting machine," Juan hollered back.

"At least this fight wasn't as short as the one with Roman," was the only positive thing I could think to say to the crew. I wondered how the TV networks that were paying big money to carry what was advertised as a super heavyweight championship would react to the ten minute broadcast of the actual fight.

Ali, who was sitting ringside, shouted colorful but potent insults at Foreman throughout the fight. I hoped Foreman could hear him.

Could I petition the gods of war that Ali-Foreman would last more than two rounds? Or should I be praying to the gods of entertainment? I'm just trying to make a living here, guys.

CHAPTER 15
GETTING THE HELL OUT OF CARACAS

After looking into Norton's dressing room at the arena to make sure he wasn't terribly hurt, I set up a victory party with a select group of US sports writers in the Hotel Avila. Foreman was met with applause when he returned to the hotel, which caused him briefly to crack a smile. He was wearing plaid slacks and a patchwork denim shirt with a matching cap and looked like he was in a good mood.

Once the applause quieted down, Foreman addressed the crowd saying, "My knee was in bad shape but I was alright because I prayed. I think I'm just blessed because when I hit a guy, you can see him crumbling down to the canvas. This was a beautiful, beautiful day."

Then Foreman went to his room and didn't appear again. The press revelers gave their attention to the buffet and to a beaming Dick Sadler. He was at the piano playing "Up a Lazy River" and singing the lyrics.

The lazy, lazy river in the noon day sun
Linger in the shade of kind ol' tree
Throw away your troubles, dream a dream with me.

The room was filled with music, laughter, and a lot of talk. Even though Foreman was absent, King provided some entertainment when he showed up in a sky blue tuxedo and didn't stop talking until he had gone through the entire crowd.

"It ain't me talking. I'm just an instrument for what's coming from on high. I'm just ebullient for what happened here and delighted that my champion did a prodigious job on Ken Norton." King kept pounding on everyone's back so they would turn around and listen. He could express the most words based on the smallest ideas of any man I ever knew.

"Don, sit down." I tugged on his sleeve.

"Aren't you hungry?" his wife Henrietta asked, pulling on the other sleeve.

But he still wouldn't shut up. I started to worry about the vice president of Video Techniques, who talked so much that he was shifting the spotlight away from the champion, the loser, and Video Techniques so that everybody would only look at him. I thought I might be able to stop King from promoting himself by pointing out that it was time to build up the Ali-Foreman heavyweight championship.

"Don, your wife's hungry."

"I'm gonna feed my wife cause I'm hungry too. I wanna go be spiritually revitalized in the land of Zaire." Oy vey!

One of the pretty latina waitresses brought over a telephone that plugged into a wall jack near my table. Norton's business manager was on the telephone. "Hank, we got a problem," he said softly.

"How's Ken feeling? Is he beat up real bad?" I thought he was calling to tell me that Norton was in bad shape and we needed a doctor.

"That's not the problem, Hank. I was told that Romero, who collected the cash from the ticket sales, has disappeared with all the money. Romero, or somebody, has left Venezuela with all the cash," Norton's manager said.

"What?! How'd you find that out?" I was in a state of disbelief.

"Somebody from the government put us under house arrest claiming that we owe them taxes on the money we earned from the fight."

"Hold on. This is serious. Let me see if I can get hold of those guys from the government and see what's going on." I left the press party quickly. King was now talking about the upcoming fight in Zaire. I was happy to see he had reversed his course and was heading down the right track. What the hell was going on with Norton and the house arrest? It was supposed to be easier to work in this country than in Jamaica.

At the Hilton I found out that there had been some drastic changes at the top levels of the Venezuelan government just a few days before the fight. My mind went immediately to the letters of credit. I had fulfilled the terms, but I had one of those gut feelings again. I decided that I better get those funds transferred immediately. Who knew what might happen? I picked up the phone and got through to one of my Angels in New York.

"Karen, did the *Post* or the *Times* carry a story on the fight in the afternoon paper?" I was worried about how my staff could document fulfillment of the terms to get the letter of credit paid.

"The fight happened too late to run the story," she told me. "First thing in the morning, I will go out and get a copy of the *Post* and clip out the write-up about the fight. I will clip it to the letter of credit and deliver it as soon as the bank offices open. I will get our $350,000." See why I call them Angels?

Karen and everyone else in my office knew that we had to put the $350,000 in our account to cover our expenses. If there was anything left over, we made a profit.

Next, I woke Juan. He was exhausted and had gone to sleep early. We had to collect the leased equipment, get it loaded onto the Hercules, and send it back to Miami right away.

"Juan, get the crew together and take the next plane out of Caracas. There has been a change of government in the last few hours. The new regime has put Norton under house arrest claiming that he needs to pay some sort of tax."

"Holy shit," Juan said. "Well, we already got everything back into the mobile unit, so that's taken care of."

"Drive it out to the airport right away. Our Hercules transporter is scheduled to come in tomorrow at 1 p.m. to pick it up."

"Who's going to slide the mobile trailer into the Hercules and take the wheels off?" Juan sounded nervous.

"Come up to my room and I'll give you a couple hundred dollars in cash. When you get to the airport, hire a couple of local guys—baggage handlers will have a sense of how this kind of thing works. You will have to show them the mechanics."

I gave Juan three hundred dollars, which was all the cash I had. "Do everything you can to get our guys out of the country now. We don't want any problems with the new government."

It took me three hours to find the attorney that I had been dealing with who represented the El Poliedro.

"Señor Schwartz, I am so sorry that this happened but it was triggered by one of our own people. Our accountants calculated that he ran away with more than $950,000 that had been paid by our citizens for the tickets. The new government decided that a small percentage of the missing gate receipts should be levied as a tax payment that should be paid by the fighters since it was their 'act' on display in the middle of the ring." This story told me it was the right time to get the hell out of Caracas.

Norton's manager called again. "Hank, we've got to pay them some money for Norton's performance at the arena. I can't get that done until tomorrow morning after the funds are transferred when his letter of credit is paid and we have some money in our account. We're stuck here for another day."

"I can't straighten this out with the new government here. It's a different group than the one I worked with before and apparently they've arbitrarily changed the rules." I had a tough time explaining this to Norton's manager. He did not understand why I couldn't get this resolved quickly and break Norton out of house arrest. I told him that I was sure Foreman had to pay the same tax. I really didn't know if Foreman had been arrested too. I had no idea how he was going to pay the tax because his letter of credit was paid to a bank outside of the United States. I didn't even want to think about it.

Juan left me a message that he had the mobile TV studio parked right next to hangar #3 and that he had paid some baggage handlers to help load the mobile trailer before the 1 p.m. flight the next day.

It was time for me to gather my things and see if the military would stop me at the airport. I took off the feathered hat I always wore and tucked it under the raincoat on my arm. Then I put on a pair of big sunglasses and messed up my hair. Despite my disguise, Ali and Gene Kilroy recognized me instantly when I ran into them at the airport.

"Hi Hank," Kilroy said, sidling up to me as we walked.

"Did you have any problems getting out of the hotel?" I asked him, because everyone knew what Ali looked like.

"A military guy came over to tell us not to leave the hotel until we paid taxes," Kilroy told me.

"You didn't even work here. Maybe they thought we were paying you to make all those comments about Foreman." I was still aggravated with Kilroy and Ali for hijacking the press conference the day before.

"Yeah, yeah. But it's OK. I slipped the guy $200 and he stepped aside as we left the hotel and got into a taxi." This place was feeling more and more like doing business in Jamaica.

I checked in for my flight and boarded the plane back to New York without a problem because nobody checked passports in Caracas. I began to decompress.

As my flight taxied down the runway for takeoff, we passed the #3 hangar. I looked out of the airplane window at the empty space next to the hanger. EMPTY! My stomach flip-flopped. The mobile TV studio had disappeared.

PART 5

THE RUMBLE ON THE ROPES: ALI-FOREMAN IN ZAIRE

CHAPTER 1
GEORGE GETS A DOG, ALI BOLTS

It took me two days to recover from the roller coaster ride of events in Caracas and clear off my desk in New York from everything that had piled up in my absence. Now I had to focus on finding the missing mobile TV studio. Each day it was missing the rental fee had to be paid—which was not a small amount. I got my lawyer, Milt, on the telephone to ask his expert opinion on how the hell I was going to find the damn thing. I was fairly certain it was the only one in Venezuela. Needless to say my blood pressure was in the danger zone.

"Milt, the Venezuelan government tried to collect taxes from everyone after the fight before letting them leave the country. Both fighters were detained. Whoever was behind this sudden tax levy probably caused my mobile TV studio to disappear. They grabbed it and moved it someplace where we're not going to be able to find it. We have already paid for one round trip for the Hercules transport plane to go pick it up. The plane showed up in Caracas but there was nothing to load, so they just turned around and flew back to Miami. We will have to pay for a second round trip once we locate it and get it back to the airport."

"I don't know anything about transporting oversized equipment by air. What do you want me to do?" Milt asked. *What the hell am I paying this guy for?*

"Milt, you gotta get creative. Start with the Venezuelan ambassador here in Washington and tell him how we're going to build up a suit against Venezuela. Tell them we have the power to enforce an embargo on their country or something like that. We'll deflate their currency."

"How the hell did this happen?"

"It has something to do with one of their own people running off with about $950,000 in cash from ticket sales. It was an enormous hit for the new political party and they must be trying to recoup their losses."

Milt had no idea how to repossess the mobile TV studio but he told me he would investigate and try to get it straightened out as soon as possible.

"Remember, every day that goes by we are paying the damn rental fee."

"You have got it covered by insurance, right Hank? Maybe the insurer can help us out?"

"That's a good idea." I gave Milt the contact info for the insurance company and the people we were dealing with in Venezuela. Milt said he was on the case. I knew that this wouldn't be straightened out in a day but I sure hoped that it would not last more than a couple of days.

I had to shift my focus to other matters; I had another fight to put on in Africa.

That night the telephone woke me up at 1 a.m. I always keep the telephone on my side of the bed at home so that it does not disturb Connie when it rings at crazy times in the night. When you're dealing with people in Jamaica, Tokyo, London, Paris, and Caracas, it often rings after we have gone to sleep and I always answer, no matter the time.

"Hey man, this is your VP," King bellowed. "I'm down in Houston waiting for a plane to bring me back to New York."

"How the hell did you end up in Houston? I thought you were coming back to New York." I was opening my eyes and trying to get my brain functioning again. My visual image of Don King was still the powder blue tuxedo and diamond pin that he wore at the press party in Caracas.

"Man, wait till you hear this story."

"Can it wait until tomorrow?" I asked.

"Man, you don't know how close we came to losing George Foreman," King said.

There was a stunned silence. "What happened? Did his plane go down?" I didn't know whether Foreman had almost died or if he just didn't like us anymore.

"We came back to the States on two different planes. My plane stopped at JFK and I had to go through customs. George's plane was continuing on to Houston."

"So how did you get on the plane going to Houston if you were supposed to get off at JFK?" I was still trying to fully wake up and find out where this whole story was going.

"There was a whole bunch of newspapermen waiting to interview George when he got off the plane… but he didn't get off at Kennedy. I knew that Foreman was pissed at us because his people had to pay somebody off so that they could get out of Venezuela. I knew I better talk to him and smooth things over. I did not even pick up my luggage in baggage claim. I went straight to the ticket counter, bought a ticket to Houston, and jumped on the plane with George so that we could talk."

I sat on the edge of the bed and hoped I wasn't being fed a load of bullshit.

"George told me to tell you to 'Go fuck yourself.' He talked with me a lot on the plane to Houston. He said, in no uncertain terms, that he is not going to fight Ali."

"If he backs out of the contract he has to return the $200,000 cash that he got up front when he signed with us," I said, trying to act like this whole thing was a minor detail.

"Hold on Hank… during the trip from New York to Houston I got George to settle down and told him that I would get him anything he wanted to make him happy."

"OK. How did you settle him down?"

"We gotta get him a white German Shepherd, something bigger than a puppy so that it will grow up real quick and be his new best friend—his pal."

"You gotta be kiddin' me… I don't understand this guy. What is he gonna call the dog—*Son, or Brother, or Friend?*" I said facetiously.

"He's gonna call the dog Diego," King said.

"OK, get back to New York and pick up your luggage from the airport and let's talk in the morning. I know a place in California where we can buy the dog and deliver it to George when he's back in Oakland… hopefully, training for the Ali fight."

I slumped back into bed. After all this shit, I had to get some sleep.

Now there were two problems that had to be solved: getting the mobile TV studio out of Caracas and finding a dog that fit Foreman's specifications.

Friday most of the Angels had the day off. Karen was working on a letter to Richard Saul regarding the UK distribution rights to the Foreman-Norton fight. She came into my office and said, "Hank, Herbert Muhammad is on the phone."

It had been a quiet day and there were not too many quiet days on my calendar. I really hoped that Herbert wasn't about to ruin it for me.

"Hello, Herbert. How are you on this beautiful day?"

"Hank. We're in trouble," he said bluntly.

"What?" I really didn't want to hear about any more problems.

"What do you mean we're in trouble, Herbert? Nobody is training yet, how can we have a problem?"

"Ali just took a flight from Chicago to London," Herbert mumbled.

"Herbert, say that again."

"Muhammad Ali got a telephone call at the training camp from a screaming, hysterical John Ali," he began. John Ali was the national secretary for the Nation of Islam.

"Gene Kilroy called me when he and Ali were already at JFK. He told me they were going to Uganda to rescue John Ali. He also said Ali is traveling without a valid passport." Herbert was talking very fast.

"Why in the hell is he doing this?"

"He said he is going to get on a plane to London so that he can take a connecting flight into Uganda and try to save John Ali's life," Herbert repeated. "Hank, I don't know whether I should tell you the rest of the story or not."

"Herbert, there's over ten million dollars riding on this fight. You don't want to piss me off and you really don't want to piss off an African military dictator. If Muhammad Ali disappears, Mobutu and every soldier in Zaire will be after me, Fred Weymar, Don King, and maybe even you. You better tell me why Ali is putting everything in jeopardy and let's see what we can do to turn this problem around." I let Herbert have it with both barrels because I was at the end of my rope and the stakes were very high.

"Hank, you know the country that's north of Zaire?"

"Yeah, that's Uganda. Idi Amin is the dictator there."

"Well, it seems that a few months ago John Ali mysteriously got his hands on some cash... this happened before you and King worked out the Foreman-Norton fight in Venezuela. Shortly after you announced the big Ali-Foreman championship—" Herbert took a deep breath and slowed down, "—John Ali went to Uganda before you completed the deal with Mobutu in Zaire.

John Ali got a large sum of money from Idi Amin because he told him that he could bring the Ali fight to Uganda."

"Herbert, where exactly is John Ali?"

"They have him in a hotel in Uganda under guard in his room. John went there, I think, to return the money Amin paid him after he found out that Ali was fighting Foreman in Zaire." Herbert was clearly stressed. "I think… they're going to execute him or keep him there for the rest of his life." Herbert didn't know what else to say.

"And Muhammad Ali and Kilroy are going to try to get John Ali out of Uganda?"

"Yeah. I think so," Herbert said.

"Shit! If Ali goes over there, they won't let him leave… He won't be able to come home. None of them will get out of the country until they sign a contract to take the fight there. You know the international press is always saying Mobutu and Idi Amin are arch rivals in a power play for Africa. How the hell did this happen?" I asked.

"I didn't know anything about this. Muhammad Ali and John Ali are old friends, going way back."

"What time does Ali arrive in London?" I needed to know, and fast.

Herbert gave me the arrival time, airline, and flight number. I had only fifty-five minutes before Ali got off the plane at Heathrow Airport. I had to figure out a way to get him to turn around and head back to the US—not get on the plane to Uganda.

"Do you have a trusted member in the Nation of Islam in or near London?" I asked.

"How many do you need, Hank?"

"I only need one. But somebody with enough clout that Muhammad Ali will believe what he says…and someone who can reach Heathrow before the plane lands. And I need him to call me immediately," I told Herbert.

My phone rang a few minutes later and a man with a British accent introduced himself and said that Herbert Muhammad instructed him to do anything I requested. I gave the man the flight number and arrival time and told him to meet Kilroy and Ali as soon as they entered customs. I told him that Ali did not have a passport and that the passport agent would probably bring Ali into the custom agency's office. I told my operative we had a confidential message from Elijah Muhammad, the founder of the Nation of Islam.

"It is incumbent that you give them the message before Muhammad starts tap dancing around and gets the authorities to give him a ticket to Uganda. It is imperative that he does not get on any plane other than one that is coming back to Chicago!"

"I understand, what is the message?"

"The message is that the Nation of Islam will arrange for the release of John Ali through its political contacts in Uganda and that Muhammad Ali is to return to Chicago immediately."

The man thanked me for giving him the privilege of delivering Elijah Muhammad's instructions from his mouth to Ali's ear.

"I am leaving right away," the man said, "and I am only thirty minutes from Heathrow. I will ask the customs agent to let me speak with Muhammad Ali confidentially as soon as he arrives and I will do exactly as I am instructed." He hung up the phone.

I knew that Kilroy would help turn Ali around but I had no idea how the Nation of Islam was going to get Idi Amin to release John Ali.

"Karen, here are the telephone numbers for Mandunga Bula in Belgium. Casey, here are the telephone numbers for Mandunga Bula in Kinshasa. We need to find him wherever he is. I've got to talk to him right away," I said.

We located Bula, and I told him that John Ali was detained

and explained that Muhammad Ali was personally trying to rescue him. Bula clearly understood the implications. "Bula, can someone with political influence in Zaire get a hold of the right person in Uganda to get John Ali released?" I asked him.

"There is no question. His Excellency Mobutu Sese Seko will reach Idi Amin directly and will arrange to have John Ali released so he can go home right away."

The assurance in Bula's voice left no doubt that Mobutu would protect his investment. I slammed the phone back in its cradle and looked out the window at the lights of Manhattan.

The close of another day—Foreman is slinging the f-word at me, Ali is in international limbo acting like he's James Bond, I am manufacturing messages in the name of the Nation of Islam, my vice president is a wild man, and the mobile TV studio is still M.I.A. in Caracas.

Jack Daniels, anyone?

CHAPTER 2

AN ARCHITECTURAL RUIN

After working at El Poliedro in Caracas, I knew that the stadium in Kinshasa must be inspected. I had to scope out what needed to be upgraded, acquired, and rebuilt by September. The stadium was old and would be difficult to renovate.

On May 3, I flew from New York to Paris-Orly Airport and picked up a passenger ticket from Air Zaire sent by Mobutu Sese Seko. To my surprise the ticket was there and the plane was on time. At this point I still had no idea what Zaire looked like.

It was dark when I arrived at Kinshasa's N'Djili Airport, which was a very modern facility. A government vehicle was waiting to take me to the Intercontinental Hotel. In the morning another military car was waiting to drive me to the Mai 20 Stadium. I anticipated a project similar to the construction on Kingston's National Stadium.

We approached a large vine-covered structure. I assumed it was an architectural ruin, perhaps a holy place. It sat in the middle of an overgrown field. The driver stopped the car and cleared some brush so that he could open the door. "Bula is waiting for you inside the stadium, Mr. Schwartz."

NO! No! No, no, no… this cannot be the stadium! I screamed inside my head.

There was no parking lot! The area surrounding the stadium would be more aptly termed a "parking meadow." Wading through the heavy brush, I approached the ruin where Bula was waiting. My only thought was *How in hell can I get out of this deal?*

Bula told me that he had been permitted by Mobutu to return to Zaire to help me meet the right Zairian people and to oversee the execution of the rebuilding of the stadium. It was an ironic use of the word "execute," since the Mai 20 Stadium was the setting for the execution of many of Mobutu's political opponents.

"No chance at all of getting this place operational and equipped to handle an event on the scale we are planning. It simply will not happen." This was my initial reaction and my concern got worse as I toured the facility. There were no operating bathrooms, human feces covered the stadium floor, and the concrete bleachers were falling apart.

"Holy hell, this could never be rebuilt in time." Video Techniques and Telemedia de Panama had signed a multimillion-dollar contract, legally binding us to broadcast the heavyweight championship fight—live, around the globe—from this facility. I started to feel ill. Did we have electricity, running water, and plumbing?

Bula interrupted my queasiness, "Schwartz, this is the stadium we use for The Leopards, Zaire's soccer team."

"Bula, we can't use this as a site for any event, never mind a championship fight. It is a hopeless mess. Is there any other stadium in Zaire that can be used?"

"This is the stadium that Mobutu Sese Seko wants to use so

that the citizens of Zaire have good seats to watch Muhammad Ali." Mobutu's primary concern was Ali and not Foreman.

I did not look around any further. After taking a deep breath and a moment to calm myself, I said quietly, "OK, Bula, who do you have helping me with this monstrosity?"

Switching between Lingala, the local language, French, and English, Bula began gathering the team that would work with me to reconstruct the stadium.

Bula introduced me to the crew. "Hank, this is Captain Unyon Pewu, who is in charge of the stadium. Anything you want to have built or changed in this building, he will take care of it for you."

"Does he fully understand the amount of work that needs to be done here? We have five months to get all of this done." Captain Pewu tried to smile and agreed that he would be able to do anything that needed to be done.

"This is Tshimpumpu, who heads the telephone company and the communications systems in Zaire. He reports directly to our Minister of Communications and will be your conduit for anything you need at the governmental level."

"And here is the engineer, Cinga."

"Does everyone on this team speak English?" I asked.

Cinga smiled and said, "Of course, Hank. We built this stadium with French and English speaking engineers from Europe." Secretly, I thought, that must have been over three decades ago.

"OK, the first thing is to clean up all this shit on the soccer field. Then we will go through step by step exactly what has to be renovated or built. Keep in mind, all of this has to be completed by September 1st, before the media and the fighters arrive."

"No prob-lem." they simultaneously responded.

I thought it best not to overwhelm them in this first meeting by asking about all of the telephone, telex, and other equipment that we would need to install.

Because I wanted to get back to the United States as soon

as possible, I worked 18 hours a day for weeks in Kinshasa getting the construction projects scoped out and underway. It was impossible to get status reports from Captain Pewu, Engineer Cinga, or Communication Director Tshimpumpu. It was frustrating and counterproductive. On my way home to New York, I reluctantly accepted that I had to return to Zaire very soon and spend weeks on-site supervising the renovation of the stadium.

Working with the stadium's staff and engineers, I realized that these people had only recently come out from under the colonial reign of the Belgians. They desperately wanted to prove they could accomplish great things without the direction of an outsider. I knew that people from my homeland were regarded as "ugly Americans." Technical people in foreign countries are envious of the American ability to efficiently accomplish things. The Zairian phrase "no prob-lem" was a patronizing way to avoid an admission that they just could not get anything done. The "ugly American" is now the supervisor. "No prob-lem."

CHAPTER 3
PRESS PARTY AT THE RAINBOW ROOM

May 15, 1974

Before leaving for Africa, a call to my public relations guy got him started on the press party which would launch the media coverage of the fight in Zaire.

"Shelly, set up the party for a month from now to announce the Ali-Foreman heavyweight championship fight. I want to hold the press conference in the Rainbow Room at Rockefeller Center. Expect a big turnout, not only from the United States but from around the world."

"That's a good spot. I'll start getting that together right away," Shelly responded.

On the flight home it occurred to me to use African art at the press conference to define the theme. I called Shelly Saltman from my office. "Shelly, is it too late to arrange the press party at the Metropolitan Museum in the African Arts section?"

"We thought of that and tried to get it there but it didn't work out. I guess the directors didn't like the idea. They were concerned that some of the fight mob might not know how to behave around precious African art objects. Instead, we're holding it at the Rainbow Room like you suggested originally," Shelly added. "It's all set for the 15th. We sent out all the invitations and I personally called most of the big media outlets."

"And Shelly, did you arrange transportation for Muhammad Ali and George Foreman?"

"One of the Angels took care of that. Connie sent over some of the art that you brought back from your last trip to Zaire. She also got some pieces on loan from the Tribal Art Gallery." Shelly's background in entertainment was one reason why he was better than most of the PR guys in the fight business.

The press party was held on Wednesday, May 15. When I arrived at the Rainbow Room it looked like everyone who ought to be there, was there. The room had been decked out with wooden statues, tribal masks, drums, and other African art. These had been arranged as a background display so that all the photographs included glimpses of the artifacts behind Ali at the microphone.

I sat on the dais next to John Daly, head of Hemdale Films. Daly was the epitome of elegance. Small and lean with a graceful athletic build. He was the personification of the Irish gentleman with a ruddy complexioned face and curly sandy-brown hair. Muhammad Ali, who was dressed handsomely in a black suit and tie, entertained the room giving his poetic rendition of how he was going to beat the crap out of Foreman.

"Where the hell is Foreman?" I asked. No one had seen him. We all started to worry that he was avoiding the media like he did in Caracas. "Was Foreman invited? Tell me he was invited, Shelly?"

"Hank, come on, of course he was invited."

"Bobby, did you hear anything from Foreman?" Bobby Goodman shrugged. No one knew where Foreman was.

Someone in the press group hollered out, "I guess Foreman didn't think it was worth his time to come. Ali would beat him at the microphone before they even get into the ring." A few members of the media laughed.

"He doesn't punch, he just pushes his opponents down. Ask Joe Frazier," Ali said as he grabbed the microphone, knowing that he had the party's attention. "A real champ don't do that. By not showing up here today, this was George Foreman's first defeat. He defeated himself. He lost a lot today."

While he had the microphone, Ali thanked the head of the Nation of Islam, Elijah Muhammad, for all his teachings and looked around the ballroom.

"Anyone have any questions?" Ali asked.

"What do you think about Foreman's style over the last two fights," one of the newspaper writers called out.

"Can't take nothin' from George Foreman," Ali answered back.

"Then why do you think you will win?"

"Why do I know I'll beat him? A few things are gonna make it happen. One is the power of Allah, who controls everything. I believe I'm in good standing with him. Two is my experience. I'll stay out of George's way for maybe four or five rounds. Nobody has seen Foreman in a good scuffle past the first two or three rounds yet. I don't rely on hittin' power because I fix it so there ain't nothin' to hit," Ali replied.

"George is a dirty fighter," Ali continued, "and I don't mean morally. I mean his style is dirty. I saw him hit Frazier on the back of his head. And he hit Roman when he was down. And he reached over and around the referee to hit Norton on the ropes. That's what I mean when I say dirty." Ali had obviously watched a lot of footage from Foreman's last three fights. "I don't want this kind of dirt in Africa. George won't try any dirty tricks when he sees all them brothers at ringside. That's Ali country."

The back-and-forth discussion went on for another half hour and Ali concluded his remarks by reading one of his poems. When he finished his verbal jabs at Foreman, I stood up to answer any questions about the agreements with Ali and Foreman.

"Why didn't Foreman come to the press party?" a writer asked.

"I don't know. I'm surprised George didn't come."

Ali came over to the lectern and interrupted my brief stint with the microphone.

"I'm not surprised," Ali said, grabbing the mic. "Foreman ain't never been in a fight. He never heard the man say, 'Round 4.'" Ali started his diatribe all over again.

"I'm the people's champ and I will win. Foreman doesn't act like a true champion." Ali did not want to stop now and I had no control over his act.

"Foreman's fight manager, Dick Sadler, didn't want George here. Sadler probably told him that I'll make him crazy by jumping circles around him. If he was here with me, he'd look like a deaf mute." We all laughed at Ali's antics, but in the back of everyone's mind remained the question: why hadn't Foreman shown up?

Ali sat down and smiled throughout the rest of the questions. King took over the podium and thanked Ali for his magnanimous feat. However, because of the way King spoke, nobody knew what the hell he was talking about.

Dick called me later that night. "Someone called Wednesday night saying we had to come to a press meeting in New York the next morning. We would have had to leave Oakland at three in the morning to get there. That's why George didn't come to the press conference."

"That's bullshit Dick, Shelly sent you an invitation and one of my Angels followed up. You just didn't want George upstaged by Ali's showbiz antics and you didn't want to sit through his poetry." I furiously slammed down the phone.

By the next day virtually all of the national newspapers and the network television stations were covering the Ali-Foreman fight. Everyone was searching for Zaire on the map. The fight, now a worldwide story, was scheduled for September 24, 1974. With all this attention and his $5 million on the line, Foreman would show up in Kinshasa. No prob-lem.

CHAPTER 4
NO PROB-LEM IN KINSHASA

Mobutu expected the stadium to hold 100,000 spectators, but when I arrived back in Kinshasa and looked at the recently finished seating, I was sure the Mai 20 Stadium couldn't hold more than 50,000 people. By the end of July the Zairian workmen had rebuilt the concrete bleachers but the communications infrastructure and bathroom facilities were not installed.

I had designed a new roof for the stadium that was large enough to keep wind-driven rain from reaching the platforms that held the TV cameras or the ring itself. It also protected the seats surrounding the ring that were to be occupied by the international media. It was designed to look like one of the thatched roofs that were common in the Zairian villages. It was completed by the time I returned. They had altered the specs in my absence, however, and it was not as large as I had originally designed it. If there was rain during the fight, and it fell in any direction other than straight down, the roof, as they had built it, would not prevent the ring or the surrounding seats from getting soaked.

Mobutu's organization was selling the VIP ringside seats for the equivalent of $250 US Dollars. I figured that the majority of these tickets would go to foreigners who would also need hotel accommodations. "No prob-lem." The foreign visitors were going to stay at local hotels and at the N'Sele government estate. The government was also commandeering a number of private villas, as well as all available rooms at the University of Kinshasa dormitories.

Most of the homes and villas located on N'Sele property were excellent. It was really more of a military compound with small and large houses designed for military officers. The estate belonged to President Mobutu and was situated along the Zaire River, previously known as Congo River, some forty-five minutes north of Kinshasa. Ali and Foreman were going to stay and train at the compound.

On this trip to Zaire, I brought with me my eldest son, Ira, who was on a college break. Ira wanted to see the natural beauty and wild life of Africa. He had gone out on a safari with a young guide while I stayed in Kinshasa to get the stadium operational. I hadn't heard from Ira since he left. His safari was supposed to last for seven days but at this point it was going on twelve. I was worried, but I didn't want to upset Connie.

I got an international line open to call Connie back home. It was 11 p.m. in Zaire and 3 p.m. in New York.

"We'll be home in a few days," I told her. I was planning another trip back to New York.

"How did Ira enjoy the safari?" she asked.

"He's having a great time. In fact, he has stayed out there a few extra days, but he'll be back in time for us to leave," I said. "No prob-lem."

The next day, Ira showed up just as happy as could be. He had great stories about his experiences, including an episode where he walked up to a group of lions and let them chase him back to the Volkswagen bus he was traveling in. I did not tell Connie

Ira's story about running with the lions. I think that's the only time the Zairian statement, "no prob-lem," ever came true.

When Ira and I left Zaire my biggest problem was getting the workmen to buy into the fact that everything had to be completed in time for the fight. "No prob-lem." is all they would say when I tried to instill a sense of urgency. The fight was scheduled for September 24th. The fighters, and their respective entourages, were arriving on September 8th or 9th.

I called Tshimpumpu to ask, "Has the road between Kinshasa and the airport been paved and the potholes filled?"

The answer: "No prob-lem."

"Have the transport buses arrived from Germany?"

The answer: "No prob-lem."

The buses were needed to transport passengers from the airport to the Kinshasa hotels and had been ordered by the Zaire government. They never arrived.

"Are the telexes, phone lines and other equipment that the newsmen need to transmit their stories installed and ready to go?"

The answer: "No prob-lem."

CHAPTER 5
A MEETING IN THE SLAMMER

September 4, 1974

By September 4th we were in jeopardy to complete everything that had to be done. After three months of doing everything in my power to rebuild the stadium and install the communications network, I had to admit we were in a crisis. I knew that if something didn't change we would not be operational in time for the fight. I called a meeting of all the investors, the government representatives, and the managers of the construction projects so I could explain the obstacles we were facing and get a solution in place.

I brought all of the key players around a conference table in London. I invited John Daly, Hemdale's attorney, Bula, Ray Nicolet (representing Mobutu and Risnelia) and several of the local contractors in Zaire. I also invited my own attorney Milton Shermett. I needed the full support of each of these players in order to do what had to be done in the little time that was left.

We spread the architectural plans of the stadium along with sketches of specific projects across the table in my suite at the

Grosvenor Hotel. Coffee and tea were brought up every few hours by room service to keep everyone alert and focused. After a particularly heated exchange with one of the contractors, I explained to Nicolet and Daly that "no prob-lem" in Zaire actually meant "we'll deal with it whenever we damn well please."

Just then there was a knock at the door.

"Are they bringing more of that Indian tea?" someone asked.

I walked to the door with a British pound in my hand to tip the waiter. When the door opened two neatly dressed men were standing there. They were not carrying tea. The pound went back into my pocket.

"Hi guys, who are you looking for?"

"We're from Scotland Yard," one of the men said.

"I'm sorry, we're not giving free tickets for the Foreman-Ali fight to anybody from Scotland Yard." I smiled and turned to go back in the room.

"We are looking for Henry Schwartz of Video Techniques?"

I stopped smiling and motioned for Milt to join me in the hallway. "Milt, they're looking for Hank Schwartz and they're from Scotland Yard."

The officer said, "If you're Henry Schwartz, we've come to arrest you and take you down to the station."

"Who wants me down at the station? Was there a murder or something?"

"No, no, no. You and Video Techniques are being sued by Richard Saul and his company." In my head I ran through all correspondence we had with Saul when he purchased the UK rights to the Foreman-Norton fight. I had no idea where the problem was. Saul was probably just trying to recover some money that he had lost.

"Alright gentlemen, this is Milt Shermett, my attorney. Give him all the documents he needs in order to respond to the allegations in regards to this claim," I turned to leave my guests in the hallway.

"Please Mr. Schwartz. We have to put these handcuffs on you and walk you out to the car."

"Milt, what the hell is going on here?"

By this time all the meeting attendees had crowded around. They found the situation hilarious and acted as if this was a game played in London by Scotland Yard.

"Where are you taking him? We are having an urgent meeting and several of the participants must return to Africa later this evening," Milt argued.

"We will keep you at the station overnight. You will appear in the High Court of Justice in the Queen's Bench Division early tomorrow morning to hear the charges. They will decide if and when they will let you out."

"Holy shit. Getting anything done around here is getting to be a real pain in the ass." I slammed my hand down on the cluttered table. Everyone laughed except for me.

"Go with them, Schwartz. We will follow and continue the meeting at the station so we can get our people back to Zaire," Daly said.

Before leaving with the Scotland Yard officials I told them, "Don't you dare put handcuffs on me and walk me through the lobby of this hotel in front of all these people. I'll walk quietly along with you and get in your car, but no handcuffs." I was getting pissed as hell.

The officers exchanged looks and a few words and finally said, "OK. No handcuffs. Let's go."

I put on my raincoat. "Let's go, guys. We will continue this meeting at the police station but let's please get a plan in place to complete this construction," I said.

They were all still laughing. I quietly entered the elevator, walked through the lobby with Scotland Yard number one on my right, number two on my left and me in the middle, hoping people would assume the suits were my body guards.

We arrived at a modern well-equipped police station. They

introduced the head bobby, who was sitting behind a desk reviewing the documents pertaining to my arrest. Several papers exchanged hands between the arresting officers and the head bobby and they walked me toward a cell.

"Wait a minute. Why are you putting me in that cell?"

"Mr. Schwartz, we have to hold you overnight and bring you to the High Court tomorrow morning. You can straighten out everything then," the head bobby told me.

"The meeting we are having is absolutely critical to the success of the Ali-Foreman fight in Zaire. How can I continue in a prison cell?" A group of ten people including Bula, Daly, and Shermett followed me toward the cell. They were still exchanging ideas as to how this could have happened.

Since the head bobby said he would help me out, I walked into the jail cell without any further objection. The bobby left the cell door open and instructed his deputies to bring a long table into the hallway on the freedom side of the bars. They centered the table in front of my cell door. I sat within the confines of the lockup while my ten "visitors" sat down in the mismatched assortment of dilapidated desk chairs that were marshaled into service. We continued our meeting as if this was a perfectly normal place to hold a corporate "war council."

We had a relatively civilized conversation, for the next two hours with no Indian tea. We put into place an action plan to salvage the millions of dollars that were at risk. Once we had a strategy formulated, everyone left and the cell door slammed shut.

Milt told me as he left that he would come back in the morning and spring me out.

"Sergeant," I called to the bobby, not knowing if he was a sergeant or not, "in the United States legal system we get one telephone call if we are held overnight. How about here in the UK? My wife should know where I am in case she starts looking for me."

"Well, since you weren't brought in here as a customer of one of these young ladies over there," he nodded to another cell that had about six enticingly dressed girls milling around, one sobbing hysterically, "I'll let you have one phone call." He chuckled. Everybody seemed to think this was funny except me.

"Hi Connie." It was about four in the afternoon in New York.

"How are you doing? It's late over there isn't it?" Connie sounded chirpy and I did not want her to be concerned. Plus, I couldn't tell her how I ended up in this mess because, at this point, I didn't know.

"Yes. It's about nine or ten o'clock here. I am tired. I think I'll go ahead and call it a night. Don't call me later." I was trying to dodge the bullet at least for the moment.

"OK Honey. Don't knock yourself out. Get a good night's sleep. Call me in the morning and let me know how it's going."

"Great idea." Yeah, right.

I walked back to the cell and with a click, I was back behind bars. The bunk felt like a lumpy pile of folded cardboard. I did not sleep. I stayed up all night worrying. How am I going to get out of here? How am I going to save this fight?

The fight is taking place in 20 days and here I am sitting in the fucking slammer.

CHAPTER 6
A BANGER BEFORE BAIL

The lowest point came the next morning when a banger, the British term for sausage, was passed through the bars for my breakfast.

About an hour later the door swung open and they took me to the Queen's Court. I rode in the back of a big van, without handcuffs. My fellow passengers were six disreputable criminals, sitting up front. All of them were handcuffed and wearing prison garb. My Brooks Brothers suit, desperately in need of a press, kept my dignity in tact. My toupee had miraculously survived the limitations of the bedding supplied by Scotland Yard.

When I entered the courtroom, Milt was there. The white-wigged judge loudly read the charges against me. The guy who was suing me, Richard Saul, was claiming that he and his company had paid for the rights to distribute the Foreman-Norton fight in the UK, with the understanding that they also had the rights to the upcoming Ali-Foreman fight. This second part was bullshit.

"Milt, who is the guy sitting next to you?"

"I am not admitted to practice in the UK, Hank, so I cannot represent you in the British court. I found you a British attorney who can represent you." That Milt is OK.

"Anthony Leader is going to represent you, get you out of here on a bail bond, and have this ridiculous claim thrown out of court."

"Hello, Hank," Leader extended his hand. "Unfortunately we've got to see this suit through to the end because, in this country, we don't have a summary dismissal process in the High Court of Justice."

"At least bail me out so I can get back to Zaire. How much do we need? I can call Connie and my bank and they will send whatever is needed by wire right away."

"I have already spoken with Mr. Beasley, the magistrate, and he has agreed to grant you the bail for 30,000 pounds."

"Connie will get this taken care of immediately."

"It is not that simple, Hank. In the US, the money for the bond can come from anybody or any source and no one cares where it came from. But here, in order to make bail, English law requires that the bond be signed by not fewer than two British citizens, currently residing in the UK."

"Jesus Christ. Let me think this through a little bit."

"How about the sports writer, Reg Gutteridge? Have you ever been involved with him?" Leader asked.

"Yes, he knows me pretty well. I'll give Reg a call."

"When you talk to him, tell him that he doesn't have to put up the money. All he has to do is sign for the bail. That is quite different from the procedure in the US." Leader was turning out to be a good lawyer. He continued, "They want a UK citizen so that they can arrest that person if you fail to show up and break the terms of the bail."

"All right, get me a phone. Let's see if we can work this through." I called four different numbers and finally reached

Reggie Gutteridge.

"Are you kidding?" he said, laughing uproariously at my predicament. "How could this guy do this to you? I'll be there in an hour to sign off on 20,000 pounds of the bail for you."

"OK now I need a second British citizen to sign off on the balance," Leader said to Milt.

"My father-in-law lives in the London suburbs. He's an older guy but once I explain everything to him he'll be here in an hour and a half," Milt offered.

Leader then turned to me, "OK, if we get Reg Gutteridge down here and Milton's father-in-law and you sign the bail yourself, we're covered by the rules and regulations of the court and you will be free to go."

Leader explained what we needed to do to handle the case Saul had filed against me. He would act as the point man in the UK and start the process. I was beginning to feel a hell of a lot better about getting this suit off my back.

My two signatories and I signed off on the bail. I promised to come back to the UK when the trial was scheduled.

My release came late in the afternoon. I took the next plane back to JFK and decided to keep this crazy 24-hour episode to myself.

On the bright side, Milt told me that he had resolved the problem with the missing mobile TV studio in Caracas. He had worked with the ambassador, who proved to be most cooperative. The tax authorities of Venezuela released the studio and agreed to pay the excess expenses created by the confiscation of the equipment. At least one bit of luck was going my way. Now I know what we pay Milt for.

CHAPTER 7
ALI ARRIVES IN ZAIRE

It took me four hours to get Bob Goodman on the telephone because the lines were still not properly configured to support the traffic that a championship fight would generate. Bobby went to Kinshasa to install the training equipment at N'Sele before the fighters arrived. He had worked with Video Techniques before on three of our international events without any problems. Poor Bobby. He found out quickly that getting things done in Zaire was not like making things happen in the rest of the world.

It was the middle of the night in Zaire when my call finally went through to the PR man. "How is it going?" I asked. "Is all the equipment operational over at N'Sele? Ali and Foreman will be arriving next week and I want to be sure they have nothing to complain about."

"Hank, did you tell this guy Chumpupu, or whatever his name is, that we were arriving with a lot of equipment?" Bobby was now wide-awake.

"We contacted the head of import customs and the hotel to

arrange transportation from the airport. They were supposed to take you wherever you had to go. What's the problem, Bobby?"

Regardless of all the telexes, there was no one at the airport when Bobby and Jack Murphy, the head of my production team, arrived and needed help getting through customs. A customs official looking for a payoff gave them trouble.

"By the time I got the equipment over to N'Sele, I had to install most of it by myself. Some help came from a couple of gardeners that were taking care of the grounds."

Good old Bobby had to take matters into his own hands to get the equipment up and running. But that's the kind of guy he is.

"Anything else I should bring with me when I come back?" I asked. It was clear that the government and their unregulated workforce were not doing us a lot of good.

"Yeah, bring some Bengay. We need it and so will you, Hank. Right now, I need to get back to sleep." Bobby yawned and hung up.

I arrived in Kinshasa on September 8th with a healthy supply of Bengay to satisfy Bobby Goodman's needs.

Ali and his entourage landed in Kinshasa late the following night. Twenty-four Watusi women, dressed in colorful purple plumage, with yellow and green skirts, lined the path welcoming Ali with a ceremonial dance. In the distance there was a chorus of drums and other percussion instruments beating an African rhythm to which the tall Watusis moved in unison. Ali made his way between an honor guard of helmeted soldiers, standing at attention.

Ali with his entourage was greeted at the terminal by a select group of government officials in a room called "His Excellency's Lounge." Ali, accompanied by his mother, Mrs. Odessa Clay, his wife, Belinda, and his business advisor, Gene Kilroy, was escorted out of the airport lounge to the front of the building where a limousine waited.

"Who is the little guy that's walking next to me?" Ali asked. Kilroy shot him a look.

"Be careful Muhammad, that little guy is your translator and he speaks English, French, and the local language, whatever that is. You don't want to offend him." For several years Kilroy had served as Ali's business manager and handled an array of external issues, including cultural protocol.

When Ali and his party exited the airport terminal, in front of the building, overflowing into the field that surrounded the airport, were more than 5,000 Zarois standing quietly. They had been waiting for hours to see Ali. Many had walked for miles. Others had come on battered bicycles and in beat up old cars. Ali was not only a sports icon, but he was also a young, charismatic African-American who represented them in the global landscape.

As soon as he walked out of the airport they began to chant in unison "Ali! Ali! Ali!"

"Are they chanting anything about George Foreman?" Kilroy asked the translator.

"No, no! They only want to see Ali because they think he has been sent by the gods," the interpreter explained.

Kilroy started to laugh. "Why don't you tell them that Foreman is a white man from Belgium?" he suggested to Ali.

"That's great!" Ali laughed and turned to the translator. "How do I say in their language that Foreman is a white Belgem[1]?" Ali was having a lot of fun.

"Foreman est Belgique blanc," the translator said, half shocked because he knew that Foreman was also African-American.

Ali climbed onto a nearby bench and put his finger to his lips, asking the crowd to be quiet and listen to him. Silence rolled over the sea of people. He faced the crowd with his arms reaching toward the night sky. *"Foreman est Belgique blanc."*

---

1 Ali's unique pronunciation of 'Belgian' and 'Belgium.'

As Ali got off the bench and started to move toward the limousine, a new chant grew louder and louder from the mass of people: *"Ali boo-ma-yea. Ali boo-ma-yea."*

"What does that chant mean? What's *boo-ma-yea*?" Ali asked the translator, who was now jumping up and down with joy.

"They are asking you to kill him."

"I feel Foreman is a stranger coming to my home to fight me," Ali called out. The translator relayed the message to the cheering crowd.

As Ali settled into the limousine, with his mother on one side and Belinda on the other, he looked across to Kilroy and proudly said, "I'll be interested in seeing how many of these brothers turn out to greet George Foreman when he arrives."

As the parade of vehicles left the airport, hundreds of people surrounded Ali's limousine and tried to reach out and touch the car carrying the young man who had an iconic significance for them. The unison chant of *"Ali boo-ma-yea"* drowned out all of the airport noise.

Foreman would arrive a couple days later but Ali knew already that he was the spiritual hero of the championship. It was a moment of triumph for Ali, who was energized and strengthened by the experience. Rallying the unqualified support of the people became a crucial factor in his strategy against Foreman. All along the drive to N'Sele, Ali held his hands high in the air, greeting the chanting crowds that lined the road for miles waving torches that shattered the darkness of the African night.

CHAPTER 8

DIEGO FLIES IN FIRST CLASS, GEORGE IS A PAIN IN THE ASS

The next day I got a call from Dick Sadler, who was at the San Francisco airport ready to get on the plane with Foreman and the rest of his group.

"Hank, we're ready to get on the plane, we have all the tickets, and our passports in order," he said.

"That's great, Dick. George didn't want to get to Kinshasa before Ali anyway."

"Hank, we got a problem," he said in a hoarse voice, indicating that he had been wrestling with this problem before he called me. "George is bringing Diego with him to Kinshasa."

"Who the hell is Diego?"

"You know, the German Shepherd you and Don got him."

"That's no problem. Just put the dog in one of those cages. It will be placed in the plane's baggage area. I'm sure the health division will need to check the dog through customs. Other than that, there should be no problem."

"No Hank, George wants the dog to sit next to him on the

plane," Sadler whispered to me.

I couldn't believe the things Foreman came up with.

"Are you kidding? That's not how it works. We got George a first-class ticket and now he wants one for his dog?" I was starting to worry that we were going to have problems similar to Caracas.

"George won't get on the plane unless the dog is sitting next to him."

"Isn't he worried about losing five million fucking dollars?" I didn't know if I wanted to shoot George or Diego. "Can't you just leave him in San Francisco?" No other solution came to me. "George won't get on the plane," he muttered again, "and the plane is scheduled to leave in an hour and fifteen minutes."

"No prob-lem. Give me the number that you are calling from and we'll see what can be done." Now I was using "no prob-lem" in the Zairian sense. I had no idea what to do, especially in such a short period of time. Twenty minutes later I had one of the top executives from American Airlines on the phone.

"Are you kidding?" laughed the executive.

It took the first five minutes to assure him that I was not kidding and the next five minutes explaining Foreman's attachment to the dog. American Airlines arranged for Foreman to take Diego on the plane and have the dog sit next to him in a first-class seat. It was a miracle!

I had five hours to find the right executive at Air France who would allow the same thing on the second leg of the flight. Of course it would be easier now that American Airlines had complied. I knew Air Zaire would have virtually no passengers on the final segment of the trip to Kinshasa and there would be plenty of seats for Diego. Hell, I don't think Air Zaire would have cared if George and Diego played fetch in the aisle.

Foreman and Diego arrived in Kinshasa and were greeted only by Bula Mandunga and three other members of the government. No one stood along the road to welcome the heavyweight champ. Looking out of his limousine window, Foreman saw only the green and yellow billboards promoting the fight. He looked at the images of himself and Ali and the words printed above in French and English.

Foreman turned to his interpreter. "What does *'boo-ma-yea'* mean?" he asked.

The interpreter knew what it meant but wisely guessed that the translation would offend Foreman. The interpreter said, "I don't know, but I'll find out and let you know tomorrow."

The translator told Foreman that they were taking him to a large stand-alone residence on the N'Sele estate and that Ali was staying at a different building also on the N'Sele property. After a moment of silence, Foreman announced that there was no way he would stay at the same site as Ali. After a heated discussion with Bula and numerous calls to other government officials, the small line of cars altered their course and headed to the Intercontinental Hotel.

George was Bula's problem. I had to deal with the crisis looming over the massive amount of media coverage we had generated and Zaire's inability to handle the technological demands of the sports writers. Several members of the press had arrived with Ali's group. Their job was to send out daily reports on the fighters' training and feature various cultural sites to boost Zaire's developing tourism industry.

The Zairian government had not anticipated the consequences of a global free press arriving with Western writers. Along with the stories highlighting the country's potential came a bit of negative coverage condemning some of Zaire's less attractive social practices. The government desperately tried to censor the material and Mobutu appointed officials to read the news stories before they were transmitted out of the country. When any of the officials found a story that was critical of any aspect of the country or Mobutu, they would tear it out of the telex and tell the writer to rewrite it without the negative content. But some of the derogatory comments leaked out.

One story described Zaire as a land of cannibals and bandits, who stalked the streets of Kinshasa at night. Other stories referred to Zaire as "the Congo," its former name under Belgian rule. This was considered an insult to the current government. Others referred to Mobutu as a dictator, and used his Christian name, Joseph-Désiré—both personal insults to Mobutu.

These problems were out of my hands. I kept a close watch on Tshimpumpu, who was responsible for the telecommunications infrastructure and the stadium redesign. The telecommunications equipment we needed in order to handle the flood of outgoing telephone and telex calls had arrived three weeks ago but was still not fully operational.

Tshimpumpu kept saying things like, "We are a young nation and we have our problems. Your news writers lack the understanding of that truth."

After one of these statements I would politely ask, "How's the installation coming along for the telephone and telex equipment?"

"No prob-lem," answered Tshimpumpu.

"Think about it this way," I countered. "The newspaper people who are here have to get their stories out so the world knows about the heavyweight title fight that is happening in this beautiful country." I tried to put a positive spin on the situation. "The success of the fight, and the share of the profit going to your country, depends on the ability of these writers to get their stories sent back to their editors so they can be printed or broadcast." I could not solve the problems of this developing African nation. I had to focus on what I could control.

Again, the answer was "No prob-lem."

I never personally witnessed the dire political situation in Zaire, but the grim reality hit me one day when I saw Don King sitting alone on a bench. I knew immediately something was wrong because King never sat by himself. Yet, there he was in a small garden at the Intercontinental Hotel. His head was down and he looked sad and troubled. I sat down next to him.

"What's bothering you, Don?"

King looked up at me. "I was walking in the center of Kinshasa shopping for some African print ties. You know how there are always two or three soldiers assigned to you and me and Ali and Foreman?"

I answered. "I don't mind that. These military guys are Mobutu's top security guards."

"Some kid, maybe ten or twelve years old, reached into my pocket and stole my wallet." He paused.

"Rotten security. Did he get away? Did he leave you anything?" Pick-pocketing was a common, everyday occurrence in Zaire.

"He didn't make it more than two or three blocks before he was caught by the security guards." King began to tear up.

"My man, what happened?" I asked.

"They caught him and got my wallet back. But then one of the guards drew out a big knife and cut off the kid's right hand just below his wrist!" At this point I could tell King felt responsible for the awful act. "I'm just sick… the kid didn't do anything that bad… they took him away screaming… I don't even know where they took him."

"They would never do something like that unless they were dealing with a bad criminal," I said, trying to justify the actions of the military guard.

"Bad criminal? He was a just a boy… and it happened right there in front of me."

I called to the waiter to bring us some beer. I had no idea how the Zairian criminal justice system worked, but I was trying to help King pull himself together. We were silent for awhile. Then I realized I had to shift King's train of thought and get him refocused on the fight.

"You know George is bringing that dog with him everywhere

he goes, even when he is training?"

"He is?"

"I met up with Jerry Izenberg this afternoon after he watched a sparring match and a workout with Ali at the training facility. After each round of the spar, Ali was yelling things to the crowd about Foreman." He had his interpreter translate word for word for the local people who had paid a few cents of their precious resources to watch him train. The average per capita income in Zaire was $70 per year.

"Ali would yell out, 'Do you know George Foreman has a dog?'"

"And everyone would yell back, '*Oui.*'"

"'Do you know that dog is white?' Ali yelled out to the audience.

"Everyone yelled back, '*Oui*' again.

"'Do you remember when the Belgians were here and they set their dogs on your people? "Ali shouted.

"This riled up the hundred who were watching Ali. They were jumping up and down and yelling, '*Oui, Ali, Oui.*'

"'Do you know that this dog is a citizen of Belgian?' Ali yelled back.

"Everyone was dancing and yelling, '*Ali, boo-ma-yea.*' They were even telling Ali that he should kill the dog," I told King, who seemed amused by the story. He was now back to his usual self.

"Izenberg said Ali smiled and raised both arms over his head and responded with the chant, '*Ali, boo-ma-yea*'. The whole country is rooting for him to regain the title."

King laughed. "My man, that is a great story." He got up and went off to relay the story to the reporters.

Later that day Sadler called me and said, "Hank, we found out what '*boo-ma-yea*' means. George is mad as hell. Also, there's an old tribal woman somewhere way in the back where George is training. We can hear her singing '*Ali, boo-ma-yea.*' She seems to be practicing voodoo. She is sticking needles into little black dolls."

"I'll try to have one of the government guys find her and get her out of there, no prob-lem," I said. I knew this was not the only witch woman working on Foreman in Kinshasa.

CHAPTER 9
LIVE WITH HOWARD COSELL

September 16, 1974

Several days before the fight I flew back to New York to oversee the final preparation, which included the worldwide marketing of what the press was now calling the "Rumble in the Jungle." I had to arrange travel for my crew and the last minute shipment of the television equipment.

Shelly had set up another press party at a hotel near JFK for members of the boxing press who had not yet left for Kinshasa. Ali and Foreman had stayed in Zaire, so I addressed the group of sports writers and passed out press kits with information about the fighters' training and details on our progress restructuring the Mai 20 Stadium and its communications facilities.

The media had their questions answered and we gave them a couple of cocktails and some nice hors d'œuvres. Those who were traveling to Kinshasa that night were given their plane tickets and sent to JFK in a limo. We felt that we had done everything possible to ensure excellent media coverage of the fight.

I went home feeling relaxed and satisfied that everything was under control. It was an unaccustomed feeling, given all that I had dealt with in the last few weeks. King had stayed in Kinshasa to look after Foreman and Ali and make sure that nothing went awry. I had been home for a week and everything seemed to be going well without me. Connie had a cocktail waiting and we were going out for a nice dinner.

As I walked into my house the phone rang. Connie and I debated whether we should answer it. "Honey, there is too much going on, I have to answer."

"Hank, I have a big favor to ask." The voice on the other end started talking in what appeared to be the middle of a conversation. "I can't get through to my office. Can I dictate my story to you and then you call the paper and ask them to send a copy boy to come to your place and pick it up?"

"Who is this?"

"Oh, this is Dick Young… of the *New York Daily News*."

"How did you get my home phone?"

It was 5 p.m. in New York and midnight in Kinshasa. Young started to dictate his story. This is how I learned that Foreman was bleeding above his right eye.

"Does that mean the fight is canceled?" the reporter asked me.

"No, no, no… It means that it will be delayed until the cut above Foreman's eye heals." I did not even know what the hell had happened. My survival instincts kicked in.

My mind started to race with questions—some rational and some irrational: How could this possibly have happened? Did someone cut it deliberately? Was this a repeat of the knee episode in Caracas? Was it a result of the voodoo woman and the chanting?

Young continued, "I've been trying to get the story out all day but I couldn't get a telephone line that would go through. I think that Mobutu's bastards have pulled the plug on every telephone line in Kinshasa. They don't want the story to get out.

They don't want the world to know that George had his eye cut and the fight is canceled."

Young's story had completely blindsided me. I had no idea how I was going to handle the media outburst that was sure to commence immediately.

"The only working phone line is at the Intercontinental Hotel. I am up in Don King's room. He has been trying to get through to you."

My other phone rang. I motioned to Connie to pick it up. She came over and whispered "Howard Cosell wants to speak to you right now. He is on a break during the Chicago Bears and NY Jets Monday Night Football broadcast."

"Hold on Dick, I'll get back to you right away. Cosell is on the other line." I gave the phone to Connie. "Keep Dick on the line while I deal with Howard."

"Hank, I just heard the Foreman-Ali championship fight has been canceled," Cosell said in his trademark voice.

"Howard, Foreman had his eye cut but nothing's canceled. We just have to move the date back a couple of days." Oh boy, I was winging it—I still was not sure what had happened.

"You really think so?"

"Absolutely. Do you think the dictator of Zaire is going to lose his $10 million? Of course we are going to reschedule."

"Great Hank! Get your ass over to the studio right away so you can tell my audience when this fight is going to happen." There was a skeptical tone in his voice.

"Get over here before we go into the fourth quarter and I'll put you on the air. Then you can tell me face-to-face the new date for the fight."

"I'll be there," I said and hung up the phone.

"Connie, hand me the other phone." I figured I better get the whole story from Dick Young.

"How long is your story, Dick? If you dictate I can take it down before I run out of here to go over to Channel 7. Howard is going to put me on before the final quarter."

"It's a couple of pages," Young said. I didn't have time for that.

"Listen Dick, I'm going to put Connie on the phone. She'll take down your story and you'll be dictating to the best 'copy boy' this side of the Prime Meridian."

Before I drove to the television studio in New York City, I got Karen on the phone.

"Karen, first thing in the morning, contact the transport company and put a hold on the shipment of the video equipment. Also call the production crew and tell them there will be a delay in our departure."

I couldn't do anything about the flight that had left New York carrying the newspapermen. But I had time to send them word of the postponement when they changed planes in Brussels. In the meantime, I still had to find out the whole story before I got to the television studio. I phoned the Intercontinental Hotel in Kinshasa and luckily got Melinda, the main switchboard operator who owed me a favor.

"Melinda, this is Hank Schwartz. I need you to find Dick Sadler and get him on the phone with me right away."

Leaving the call connected, she ran around the hotel until she found Sadler who was tinkling on the keys of the piano in the hotel bar. I knew Dick well enough to be sure he was playing to calm himself down. It took Melinda about fifteen minutes to find him and get him connected on the nearest phone.

"Dick, this is Hank, give me the low down. Has a new date been selected?"

Sadler's speech was slurred; he had had a drink or two. "The figh is gonna haf t'be moved ta late Octover so da cut can heal," he told me. Then he filled me in with all the details I was missing. "But… I think it's gonna be canceled," he concluded.

"Not a chance," I told him and hung up. By that time I was dressed and heading for the door.

When I arrived at the television studio I asked for some cosmetics, so I would look wide-awake and camera ready. They tossed me on camera with Cosell.

"Gentleman, you are on the air in 5…4…3…2…"

"Ladies and gentleman, we are here with a live report on the Ali-Foreman fight scheduled for September 24th in Zaire. We are joined by Hank Schwartz of Video Techniques—one of the promoters of the event. What happened with George Foreman's eye, Hank?" Cosell asked.

Goddamn Cosell. There were no pleasantries exchanged or softball questions leading in. He just went right for the jugular.

"Foreman just got a little cut above his right eye while training… during a sparring round. It will take a week or two to heal."

"Do you expect the fight to be canceled?"

"For heaven's sake, Howard, nothing is being canceled. It's a minor complication. We just have to move the date of the fight forward. The world will still be able to see one of the greatest sporting events of all time."

"Tell us, Hank, if it's not canceled, what is the new date?"

I had been talking general bullshit but Cosell was pushing for specifics. I did a quick computation in my head.

"It's going to happen at 4 a.m. Zaire time, 10 p.m. here in the states, on October 30th. We will broadcast as planned from the newly reconstructed Mai 20 Stadium in Kinshasa." I clenched my teeth and smiled into the camera.

Everyone in WABC's TV studio was happy to hear a new date set so quickly after Foreman's injury. I was happy that the football game was ready to resume and cut off my conversation with Cosell.

By the time I finished my segment on Monday Night Football and returned home, it was close to six in the morning in Zaire. I had to talk with someone in Ali's camp to see what their position was. I had a phone line that was open in Ali's N'Sele villa after 5 a.m. I hoped to get someone up and about who had an idea of what was going on.

"Who've I got?" I asked. I had not as yet sorted out the various voices that traveled with Muhammad Ali.

"Hank, this is Gene Kilroy. Why are you calling so early in the morning?" He was fuzzy but awake.

"I don't know if you heard yet… we've agreed to postpone the fight to October 30th at four in the morning." I didn't know whether the 30th was really a good date or not.

"Yeah, we heard that," Kilroy responded.

"Does Ali agree to that?"

"Listen Hank, Ali is comfortable here. He doesn't mind being here another four or five weeks. He would not want the fight canceled. In fact, he wants to buy a house here so he can live among his brothers."

"Well we can't cancel and we can't move it out of Zaire."

"I got to tell you a joke we played on Dick Sadler. I called him in his room over at the hotel and I mimicked Cosell's voice and accent," Kilroy stated.

"How did that work out?" I knew there would be something to smile about as Kilroy continued.

"I said, 'this is Howard Cosell. I am going on the air with you right now. Start counting back from ten, Mr. Sadler."

"Sadler started, ten, nine, eight, seven… and when he got to one I said, still talking like Cosell, 'I understand the fight is canceled,' and he stuttered 'N-n-n-no. It's not canceled at all.' So Sadler thought he was telling the world that the fight is not going to be canceled. That made everybody on our side feel much better."

I was laughing by the time Kilroy ended his story. After saying goodbye I reflected on the consequences of a decision to cancel the fight, feeling relatively confident that the Rumble in the Jungle would occur. I knew that a cancellation would most likely cost lives. And if Foreman decided not to fight, even he would not be able to escape the reach of Mobutu.

CHAPTER 10
WHIRLYBIRD JITTERS

While Karen worked to turn the newspaper group around at Brussels and head them back to the United States, the other Angels were calling Video Techniques' production crew to inform them that they were not going to Kinshasa until a later date. I, on the other hand, had to get on a flight back to Zaire as soon as possible.

A great race was on. If we delayed the fight, the media would assume it was canceled. Plus, the rainy season was fast approaching in Zaire. Unless there was some way to convince Mobutu to move the fight out of Kinshasa, which was a long shot, the successful production of the championship fight was literally a time bomb.

These dilemmas, in addition to my numerous flights back and forth from New York to Zaire, were just about to put me over the edge. It must have been obvious because people were now referring to me as "Crazy Henry." That's how I looked to the uninitiated who were unaware of all that had gone into putting this extravaganza together.

I was picked up at the N'Djili Airport by a military vehicle. A lieutenant sat in the front seat next to the driver. Neither of them looked at me. I got in and we headed toward my hotel.

"Mister Hank, I was given the charge to tell you, when you arrived, that you have an appointment with our President," the lieutenant said while looking sternly ahead at the road. He delivered this message in a way that I understood it to be an order rather than a request.

Mobutu's summons came as a surprise. I had to figure out exactly what to say to the Honorable Mobutu Sese Seko when I met him face-to-face for the first time. I needed to be clear with him that the constant repetition of "no prob-lem" was not producing solutions to our very real problems.

"When is the meeting?" I asked.

"Two days from now, at five in the afternoon."

I had about 58 hours to find out what new problems had arisen in my absence besides Foreman's cut. Among the more troublesome issues was the communications connection with the new microwave that had been installed. I needed to determine how well the satellite uplink was working and see if it would accept video programming. It never showed through my jacket, but I was sweating buckets.

As the military jeep drove up the ramp to the front of the Intercontinental Hotel, I spotted a group of newspaper reporters trying to interview Foreman. Diego, who looked to be fully-grown now, was sitting beside Foreman enjoying the attention.

As I got out of the jeep and walked toward the group in front of the hotel, I could hear Foreman telling the reporters stories about himself and his pal, Diego. While Diego sat by the front doors, Foreman walked across the road leading up to the hotel. He leaned against the low concrete fence that separated the upper platform from the hotel's parking lot located about twenty feet below.

"Sit!" Foreman ordered Diego. I guessed that Foreman was showing off Diego's training.

"Come, Diego!" Foreman hollered across the narrow roadway while thumping his chest. Foreman, now with his arms outstretched, was going to show the news media that besides being in control of the heavyweight title, he was also in control of his dog.

Diego cocked his head as he listened to the instructions shouted by Foreman. Diego ambled across the road and prepared to jump into Foreman's huge outstretched arms. Unfortunately, Diego either did not see or misjudged the distance between where he was and where Foreman stood calling to him "Come!" Diego took a flying leap toward the enormous target, sailed past Foreman, and tumbled over the concrete barrier, landing on the black asphalt in the parking lot below.

Foreman didn't say a word as he ran past me down the ramp and into the parking lot. The entire group of reporters followed him. I ran into the herd of newsmen trying to reach Foreman. Diego laid on his side on the floor of the parking lot, out cold. He didn't look too good and neither did George. Everyone crowded around as George tended to his pal. I pushed my way through and was relieved to see Diego start moving.

Foreman looked up at me, his eyes glistening with tears, and growled, "If my dog is not OK, I will not fight Ali."

"George, he looks OK." He didn't. "But if you need a veterinarian we will find one to check him out," I said, smiling to combat Foreman's weepy glare.

"Not just any doctor, especially not one from this country... not for my dog," he said. I was sure that he was thinking about the voodoo witch that was chanting behind him during his training.

"We will fly in a vet from Brussels, but let's see how the dog is doing first."

Diego got up and hobbled around with a slight limp in his

rear left leg. Foreman relaxed a little but he was still visibly worried. He decided the interview was over. The two buddies, George and Diego, retreated into the hotel.

As the newspapermen disbursed, I turned to the lieutenant who was still at my side.

"Can you get me a call with Mandunga Bula so he knows I'm back in Zaire?"

"I will try. What room are you in tonight?"

"I don't know yet but I will let you know after I check in."

Bula already knew what room I was going to be given and was on the phone by the time I opened the door to my suite.

"Bula, I need to check out the communications systems from the stadium to all the connections, right down to the uplink. The tower is somewhere in a valley near here. I need to get out there so we can test the signal. Can we drive there?"

"No, Hank. It's too far away. I'm told that all the equipment is operating," Bula responded with the customary Zairian complacency.

"No prob-lem, eh Bula?" I laughed.

Bula caught the inuendo. "OK, I'll ask the military and see if we can get a helicopter to fly you over there tomorrow morning. It's located in the central part of the Rift Valley. It's about 100 miles away."

"Tomorrow morning?" I asked.

"I'll try," Bula said.

"You know I have to meet with Mobutu in a couple days?"

Bula was uncharacteristically quiet. I sensed he had no knowledge of my meeting with the President.

"I will find Don King and see if he will travel with us," I said, knowing that Bula liked King from the time we spent together in Paris. "I don't think he's ever been in a helicopter before, so it will be a fun excursion for him."

"OK. We'll pick you up in the morning," he said, ending the conversation.

Next, I got King on the phone. "Don, why the hell did Dick Young go to your room to call me that day when Foreman cut his eye?"

"Man, you know the problems with the phone lines—the news guys are not able to get anything out of here on the telex. Some of the stories are even being pulled out of the machines and torn up before they are sent. It is a nightmare. If we don't get this fixed we are going to lose all the momentum we have drummed up in the media."

"Couldn't Tshimpumpu get in touch with the Minister of Communications?" I asked, "That guy is worthless. Listen Don, I'm going to take you out on a helicopter trip tomorrow morning."

"What? No way, man. They might leave me out there as a snack for the lions." King was nervous.

"If they're going to leave anyone out there with the animals, it should be Foreman. I'll bet he cut his eye on purpose thinking he could get out of the country. He is still in a panic about the voodoo lady who's been dancing around him. I'll meet you at 10 a.m. with a military vehicle to take us out to a field where the helicopter will pick us up."

"Oh man, I don't think I should go on this trip. Do I really need to do this?"

"Don, this is a chance for you to learn how the technology works."

I didn't tell King about the meeting with Mobutu. I wanted to make sure he was focused on keeping Foreman and Ali in Zaire while I tried to convince Mobutu to get the fight moved somewhere else.

The military jeep picked me up at 7 a.m. and took me to a gymnasium which contained a small TV studio that was hopefully connected to the uplink antenna in the Rift Valley. I had to make sure that the video test signal from our equipment could reach the uplink. A new piece of microwave equipment with smaller antennas was being installed at the Mai 20 Stadium. It would be connected to the gym's TV studio. Then we could broadcast from the stadium to the uplink and from there beam up to the INTELSAT satellite that would send our TV picture to the rest of the world.

We picked up King after my visit to the TV studio. The military jeep took us to the field where several members of the Zairian Air Force were waiting with a rather large, olive green helicopter.

"Man, I don't like to fly in these whirlybirds," King protested. He was shaky about getting in the copter. His over-sized personality was taking a backseat to his nerves.

"Come on Don, it's important for you to understand how the rest of the system works. If there's no uplink, or if it's not working right, it'll give us a legitimate reason to move the fight out of the country. Now sit back and relax. You can sit in the front seat next to the pilot. You will have a good view of where we're going."

As they stretched the strap across King's chest, the big blades began to rotate. When the whirlybird started to lift off the ground, I watched Video Techniques' big African-American vice president turn pale.

There was a lot of noise as we skimmed over the villages and headed out to the Rift Valley. Once over the jungle the forest canopy below was gorgeous. We approached Stanley Falls and hovered over small prides of lions, large herds of zebra, and groupings of fast running giraffes. The closer the helicopter got to the ground, the faster any form of life scattered in all directions. It was a great experience to see the elements of nature, at home for thousands of years in this part of Africa, while traveling in this century's flying technology.

The helicopter set down fifty feet from the uplink control building.

"You don't have to get out, Don," I said. "If it's going to take me long, I'll let you know. I've just got to see if we're receiving a clean signal from the studio in Kinshasa."

"Man, take your time." King was glad to be on the ground again.

The contractor who had designed and installed the uplink had done an excellent job. It could transmit a clear video signal and the studio was well-staffed. I was warmly received by the technicians, an engineering group from Israel, who lived in modern houses near the uplink. The screens received the test signal from the studio in Kinshasa and everyone, including me, was satisfied. It took less than an hour on the ground to check the connection and have the technicians explain their methodology.

"Hank, let's go home." King hadn't gotten out of the helicopter. He was being watched by a small herd of zebras nearby, feeding on the grassland.

"We can't use the excuse that the uplink is a problem because it's working perfectly. Don, let's finish the day with a nice trip home in the whirlybird." I saw that King was closing his eyes as the big blades started to rotate again. He was very happy to get out of the helicopter when it landed near the hotel.

CHAPTER 11
STAYIN' ALIVE

The next day, I had a sit down with Dick Sadler. We met in the corner of the outdoor patio and talked over a pot of coffee.

"How's George? And how's the dog doing?" I asked Sadler.

"Ah Hank, you know he's very introverted. He only talks to Diego. But he does want to get the fight back on track."

Face-to-face conversations with Sadler were much easier than over the telephone.

"I won't ask you how he got the cut over the eye, but I need to know how bad it is and how long it's going to take to heal?"

"It happened during a sparring match. It didn't need any stitches. One of the doctors used a butterfly bandage to keep the two sides together and it's healing well. But it's going to take at least another four weeks."

"We've got to hold the fight together, Dick, there's too much at stake for all of us. I have a meeting early this evening with Mobutu Sese Seko to see if we can regroup here or should move it elsewhere."

"Yeah, I know it's a tough decision, the fight still could be canceled. Or it could be moved to another date," Dick said.

"No matter how this gets resolved, we've got to set a firm date. If all the players and the media keep saying it's going to be moved around or canceled, we're going to lose the whole fucking thing. And a lot of money. George will take a huge loss, he will lose a fortune."

"Yeah Hank. I know that's a problem."

"You've got to get George to cooperate with me. We have to commit to a date that's for real. I don't think Mobutu is going to let any of us out of the country until the fight comes off. Hell, at this point, we're lucky we're still alive."

Sadler was looking at some distant clouds as I continued. "Dick, I picked a date that's about a week later from the dates you chose to make sure that the eye would be completely healed. I picked October 30th at four in the morning Zaire time. That should make everything work. Do you agree?"

His gaze returned to my face. "You picked that date?"

"Dick, I had to give the media a set date. Cosell put me on Monday Night Football live when this whole mess hit. I had to make it look like we had everything under control. If you can keep George in line we may stay alive. Get him back on a training schedule. Give me your word, Dick and cooperate with the plan. If I know you are with me, I can meet with the Honorable Mobutu Sese Seko and give him the October 30th date. Otherwise, we may never get our passports back and we may never get out of this country alive."

"You think this is going to work?"

"From what I can see right now, I think it will work," I said. "What's your call, do you think we can work it out with George?"

"Is it going to work with Ali?" Dick asked.

"I talked to Herbert Muhammad this morning and Don is going over there to speak with them. Muhammad is content here and I think we can get them both to agree to the Oct. 30 date."

"What should I tell George?" Dick asked.

"George has a history with us: the Jamaica fight with Frazier, the Roman fight in Japan, and Norton in Caracas. He knows we can produce a great fight. I feel sure that he will accept the October 30th date. He stands to lose his life here otherwise, never mind the $4.8 million dollars."

"I'll tell George that Ali has agreed to the date." Dick was relieved that the responsibility of picking the new date was no longer his. He looked more relaxed.

"Good idea," I said, and we finished our coffee.

My next concern was the rainy season, which might descend upon us at any moment.

CHAPTER 12
ACROSS THE TABLE FROM MOBUTU

I brought Jack Murphy, my technical producer, with me to be my backup at the meeting with President Mobutu. The meeting was held at a building that was near N'Sele, and Murphy and I were brought into a room that contained a rectangular conference table with three chairs on each side. Murphy sat down on my left. A third person, a rumpled young Zairean official, came into the room.

"Schwartz, I am the Minister of Communications," the young man said. "I take care of all the communications systems in this country." We shook hands as we sat down but he did not tell me his name.

"Does Tshimpumpu report to you? " I asked.

"Yes."

"Has Tshimpumpu told you how many problems we're having trying to get everything ready for this fight? And nothing's been done to solve them!"

The Minister of Communications did not answer the

question. He looked straight ahead and tried to pretend he was deaf. I glared at him but he wouldn't look at me. My impression was that he knew he was the major problem.

I had been told several times by Tshimpumpu that the Minister of Communications could not see to our requests because he was out of the office with his girlfriend. I knew this guy was in deep shit.

We all stood up when the Honorable Mobutu Sese Seko arrived, accompanied by two military officers—a general and a captain. We introduced ourselves and Mobutu sat down across from me. The captain stood in the corner of the room.

"Monsieur Schwartz, it is good to meet you. I normally speak only in French, but at this meeting I will speak to you in English," Mobutu said. He looked calm and friendly.

"Honorable Mobutu Sese Seko, we have substantial problems that we have to correct if we're going to make this championship fight a success and repay your country's investment." I paused. "You know that George Foreman received a cut above his right eye and the fight cannot take place until the eye is healed."

Mobutu answered, "I am sure that you will get everyone to agree to a new date as soon as possible."

"My company and our associates have approved the date of October 30th. This will give Foreman enough time to heal."

"Yes?" Mobutu asked and left me in silence to continue.

"Sir, I am sure that you know the rainy season is likely to commence prior to October 30th."

"Yes."

"In order to protect your investment and that of the government, I suggest that we move the fight out of Zaire and into a site in the United States."

My goal was to propose a compromise that would protect the $9.8 million they had invested in Ali and Foreman, as well as the additional $3 million they had spent rebuilding the Mai 20 Stadium and on the supporting communications infrastructure installed to enable the broadcast.

"That is not possible. I have brought this championship fight to my country and I want it to be held here. I am a decisive leader. I am respected in other countries on this continent. The fight must be held in the capital of my country. It cannot be moved." Mobutu made his statement very clear. I knew, in that moment, that my staff, my equipment, and my reputation were trapped in Zaire.

"If it rains during the actual fight, it will cause complete havoc. The downpour will reach the spectators sitting around the ring and the rain would flood onto the canvas and disrupt the fight. Perhaps we can move the fight into a local gymnasium where you could seat maybe… 2,500 people," I said optimistically.

"I give you the authority to expand the roof sufficiently so that in the event of heavy rain, no water will reach the ring or the seats surrounding it."

I wasn't getting very far trying to move the fight to another venue. During our entire conversation Mobutu had looked me straight in the eye with the same blank expression. I decided to make one more attempt from a different angle.

"Sir, every newspaper reporter that has come to Zaire from the United States and Europe has found it impossible to send a story out of the country. They have experienced censorship by your Communications Minister, through his assistant Tshimpumpu. They have been unable to promote Zaire as an attractive tourist destination as you hoped."

Pointing directly at the silent man to my right, I said, "This Minister of Communications has not been available to solve the tremendous problems that have affected our ability to transmit video signals from the stadium. These issues may even make it impossible for us to broadcast a clear television picture during the fight."

Mobutu kept his gaze on me and I turned to look at the Minister of Communications. "I am told he has been on social travel or focused on other projects. This has created a major problem for us. It has made it very difficult to market this event and to protect your country's investment. Under these circumstances, I cannot ensure the proper financial return to Risnelia and Zaire."

With his gaze still locked on me, Mobutu leaned over to his left and said something into the general's right ear. The general summoned the captain with a finger gesture and gave him instructions in Lingala. I assumed that the instructions would allow me to move ahead and undertake the additional construction programs without much resistance. Unfortunately, that was not what passed from Mobutu to his general to his captain.

The captain drew a pistol from his holster with a large silencer attached to its short barrel. In the next instant there was a quiet *"bang."* The Minister of Communications had started to stand up when he saw the captain coming toward him. He never made it off his chair. Murphy promptly fainted.

Mobutu, who briefly broke his lock on me to watch the shooting, turned back to me.

"Monsieur Schwartz, vous êtes le Ministeur d'Informations maintenant. Vous avez compris?"

Mobutu had found the dead man's replacement. That amount of French I understood. I found it impossible to decline the offer.

Mobutu stood and continued in English. "I will arrange a meeting with George Foreman and Muhammad Ali in the stadium within the next few days. I want to be sure we are all in agreement as to how we will move forward."

"Sir, October 30th has been approved by George Foreman and Muhammad Ali. Is it approved by you?"

As he turned to leave Mobutu said, "Will our investment be protected on that date? If so, it is approved." He left the room with his general. The captain remained.

I had to help Jack Murphy, who stands six feet two inches,

leave the room after he regained consciousness. "Jack, I think it would be in our best interest if we forget what actually happened during this meeting—with the exception that the October 30th date is a go." We both knew we were going to be in Zaire until the fight was over.

CHAPTER 13
DON SELLS LEMONADE, WHILE I WORK ON THE LEMONS

Jack Murphy and I adjourned to the hotel bar for a meeting with Jack Daniels—it was the first murder for both of us. After a couple of stiff ones, Murphy went upstairs to rest. I decided it was a good time to get a hold of King and bring him up to date.

I was concerned King and I were drifting apart as a team because of the different angles we were working. I wanted to reconnect with him so that both sides of the operation were singing from the same songbook.

"Don, we've got to talk."

I sat down with King on the patio outside of the hotel where there was nobody near us who could hear our conversation.

"Hey I'm glad you are back, man," he said in his big, booming voice.

"I know you've been trying to keep Ali and Foreman comfortable… maybe we both know why Foreman's eye got cut," I said in a more hushed tone. "Listen Don, if we're going to talk, you need to keep your voice down so we don't have any newspaper guys picking up information as to where this fight is headed."

King seemed to understand it was important not to let the world know what we were discussing. I'm sure he also picked up that the meeting with Mobutu didn't go as I had hoped.

"What happened? Where are we? Do we have a firm date for the fight?" King's eyes were shifting back and forth as he tried to make sure that nobody was close enough to hear his questions. No one was around, luckily. Even King's quiet voice could be heard fifty feet away.

"Would you shut up for a minute. I'll give you some highlights and spare you the bad shit. The fight's going to be held on October 30th at four o'clock in the morning. I have to keep it in the fucking stadium here in Kinshasa. In the next few days, I have to redesign and rebuild the roof in case the heavy rain comes."

"Man, that's more than five weeks from now!"

"We have to get Foreman and his doctor to agree to that date. Dick told me it won't take too long for the cut to heal. I need you to talk to Foreman."

I could tell King was wondering whether this would work. "I have to make a quick trip back to New York to change the payment dates on the letters of credit. We have to find out where we are on sales. Madison Square Garden cannot carry the fight on the 29th. They've got something else booked that night. But before I can leave I have to get the construction guys started on the roof expansion."

"Holy shit! No Madison Square Garden. That's a hell of a loss right there. How are we going to get all this done, Hank?"

"We're in a tough spot with a line through the middle. On the one side, you can think that this is impossible. Screw that side." I drew a big 'X' on the patio table where we had settled. "On the other side, we know what has to be done." Keeping everyone working toward the same goal with full knowledge of all the facts was imperative. I was making an effort to get King to understand all the possible ramifications so that he was up to speed enough to help me out.

"I don't understand why we can't move the fight out of here?"

"It's not an option. If I had taken the position that it was impossible to stage the fight here, we would never get our passports back. If I had gone down that path, I sincerely doubt that I would be sitting here alive. Same goes for you. We are dealing in extremely high stakes." I laughed because I didn't know what else to do.

"My man, that's a lot to get done in five weeks."

"If I have to change the fight to a later date two things are going to happen: first of all, we will lose all the closed-circuit TV broadcast business and all the revenue that goes with it. Everybody will think that the fight is never going to happen. Second, you and I will become permanent residents of Zaire. And we will not be housed at the Intercontinental, assuming we're still alive."

"Man, those are not good outcomes," King mumbled.

"Alright. Then let's forget that the situation is impossible and get started making it work."

"Yeah, OK. Am I going back to New York with you?"

"No man. We turned around some of the sports writers when they landed in Brussels two nights ago, but we still have lots of newsmen here who are going to write stories and send them back. You must keep these positive stories coming. If we don't keep the energy up in the press, we will never be able to renegotiate the distribution deals. Your job is to make sure the press understands all the players have agreed to the October 30th date. Show them this fight is definitely going to happen." King started to perk up as I shifted the focus to how we were going to move forward. "You also have to keep Foreman feeling good about being in Africa," I told him. "Use your big booming voice for that, my man." We both laughed.

I felt sure King was delighted to have an opportunity to flaunt his huge personality to the media as the representative of the promoter. His relationship with the fighters was solid, so I knew he could handle Foreman. Ali, on the other hand, was no prob-lem.

There was another issue lurking in the back of my mind, however. Muhammad Ali liked to wander through the streets of Kinshasa a couple of times a week. He was cultivating a personal relationship with hundreds of locals, who would approach him hoping to touch their hero while chanting *"Ali boo-ma-yea."*

His success in becoming the people's champion was increasingly a cause for concern. If Foreman laid out Ali the way he had Frazier, Roman, and Norton, security was going to be an issue. We were fearful of the crowd's reaction. But I would worry about that when the time came. Saving my own neck was the next item on my agenda.

Video Techniques had produced television events in the United States, Jamaica, Japan, and Venezuela, but never had we faced as many problems as in the developing country of Zaire. Real problems existed in this country. I hoped that the fight would have some positive impact on the plight of the general population.

Later that day I could hear Don King almost singing "October 30th" as he wandered through the gang of sports writers hanging out in the hotel lobby. Nobody can work a crowd like Don King. I went up to my room for a moment to process everything that had happened in the last 72 hours… and to make a reasonably heart-felt prayer.

CHAPTER 14

FAILURE IS NOT AN OPTION

By the time I returned to New York, the roof had been redesigned and the process of reconstructing and enlarging it was well under way. No prob-lem getting my passport back for this trip. Mobutu wanted Video Techniques to protect Risnalia's investment and he knew that my international mobility was necessary to accomplish that.

"What the hell happened?" Karen said, greeting me as I walked into the office.

"Never mind what happened, how are the sales going?" We had no time to lose.

"As soon as the *Post* and the *Star Ledger* carried the story that the fight was still on but changed to the new date, we got a lot of negative feedback."

"Hank, we lost the Nassau County Coliseum," Dolly added. Another salvo!

We had lost two major venues in greater New York. We couldn't continue losing locations and hope to make a profit on the fight. We had to expand the market around the new date and make sure the media knew that the championship was rescheduled, not canceled.

Part of the problem was the transmission difficulty the journalists were having getting their stories out. After Dick Young called me the night of the cancellation when he couldn't get through to New York, I knew we had big problems publicizing the event.

The reasoning in Zaire was that Mobutu had eliminated the communications problem by appointing me Minister of Communications.

Reading over the stories that had found their way out of Kinshasa, I was surprised at the topics some writers chose to cover. In addition to reports of cannibals eating people and bandits jumping out of trees, I also read about the Michengo worm, a parasite that gets under the skin through the soft soles of your feet and eats its way into your organs and puts your bodily functions out of operation.

I gathered the Angels and we formulated a crisis communications strategy. There were no more than fifty journalists in Zaire, instead of the two hundred we had anticipated. We decided to plaster the western world with press releases packed with fascinating information about Zaire and the championship title bout.

"OK, my lovely Angels, we need to spread some positive information about Zaire to the rest of the world. Everybody should know that Kinshasa is one of the three most modern cities on the African continent. They have three universities, a museum with exhibits on the natural history of the country, and a fantastic array of flora and fauna that cannot be seen anywhere else in the world. Zaire should be looked at as an ideal tourist destination. Sure, it's operated by a military government led by a president who represents a single political party... uh, strike that last part."

"When are you going back to Kinshasa to finish production?" Dolly asked.

The Angels expected an answer in terms of days or weeks, which is why they all laughed when I looked at my watch.

"In a few hours," I told them.

Back in Kinshasa, I met up with King, who looked tired. His previously flat hair was all of a sudden standing straight up. Africa had a profound effect on him. King was going through an interesting transformation.

King told me that the number of journalists arriving in Kinshasa was increasing by the day. He also said that Tshimpumpu's people in the press headquarters at the Memling Hotel had stopped reading, censoring, and tearing up news stories that were put into the telex machines. I had been Minister of Communications for only a week or so but I seemed to be making progress already.

Checking in with the fighters' camps I couldn't get hold of Dick Sadler, so I made a call to Angelo Dundee, Ali's trainer.

"Angie, we've got three weeks 'til the fight. How does it look from your perspective?"

"Well, Foreman's bandages are off and Dick Sadler says the cut looks like it is healing. George keeps talking as if he wants more time. It will be a miracle if the fight comes off on time."

"We don't have any more time, Angelo. If we bump the fight to another date, it will never happen. I don't think any of us will be able to get out of Zaire until Ali and Foreman go into the ring. We don't want to go down that road."

"Yeah, I know," Dundee said.

"We must make sure that Ali is in good shape and we have to keep the pressure on the champ."

"Ali's in tremendous condition. We're eating well. We get steaks every few days flown in from Chicago. We don't eat the tribal stuff. They say it's monkey meat."

"Great, Angelo. If we keep both camps happy until the fight

comes off, it'll be OK."

A driver took me to the airport to pick up Connie, who was arriving with the rest of the production staff. I had to be there to make sure everyone got through customs. I wanted to be certain the equipment got off the plane and onto a truck accompanied by military personnel. We didn't want anyone jumping out of a tree and robbing us. Everything ran smoothly through the military checkpoints and we settled in at the Intercontinental Hotel.

It was a chore getting the staff back and forth from the hotel to the stadium, moving quickly under heavy military security. But it wasn't any worse than our experience in Jamaica.

The following day I preached an inspirational sermon. It was the same thing I had said to King: failure is not an option.

The technicians checked out each platform that was wired to the small television studio located in the lowest level of the stadium. They also inspected the grid that had been mounted over the ring to hold the lighting fixtures and spot lights.

The newly-expanded roof would be finished in a few days and a standby generator backing up the power system in the stadium was in transit from France. In the event that the local power shut down we would have a stand-by source of power. Nothing must fall through the cracks. We were prepared.

Bula was standing with me and listening to the instructions I was giving my team. I explained to them that everything needed to be finished in time for the weigh-in.

"In the next three days, technicians will wire the stadium and connect the cameras to the studio in the bottom of the arena." I pointed out the locations.

"As soon as the ring is in place we will build the special seating box for the Honorable Mobutu Sese Seko and his guests. He will be sitting close to the ring and high enough to see and be seen by everyone," I said to Bula as he scanned the rebuilt roof. "There will be sufficient room for Mobutu's body guards."

"Schwartz, our Honorable President Mobutu has decided to stay in the palace the night of the fight and would like to be sure that you have a connection, or whatever you call it, so he can see the fight on his television set," Bula explained.

"No prob-lem!" That was a surprise. Maybe Mobutu was concerned about getting assassinated sitting front and center among so many of his people.

"OK, we'll figure this out and see what we can do."

"Anything else you need?" Bula asked.

"Send me about twenty big guys to help us put up the ring and hang the lighting grid and fixtures."

Bula smiled as he said, "Minister Schwartz, no prob-lem." Then he nodded and left the stadium.

I wondered whether Mobutu told anyone that the former Minister of Communications was no longer with us and that I now held the office. I fantasized he might have told them that the former minister had an unexpected heart attack and I had been forced into his position. Now, I was accountable for all the problems. Be careful what you ask for.

In any case, the communications network was finally operational and I was able to talk with Karen several times each day.

"Karen, ask Shelly Saltman to distribute a press release telling the world we can broadcast live from the heart of Africa. Most of the world still has a lot of questions about satellite technology and how we will get the picture out of Zaire and into the theaters. This might help the distribution. We need to make a few more sales to break even."

A call came through at 2 a.m. the next morning. Shelly thought a press conference featuring Ali and Foreman together, broadcast live from Kinshasa, would help boost sales of the championship.

It took two days to set up a telecast in the small studio we built in the stadium. Ali and his group were there but, once again, Foreman didn't show. Instead he sent his sparring partner,

Henry Clark, who tried, awkwardly, to explain the champion's absence.

"George does not want to come into the studio with Ali only to have Ali verbally hurling insults at him and tearing him down. George says this would cause the fight to happen right then and there before the cameras without the five million dollar purse."

All of Ali's people got off their chairs and started to move toward Clark, which scared the shit out of him.

"George wants this fight to come off without any setbacks, that's why he's not here." Clark tried to back them off. He kept shifting in his chair so he could keep his eyes on Ali's group who was circling around him.

I stepped in and tried to calm down the members of Ali's camp who were clearly contemplating an attack. Clark was only the messenger for Foreman's ridiculous excuse.

"Come on, everybody, calm down and focus on the telecast," I said. "We've got to get this up and running so we can transmit to the studio in Manhattan. This is being broadcast not only to feature the fighters, minus one, but also as a test to show that we can deliver a great picture from over here in Zaire."

Once we got the cameras rolling we anxiously watched the monitors and were relieved to see that we were broadcasting Ali's voice and fine crisp image all the way to New York City. Ali was made for media. He fills the screen and commands the attention of the audience.

There were a number of journalists in the studio throwing questions at Ali, who threw comments right back.

"Is this in color?" he asked. "I'm beautiful in color. I'm beautiful in Africa. How long will this interview be?"

"We bought only ten minutes of satellite time," I said.

"That's all?" he asked, sounding disappointed.

"How is Foreman doing?" asked one of the writers from the New York side of the teleconference.

"The champ wouldn't even show up. He's doing everything he

can do to get out of this fight. He gets himself cut. He's already lost the first five rounds of the championship," Ali answered. "The stage is set. I'm still the fastest, the greatest fighter of all time. The delay helped me and hurt George. He's flabby. We spied on him. The man has no skills. The man has no class. The man has no strength. The man has no footwork. He's a gangster. He's a barroom brawler."

I was watching the studio monitors and Ali's mouth was working extraordinarily fast to fit in as many knocks on the champ as possible in the ten minutes of air time we had purchased.

"They've been saying that I'm thirty-two and my legs are gone. Well my legs are gonna be in great shape the morning of October 30th."

It was a perfect communication link. I had produced an image of Ali that was six thousand miles away from New York City but was free of snow, totally real, and clearly audible. It was as if he were in the next room at 30 Rock.

It was the first live telecast ever from Zaire and it confirmed that Video Techniques would be able to broadcast the fight live. The picture connected to the uplink station in the Rift Valley, was sent up onto a selected group of transponders in the satellite, traveled across the Atlantic Ocean, and shot down to the station in New York, delivering one hell of a terrific picture. I knew that we had accomplished something truly innovative and was terribly proud of what we had done.

Ali finally took a break from his abuse of Foreman and talked about his activities in Kinshasa. When asked how he spent his days, he said that after spending his non-training time running around with the Kinshasan people, he would go back to the estate where he was staying to rest and watch films sent to him from New York.

"I like to watch 'Return of Dracula' and 'Frankenstein Meets the Wolf Man' and 'The Mummy,'" he said. "And you know that George Foreman is 'The Mummy…'" Ali couldn't stop his verbal jabs at Foreman.

For a brief moment now and then I forgot that I was producing a live telecast and just watched Ali. His charisma was as powerful on the screen as it was in person. I had seen very few people in any profession with the presence this fighter had.

CHAPTER 15
THE FLIP OF A SWITCH AT THE WEIGH-IN

Right after the history-making telecast I set aside two days to travel with Connie.

"I knew you would want to see the flowers and the jungle growth so you could get ideas for your paintings," I told her. "Let's see if I can get some security to move us around outside of Kinshasa."

Connie wanted to see the third largest waterfall in the world. It was previously known as Boyoma Falls, then renamed Stanley Falls, and now was called Inkisi Water Falls.

It was enormous and it was beautiful. Small monkeys and other strange little animals living around the waterfall had to be chased away with long sticks by our traveling security group because they were hassling us. It was like we were in one of those old Hollywood films where the production teams shot in remote locations and had to deal with a lot of animals who lived on the set. The trip was a pleasant break and allowed me to think about something other than the fight.

As we approached the date for the Rumble, most of the "no prob-lems" had been solved. Foreign tourists finally began to enter the country. Tourism produced unanticipated complications because of Zaire's strict currency rules. A visitor could not leave the country with more foreign cash than he or she entered with. The official exchange rate was about .50 Zaires to each US dollar and there was a significant currency black market. The locals involved in the shady business were having a field day with the white tourists.

Connie and I flew back to Kinshasa the day before the weigh-in. I went to bed that night thinking that everything was under control. The next morning I learned that Foreman was telling everyone that he was going to pull out of the fight. We had yet another issue with Foreman. John Daly wanted to have a meeting with me because he had a few ideas how to handle this latest problem.

"Foreman wants an additional $500,000 to enter the ring. His spokesperson came to me and said that it was in Hemdale's best interest to keep Foreman happy. He wants cash under the table," Daly said.

"When did this happen?" I asked.

"A couple days ago, about the same time your production crew arrived."

"How the hell are we going to handle this?"

"I asked Foreman if he would go forward with the fight if we paid him the additional money. He said yes. I tried to negotiate something with him so that he worked with us on the next fight, but he would have nothing of it. The money is to be a "gift" to secure his future cooperation. I asked him if he cared who gave him the $500,000 and he said no."

"Did you ask anybody if Mobutu would take care of another half a million dollars?"

"I wouldn't dare do that, too risky," Daly said.

"Well, he didn't show for the television broadcast… people

are still suspect whether this fight will happen. If we can just get him to the weigh-in, he will be seen worldwide on the broadcast. He won't be able to back out then."

"Hank, I think we need to stall for time and get him to the weigh-in. Why don't we get Foreman to send someone to my London office with an empty suitcase. We need to act immediately... before the weigh-in."

"What are you going to do when he gets there? Pay the $500,000?" I asked.

Daly looked at me very calmly and said, "Hank, we'll stall Foreman's bag man while he's in London. We'll keep the guy busy until after the weigh-in. Maybe we won't be able to come up with the cash after the weigh-in."

I wasn't nearly as relaxed as Daly was. "I think George is trying to shake us down, John. Maybe we should lock the bag man in a closet in your office until the weigh-in is over."

"What a nasty approach," Daly said facetiously. "OK, I'll tell George to send someone with an empty suitcase to my London office right away. Think of this as a double-reverse shakedown."

"The weigh-in is going to take place at about midnight tonight Zaire time. It will be televised over the ABC network at about 6 p.m. in New York, and several networks in the UK. Once Foreman is on camera and broadcast to the world, he's committed."

Daly looked around self-consciously and said, "Keeping this fight together has been one of the most challenging experiences of my life."

"Maybe we should sell George's dog, Diego to some rich guy here for $500,000," I said, trying to make the situation seem less dire, but Daly didn't smile.

Just before the weigh-in took place, I was brought into Bula's office and told that there was a problem. Don King had printed some posters that contained caricatures of Ali and Foreman strung together with chains and neck clamps. The poster contained the text "Historic Souvenir And Timely Message From Don King" and "From Slave Ship To Championship." The posters even had an image of King in the lower left-hand corner. It was my job to explain to him that these posters were unacceptable.

I put in a call to Don. "Your posters have upset the Honorable Mobutu and Bula and a lot of other politicos on the continent. All of these posters will be taken down and destroyed. We have received a memorandum from the government giving instructions as to what must happen."

"Why do we have to do that?" he asked.

"This is not bullshit, Don. They don't want to be looking backwards. You could have talked about how Zaire's money and resources made the championship title bout possible, but *not* about a slave ship! That was a place you should not have gone." I was really exasperated.

The government had opened the stadium's gates trying to attract a large number of locals to see Foreman and Ali weigh-in. Ten thousand people showed up. I hoped the chanting of *"Ali boo-ma-yea"* would not be heard.

I dressed in white shirt, white pants, and white shoes. I wanted to be easily seen whether I was in the studio, on the field working on the lighting, or making sure the cameras were in place and functioning.

Ali arrived at the stadium on time and bounced down the aisle wearing a white satin robe that matched his trunks. From the minute he climbed into the ring to be weighed he was dancing to the chanting music, *"Ali boo-ma-yea, Ali boo-ma-yea."* There was no stopping the Ali loyalists.

Foreman solemnly walked down the same aisle accompanied by his entourage and Diego, who trotted at his side. The television signal traveled its path and streamed down to the ABC studio in the middle of New York City. It looked and sounded like a 35 mm film in a theater.

Roone Arledge, who was piloting the broadcast for ABC, called me on a direct telephone link from their studio in New York to one of the commentator's stations next to the ring.

"Hank, the picture looks great," he said. "We can see Ali dancing around the ring getting ready for the weigh-in and we can see the big scale and all of the people, but where is George Foreman?"

"Foreman is approaching the ring now, moving slowly through the crowd trying to draw the attention away from Ali toward himself."

"Roone, hold on a minute." I put down the phone because I saw a commotion in the stadium. A man near the ring had kicked Diego as the dog walked passed him. Foreman stopped abruptly at the edge of the stairs leading up to the ring and looked around for Diego.

"Where's my dog? Diego!" he hollered out.

One of Foreman's trainers looked around but Diego had run off.

"Somebody spooked your dog. We are going to catch Diego and eat him for dinner!" some smart-ass yelled to Foreman. The Belgians had used the same type of dog for crowd control during their occupation and after they left, the Zairois ate the remaining dogs in a stew.

"My dog! Where did Diego go?" Foreman yelled again.

Kilroy and Dundee were standing in the ring just above me. Dundee couldn't hear anything over the chant of *"Ali boo-ma-yea."* Dundee turned to Kilroy and asked, "Was Foreman saying something to me?"

Kilroy turned to Angelo and said, "He called you a *dago*, Ang."

Dundee tried to get into a better position and shouted, "Fuck you, George!"

"I'm looking for my dog!" Foreman replied.

"Kilroy, what did he say?"

"Now he called you a dog."

"Kiss my ass, you big son of a bitch!" Dundee yelled back to Foreman.

Foreman refused to get into the ring to be weighed until they found Diego.

I picked up the phone to speak with Roone Arledge. "I hope you didn't hear all that and I hope it wasn't on the network."

"I didn't hear anything. Hank, the picture has disappeared!" Arledge was screaming at me through the phone.

"What?"

"The signal is completely gone."

"Don't go away, Roone."

I dropped the phone on the table and ran down to the studio. Before I even got to the studio to look at the screens I heard everyone on my staff yelling, "It looks OK here, Hank." I ran out of the stadium and jumped into the first military looking car that had keys in the ignition. The driver was napping.

"Get up! Get up!" I yelled. "Captain, look alive. Take me to the Kinshasa Gym immediately and don't give me any hassle."

The captain looked at me, standing out against the black night, and he was frightened. I knew the white outfit had worked to commandeer the car. We took off in a flash and covered the five blocks to the gym in less than two minutes.

I ran up the stairs and around the track that led to the door to the studio. When I threw the heavily padded door open, it hit the wall and flew back at me, catching me in the face. I pushed the door open, carefully this time. Three young Zairois were manning the studio and watching the monitors. When the door hit the wall and made a loud bang, all three young men jumped out of their seats and ran passed me out the door. I felt blood start to trickle out of my nose.

Most of the monitors displayed a clear picture of Ali still bobbing from foot to foot while Foreman lumbered into the ring. The two that were dead center, however, were the blackish navy color that all video production people fear. I could feel the warmth of my own blood streaming down my face.

The old equipment in the studio was not too complicated. There was a simple toggle switch used to send the signal from the studio up to the roof of the gym. This sent the video picture to the old microwave equipment that broadcast to the Earth Station so it could beam down into the US. One of the young technicians had decided to show off and send the TV signal to his friends. He inadvertently pushed the switch to "Off." I pushed it back to "On" and the two dead monitors immediately lit up. The picture reconnected to the microwave network and began functioning again.

My face and my white shirt were covered with blood. When I walked out of the building, the captain figured he had a reason to be scared. He had seen the three young technicians evacuate the studio. He stared at me without asking what happened. I was stunned he had waited around. We slowly drove back to the stadium where he dropped me at the entrance. As soon as I slammed the door to the car he floored it and took off.

"Have you been shot?" Murphy asked as I re-entered the TV studio. He had been at the Mobutu meeting with me so it was a legitimate question. By this time, my white clothes were splotched in red.

"Give me a handkerchief, Jack."

I had missed the weigh-in and had no idea what part of the telecast made it through to ABC. I pinched my nose to stop the bleeding, and with a nasally voice, got Arledge back on the phone. Before I started to explain anything he started talking.

"Hank, it was a great picture. I'm sure we'll get a terrific TV broadcast when the fight starts."

"Did you get the picture up in time?" I asked.

"Just about ten seconds before the weigh-in actually started," he said.

"So everything's OK on your side?"

"It came out just fine. But next time, you should be up on the satellite at least fifteen minutes before the program starts, not ten seconds. That is cutting it too close."

"Yeah, you're right. We can talk this over tomorrow," I said. There was no way I wanted to explain to the head of ABC why the TV broadcast disappeared and miraculously came back up in time. It was just the flip of a switch.

CHAPTER 16
"JUST ANOTHER DAY IN THE GYM"
—Muhammad Ali, an hour
before the Rumble in the Jungle

October 30, 1974

It is midnight in Zaire, four hours before the Rumble. As far as I know, I have two fighters, a working video transmission, and no one is bleeding. There are 60,000 people in the Stade du 20 Mai, including most of the medicine men and spell casters who reside in Africa. Their services have been hired for the night in an effort to affect the outcome of the fight… and the wagers that constitute a large segment of the underground economy in Zaire. The humidity is near 100%. The broadcast is going to be seen in over 300 theaters and a number of stadiums in the United States and the United Kingdom. It is a sporting event like nothing that has ever been produced before. It is a technological achievement like nothing that has ever been produced before.

David Frost is in Kinshasa to do the commentary for the UK. Bob Sheridan is the commentator for the broadcast in the United States.

The rain looks like it will hold off.

Before the fight, the word was that Ali was going to dance

using his grace to escape Foreman's punches. In the dressing room Ali had yelled "Bundini, we gonna dance?" Ali pulled the long white satin robe, trimmed with traditional African patterns, over his body as he prepared to enter the stadium. "Ain't we gonna dance Bundini?" he called out even louder. And Bundini responded, "All night long, Muhammad." Many people question Bundini's role in Ali's camp, but anyone who has ever witnessed the energy that transfers between them in moments like this understands that Bundini is the battery charger.

Ali is sucking energy from the Zairian spectators with whom he has developed a huge rapport in the eight weeks he has spent in Africa. He arrives just a few minutes before 4:00. After a quick peek inside, he enters the stadium with his entourage and makes his way into the ring. He is still considered a heavy underdog, a has-been, likely to retire after this match. Only Floyd Patterson has ever regained the heavyweight title after losing it. The odds are 3 to 1 against him. The thousands of Zairois, who have paid the equivalent of $10 to see him, will not be persuaded that Ali is anything less than a champion.

Foreman keeps Ali waiting in the ring, as he planned. Ten minutes pass while Ali entertains the crowd and does the shuffle in all four corners. The undefeated champion comes out of the locker room and slowly jogs down the aisle in his red velvet robe. He climbs into the ring supported by his corner men. This time, no Diego. The champ is already dripping with sweat.

The fighters and referee Zack Clayton stand in front of flags facing the camera as the national anthems for Zaire and the United States are played. "You been hearing about how bad I am since you were a little kid with mess in your pants! Tonight, I'm gonna whip you till you cry like a baby," Ali screamed over the music. We chose Clayton, the ex-Harlem Globe Trotter, as the referee because we thought Foreman would listen to his counts.

As the Star Spangled Banner concludes, the opponents are standing opposite each other, center ring while Clayton states the rules. The venom in Foreman's stare is palpable. Ali is jabbering, spewing verbal taunts at Foreman. Clayton tells Ali if he doesn't shut up he will stop the fight. "That's the only way you gonna save this sucker. He's doomed." I cannot hear the words but I see the lips moving on the monitor and tell the cameraman to go in for a close up. I see the look in his eyes. I see the wheels turning in his mind. Even with his mouth guard in, he does not stop slinging phrases that do more damage than his jab. Ali and Foreman barely tap gloves and return to their corners.

Ali looks down at David Frost who is broadcasting from the floor. He feigns fear in the presence of Foreman. He trembles his hands, he knocks his knees. He laughs. He points his glove at Foreman and spits his mouth guard so that Foreman can clearly hear him say, "I'll get your ass, George."

The bell rings—Round one! In the first seconds, I realize Ali is playing with Foreman.

After a meaningful jab at center, Ali reverses and steps toward the ropes as his corner screams hysterically. Ali allows Foreman to club his body. Leaning backwards—way out so his head is over the typewriters of the newspapermen sitting ringside—but supported by the ropes, Ali taunts Foreman. The verbal fuselage never misses a measure.

Foreman gives his all to Ali's body. Ali holds his gloves high and near his face to protect his head. When Foreman moves in close Ali whispers, "Is that all you got, George?"

At the end of round two, Ali waltzes back to his corner with his head held high. "What are you doin?" Dundee screams. "Why don't you dance?" Bundini screams.

"Don't talk. I know what I'm doin'."

Round three. "This is the wrong place to get tired," Ali hollers at Foreman. He throws verbal punches that, at this moment, are far more powerful than any physical punishment he could inflict.

"Who loosened the ropes like that?" Jerry Izenberg yells up

to Angelo Dundee. The ropes look like the tension has been released at the joints giving them an unusual flexibility.

"I didn't loosen them. Bobby Goodman and I tightened them earlier so Ali wouldn't fall through. I think the humidity has made them slack," he calls back.

Flexibility in the ring ropes allows Ali to reduce some of the direct impact of Foreman's blows. As his body bounces back and forth on the elasticity of the ropes he disburses some of the thrust of the punches. Watching Ali's eyes in the camera close-up, it seems that he did not make up his mind to pursue this strategy until sometime during the first round when he realized that dancing was not going to save him from the ferocity of Foreman's sledge hammer attacks. I was aware that he had considered this approach, however, because he had spent hours of training being pounded by his sparring partners learning to take the pain while calculating ways to avoid and dilute the impact. He had perfected the art of making his opponent miss.

After the bell following the third round Ali did not sit down on the stool in his corner. He walked over to the TV camera and made a funny face for all the world to see.

Round five. "Is that the best you can do?" He questions as he leans backwards on the astonishingly loose ropes. "That's a sissy punch, George."

A Zairian official jumps on the ring apron and tries to adjust the ropes. Intending to tighten them, he moves the turnbuckle the wrong way and loosens them further. Dundee runs over and they exchange words.

Ali flirts with the roaring crowd. He raises his arms in the air in response to the chant. The stadium is filled with the beat of sixty thousand Zairois singing *"Ali boo-ma-yea,"* a percussive soundtrack to the psychological drama that is unfolding inside the ring.

Between the ineffectiveness of his body shots and the incessant chanting of *"Ali boo-ma-yea,"* Foreman's confidence starts to fade. He has always used intimidation as a component of his strategy, now he is on the receiving end.

Ali decided to lay on the ropes, apparently without consulting his corner. He altered his strategy and turned what has been considered a weak defensive technique throughout the history of boxing into a winning offense. He quite simply let Foreman wear himself out. Round after round Foreman came out of his corner and slugged with all his might.

During the sixth round Ali spits these words: "Now it's my turn, George." Then Ali lets loose with all he has when Foreman can no longer take the mental or the physical punishment.

It is the eighth round... Foreman has become mechanical with his attack. Ali has completely psyched him out. Foreman is confused and drained of energy. Ali lands a left-right combination on the point of Foreman's jaw. Ali reels him around and Foreman falls backwards onto the blue canvas. Foreman cannot handle the mental confusion and physical pain of being knocked down. The fall actually shakes the ring and we hear a big thud through the headphones.

Foreman's eyes look like marbles. He holds is head up, but his body is down. Three. Four. His chest heaves with exhausted breathing. He is gasping for oxygen, trying to clear his head.

Archie Moore, who is in Foreman's corner, runs around the ring apron and shouts something. Foreman raises himself one last time. He is up on his haunches. Ali paces in the neutral corner. Six. Seven. Foreman cannot get up. Eight. Zack Clayton swings his arms over Foreman. Eight-count knock-out.

Ali lifts both arms in the air. The crowd erupts. His corner surrounds him. The crowd charges the ring. Don King is the first one in.

I remove the headphones and step out of the broadcast booth at the bottom of the stadium.

The heat is oppressive. People are running, jumping, screaming, throwing themselves in the arms of perfect strangers. The crowd is so thick it is hard to move. I need a moment to digest all that has just happened. I step out from under the roof we built over the stadium and look up into the African sky. I take off my glasses and rub my face with both my hands. It is absolute chaos behind me. A deafening roar of celebration. The cloud cover has obscured the normally brilliant stars. The fight started on time, it is now 5:15. I spread my fingers so I can see the horizon which is just beginning the gradual migration from deepest navy to the pinky gold of daylight… and the first drop fell.

CHAPTER 17

THE RAIN COMES

As I held my champagne glass to be filled for the first time, the skies opened up. It descended with a ferocity that I had never imagined. The impact of the torrential rain was intensified by heavy winds. I was grateful to the weather goddess, Shango, that she had kept the rains away until the end of the fight. I thanked her with all my heart.

The Rumble in the Jungle was over in 8 rounds—Ali's mind over Foreman's matter. Ali had regained the title as the world heavyweight champion, just as I believed he would.

While people were congratulating each other over a successful broadcast, Tshimpumpu came up to me and said, "Our president is inviting you and your staff to a breakfast at seven o'clock this morning in the Intercontinental Hotel ballroom."

I was on top of the world. I had worked my way from Madison Square Garden, to Jamaica, to Japan, to Venezuela, and now, here in Zaire. We had achieved something great. I had not only witnessed, but produced a once-in-a-lifetime event.

Connie and I went to Mobutu's champagne brunch. Having slept only a few hours between the weigh-in and the fight, I was still running on the adrenaline that had been coursing through my veins for the last 48 hours. As my glass was refilled again, one of my cameramen grabbed me and pulled me into a corner.

"Hank, are you ready for this? That fuckin' roof that you made so big to keep the rain off the ring…" I thought he was going to follow with a compliment. "Well, it kept the rain off the ring but it has all run down onto the track, which doesn't absorb water. Now it's flooding the basement level of the stadium."

"Do we need to deal with this now?" I asked.

"The production room is totally flooded. If we don't get the TV equipment out immediately it will all be ruined by the fuckin' water," he finished.

I put my champagne glass down turned to Connie and said, "I'm sure you can take care of yourself for an hour or so."

We hurriedly exited the ballroom and I asked, "Can you still drive in this weather?" He nodded yes. "Let's get over there so we can save the equipment."

I guess the message from the weather goddess was that she was a fan of the fight, but after it was over the protection was lifted. Shango was apparently not a fan of television and she was going after my equipment.

It wasn't easy driving back to the stadium with buckets of water hitting the windshield but we made it safely and not a minute too soon. By the time we reached the lowest point of the building, where the production studio was located, we were wading in water up to our knees. We had to carry each piece of equipment out of the studio and move it to a higher floor in the stadium.

I went back to the party and found Connie enjoying herself with all the new friends she had made in Africa. It was a thrill to be congratulated by the journalists and government officials. I loved hearing that the picture quality had been wonderful and the broadcast was a huge success.

Ali showed up and spent a good deal of time with the press colorfully describing how he won the fight by outfoxing Foreman. They surrounded him, shoving their tape recorder microphones in his smiling face.

"I leaned against the ropes so my body could take the punches and I could bounce back and forth with them. You guys thought I was a dope letting him land punches all over my body," he said. "So who was the dope? George used up all his strength working the body."

"What do you call that technique?" asked one of the journalists.

"I call it the rope-a-dope. That's what it is—rope-a-dope."

Ali continued to regale the press about his rope-a-dope strategy and even put it into a poem. Everyone was drunk from the continuous flow of champagne. We laughed at the rain and wind as it howled outside. We shook hands, had our backs pounded, and told each other that the Rumble in the Jungle was one of the greatest sporting events that had ever happened. Everyone was thrilled to have been a part of it.

"Who loosened the ropes so that you could lean against them like that?" another journalist asked Ali.

Ali didn't respond to the question and the mystery has never been solved.

Ali looked around the room with his smiling eyes and hollered back, "You figure it out." Then he turned and raised his hands up and started to chant, "Ali, nearly bomaye."

After all we had been through, it was time to celebrate. We danced all day long. The party just wouldn't quit.

CHAPTER 18
DANCING WITH THE WATUSI

"Don, Mobutu's people have given me a schedule and a couple of airline tickets to Goma to take in the scenery and to check out the Watusi tribe, as the government's guests. I don't think they want to give us back our passports until the money from the fight starts rolling in."

"We are going to fly up to Goma with friends for a couple of days. Our passports should be back in our hands in about a week."

"I'm talking with Ali to figure out the options for his next fight," King said.

"Alright, you can wait for me here or go back to New York and we'll get together as soon as I am back in the office."

For weeks everyone had been aware that King was building strong relationships with both Ali and Foreman so that he had his bases covered regardless of who won the title. He had also effectively built up the visibility of his own company, Don King Productions, as he spoke with newsmen and took credit for the production. By the time the fight took place Don King had become the face and the spokesperson for the promotion of the fight and he rarely if ever mentioned Video Techniques. I sensed that King was drifting away and that he would not remain the vice president of Video Techniques much longer. His name and oversized personality were linked to the Rumble in the Jungle and I was sure he would use his newfound celebrity to propel his own company to a higher profile in the business of boxing. When he left the champagne breakfast, he was already working out his next move.

Connie and I and two of my financial advisers took the trip to Goma. We had a great time exploring the area and partying in the small regional hotel. We took a short safari where we saw chimpanzees, antelopes, and a variety of birds. We had hoped to see one of the Western Lowland Gorillas, the same species as in the zoo in New York. The gorillas were in hiding or stayed away because of the drumming and thumping sounds that our guides made to keep the animals far enough away from us so we felt safe.

We were invited to a presentation of Watusi tribal dancing. A guide led us down a narrow trail to the top of a plateau high above the forest canopy. When we arrived the place was deserted.

"Can anything go right with these government guys?" I asked jokingly as I surveyed the breathtaking landscape from the ridge of the plateau. I was a little worn down from all the challenges of the Zairois bureaucracy.

"The least they could have done was offer us a few drinks before we came out here. It would've been nice to see the Watusi after a couple of martinis."

Then suddenly we heard drum beats drifting up from the valley. As the sound of the drums got louder a procession of Watusi all dressed alike came into view. They wore yellow and green skirted trousers with splotches of red dabbled here and there, reflecting the colors of their country's flag. The long line of male dancers were all naked above the waist except for elaborate necklaces and long lengths of fabric that crisscrossed around their torso from shoulder to waist. All of the Watusi carried six or seven foot long spears in one hand and small colorfully decorated shields in the other. They wore leather ankle bracelets with noise makers on both feet but otherwise were barefoot. I couldn't imagine how they came up the trail to the top of the plateau with no shoes on.

"Connie, what do you think of this group?" I asked.

"Look at the head dress they're wearing. It looks like a flowing lion's mane." Connie was in awe as she watched them begin to dance.

They danced and they danced and they danced, with fantastic lifting, swirling, pivoting, and high-stepping movements. Because they were so graceful, it took a while to notice that the average height of the Watusi was more than seven feet. Their height is part of their tribal genetics.

The leader of the Watusi tribe approached me, handed me his spear, and indicated with his arms that he wanted me to dance with them.

"Are you kidding? You're not going to join them are you?" Connie asked me.

My buddy hollered, "Don't do it, Hank. You can't move that way."

I looked back at the dancing group behind me. I didn't want to offend them, plus I was drawn in by the graciousness of their leader. I was seduced by the exhilarating repetition of the primal beat. I pointed the tip of the spear away from me, and held the long pole close to my body. I started to swirl and dip in rhythm with the drums hoping it would be acceptable to the Watusi. The more I danced the better I got, until I began to feel I was one of the tribe.

"Stop Hank! You're going to hurt yourself!" Connie cried

out after I didn't know how long. I was reveling in my oneness dancing with my Watusi brothers. *Dum, dum-dum, dum da dum-dum. Dum, dum-dum, dum da dum-dum.* Over and over again. I actually started to feel my heartbeat synchronize with the rhythmic pattern.

"You're going to stick someone with the spear and they'll put you in jail," Connie lobbed in with a reality check. At this moment in time I had not yet told Connie that I had been appointed the temporary Minister of Communications of Zaire. I thought it best not to share the circumstances of how the office came to be vacant until we were safely back in New York. She had no idea I was a government official of the country.

"Don't worry, darling, there's at least twenty feet between me and them. I am sure they realize I am not accustomed to dancing with a lethal weapon." *Dum, dum-dum, dum da dum-dum. Dum, dum-dum, dum da dum-dum.*

It was one hell of an afternoon and a moment I will never forget. Dancing with the Watusi was a perfect way to end my time in Zaire.

On our last evening in Goma the local government honored us with a dinner and the hotel presented us with a special menu of local delicacies. Our meals were placed in front of us served under a domed silver plate cover. I lifted the lid, inspected the dish, and turned to the chief government official, "What is this?"

"That is the culinary hallmark of our region. It is the hand of a gorilla."

We all put our knives and forks back down almost in unison. We couldn't even look at each other. After that we decided to pass on the other dishes as well. Instead, "How about another Jack Daniels."

We returned to our rooms, looking forward to catching the plane out of Goma as early as possible the next morning. When we arrived at the airport we learned that the flight we were taking back to Kinshasa had been canceled and we had to wait until later that evening for the next plane. When we were told that our plane was about to land in Goma, we found ourselves standing in line with a large number of other passengers. Luckily the government had made it possible for us to move to the front of what was becoming an unruly melee of people pushing and shoving to get on the flight.

"Mr. Schwartz, stand on this scale so we can read your weight," the Air Zaire pilot told me.

"What is this? Do you want to find out whether or not I'm a heavyweight like Muhammad Ali and George Foreman?" I joked.

"No, no, we have low fuel and high wind problems. We have to lift the plane off of a very short runway to prevent the plane from crashing in the valley below."

"Are you going to weigh everybody?" I asked starting to worry.

"Yes, yes, yes. We have to weigh everybody and add all that weight together with the luggage to make sure that we can take off safely," he answered.

After I got off the scale, I turned to Connie and said, "Now it's your turn," motioning for her to get on the scale.

"Don't be ridiculous!" Connie said. "Nobody is going to find out what my weight is."

"Do you want to get out of here before we become dinner for the gorillas?" I retorted. "Get on the scale."

Over a hundred people were left behind. Most of the passengers on the flight were local farmers or people living in extremely poor communities.

"It doesn't smell too good on this plane," Connie said after everyone was seated in the small jet. The bathing habits of rural Africa are quite different from what Americans are accustomed to.

I reached into my carry-on bag and removed my bottle of

"Brut" and handed it to Connie. "Pour this on your handkerchief and you can hold it up to your nose to cover the smell."

We landed in Kinshasa, went to the Intercontinental Hotel, and found our passports were available at the reception desk.

"Were there any other passports released?" I asked the desk clerk.

"Oui, oui, Monsieur Schwartz. Muhammad Ali has left with his group, George Foreman has left with his group, and your associate Monsieur King has also left our country."

After I showered, I got Tshimpumpu on the phone.

"Have the crew pack the equipment. It has to be on the same Air Zaire plane that we are leaving on tomorrow morning," I told him.

"No prob-lem Minister. We have already packed all the equipment and it is ready to be picked up later today and sent to the N'Djili Airport." Tshimpumpu laughed into his end of the phone. Even though the fight was over he knew that whenever he said "no prob-lem" I would start to worry.

"Does the crew have their passports? I want them to leave on the same plane," I asked, questioning what his no prob-lem really meant.

His laughter continued. "Did you see the chair that President Mobutu has given you as a gift for being our new Minister of Communications? It's big enough for two people and it has water buffalo horns on it."

I didn't know anything about a chair. I thought Tshimpumpu was just pulling my leg to see if I was still worried by his "no prob-lem."

"No I haven't, but I'll keep a lookout for it," I said, trying to be friendly.

"I had my people work with your staff to pack the chair and the other African art pieces that your wife purchased. I had a whole crate put together with the television equipment." I realized then that he was serious. After all of our difficulties I wanted to express my appreciation for everything he had contributed to the success of the production.

"Thank you, my friend," I said and hung up the phone.

I left Connie taking a nap and went downstairs to have a farewell drink with the TV crew.

"Wait till you see the size of the chair that Mobutu Sese Seko sent over for you. It is like an African throne," one of the crew said as we toasted ourselves one final time.

I was ready to go home. I finished my Jack Daniels and went upstairs to get ready for bed. I didn't ask any other questions about what happened while I was away in Goma. But as I got into bed I was struck with curiosity as to what happened when Foreman flew home—was Diego sitting with him in first class?

I hadn't seen the magnificent chair yet, but as I drifted off to sleep I had fun imagining what it looked like, especially with me sitting on it. I wondered if I would be able to use it as my desk chair at work. Perhaps I would have to get a bigger office.

PART 6

THE POWER SHIFT: BOXING BECOMES KING

CHAPTER 1
A VISIT FROM THE TREASURY

It was great being back in the US, looking out through the security bars of my office window in beautiful New York City. Seeing the cityscape was a tremendous relief. I was still recovering from all that it took to produce and distribute the Rumble in the Jungle. Hank's Angels were busy following through with the paperwork, collecting the revenues to be sent to Risnalia and Hemdale, and determining what our piece of the action would be.

On an otherwise quiet day, Karen broke the silence by telling me that there were two men here to see me. I stopped sorting the papers on my desk and looked up.

"Who are they?" I asked.

"They say they're from the government, the Department of the Treasury," Karen answered.

I racked my brain to see if anything could have gone wrong but came up blank.

"Show them in," I said.

They walked into my office. One of them must have weighed 250 pounds and seemed to overtake the space in the limited square footage of office.

"Hi guys. Can you show me your government identification." I smiled and held out my hand.

They had no problem producing identification from the US Department of the Treasury.

"We're here to suggest an amendment to the agreement between your companies and Risnalia," said the smaller of the two agents.

I sat on the edge of my desk and waited for the next line. They proceeded in a friendly, relaxed manner. But the silence took all the air out of the office and I felt I was suffocating.

Finally the heavy agent said, "This is only a suggestion from the Secretary of State… because of the relationship between our country and the government of Zaire…"

"Yeah, OK, only a suggestion. Let's have it," I said, wanting them to get to the point. I was glad that these agents weren't dressed in fatigues like the military officials in Jamaica or Caracas, or brandishing firearms like the captain in Zaire.

"Look, Mr. Schwartz, we're only here to suggest that you change the wording in your contract with Risnalia to read 'and the Office of the President of Zaire.'"

"Thanks. I will look into that and see if it can be done without shaking up any of the paperwork that's already in place."

Both nodded goodbye and left me sitting on the edge of my desk. After a minute or two I figured out that the issue must be that if the money collected in the United States was to be transferred to Risnalia in Switzerland, which was really the office of the President of Zaire, then our government would not have to withhold taxes from the income paid to the Zaire government. Mobutu Sese Seko or Raymond Nicolet must have talked to the US Ambassador to Zaire to get this change implemented before the majority of proceeds from the Rumble were transferred back to Risnalia.

It was a transaction that Video Techniques would perform on Telemedia de Panama's behalf. Since the money was already coming in, I had to get it done right away. We had done well in Zaire, in spite of all the challenges.

CHAPTER 2
ALI DEFENDS HIS TITLE

May 16, 1975

I hadn't heard from Don King for several weeks. The phone rang and I was told that King was on the line. I knew he needed something.

"My man, how are we doing?" King shouted into the phone.

"Where are you?" I asked.

"Did you see my picture in the *New York Times?*"

"No, I didn't see the *Times.*" I was perfectly happy not to read anything about King, Ali or Foreman, at the moment. I was more interested in finding out why my vice president had been out of contact for three weeks.

"You didn't see me on the balcony at the Beverly Hills Hotel? I'm out there with my hands raised over the city of L.A. making a prayer." King was nothing if not self-centered. "You didn't see the robe I'm wearing? The picture is in black and white but the robe is striped in orange and black and it's like a preacher's robe."

"No, I didn't see that."

"I got one of those robes for me, one for you, and one for Foreman. I'm shipping it to you."

"That sounds great, Don. Now, what's going on?"

"I'm gonna set up another fight and Telemedia de Panama will act as the promoter."

"What kind of fight are you settting up?"

"I got Al Braverman to line up Chuck Wepner—that big white heavyweight—and I'm gonna get Ali to give Wepner a shot at the championship."

"I haven't seen any contract with Chuck Wepner on behalf of Telemedia."

"Don't worry about that, man. I signed it."

"It doesn't work that way, Don. You are not a legal agent for the company."

"Don't worry about that man. The money is there and Video Techniques will do the production and distribution."

"Send me the contract you signed with Wepner. I want my lawyer to take a look at it."

"Yeah, yeah, OK, I'll send it… Listen, I've decided I am going to move to New York. Henrietta and I will be looking for a house. I also need an office in Manhattan. We need your help."

A couple days later a UPS package arrived with the orange and black striped robe, which was big enough for Foreman, Connie, and me all together. Video Techniques received the bill for all three robes.

The Ali-Wepner fight was set to take place on March 24th, 1975 at the Richfield Coliseum in Cleveland, OH, a site chosen by King. Since it was essentially a rehearsal fight to keep Ali warmed up for his next major opponent, it was easy to obtain the financing. Wepner bled terribly through all fifteen rounds. Ali retained his title, a TKO two minutes and fourteen seconds before the final bell. Wepner was greatly overmatched. This fight supposedly inspired Sylvester Stallone to write the screenplay for *Rocky*. The production was effortless compared to what we had been through producing bouts in foreign countries. Everybody in the office was glad to have an easy time of it.

Soon after, one of the Angels danced into my office and said, "Hank, there's a stranger on the telephone."

"Is it one of the strange guys who has called before or is it a new strange guy?" I asked.

"I think it is a new one. This guy sounds like a Chinese waiter."

"OK, let's see what he has to say."

"Is this Mr. Shortz?"

"This is Hank Schwartz. Who am I talking to?"

"My name is Mike Ong. I would like to speak with you to do a championship fight in Kuala Lumpur," he said in heavily accented English. He was difficult to understand, but I heard Kuala Lumpur clearly and knew it was somewhere in Malaysia. "Can you make an Ali fight in Kuala Lumpur?" Ong asked.

"I'm sure if the money is there and you pay in US dollars, we can make a fight with Ali."

"Mr. Shortz, can you broadcast it worldwide?"

"Yes we can. But you have to understand that when we did the broadcast from Zaire, we had to put the fight on at four in the morning because of the time difference between here and there."

"The fight could be in the early part of the day at a big outdoor stadium. Malaysia time is many hours ahead of American time."

"OK. Let's talk more about this and I'll see if we can line up another championship event. Are you in the United States now?"

"Yes, yes. I am in San Francisco and I would like to meet with you," Ong said.

"I am on my way to Las Vegas to see Muhammad Ali fight Ron Lyle. We will start planning his next championship once I get there."

"Shortz, you are coming to Las Vegas? I come there to spend an hour with you. We will discuss putting an Ali championship in Kuala Lumpur."

"OK, call my secretary later today. She will tell you where I will be staying in Vegas. But don't waste your time or my time if the money is not available."

"Shortz, do not worry. The money in Kuala Lumpur is from the government… and elsewhere."

I wondered what Ong meant by "elsewhere." Sharing the news with King on the telephone, I explained, "I'm gonna meet a guy in Vegas who says he wants to mount an Ali championship fight in Kuala Lumpur."

"Where is Kuala Lumpur?"

"It's somewhere near China."

"No shit, man."

"He wants Ali to fight a big white guy. Who do you think Ali would be willing to fight? What deal do you think we could make?"

"Well, maybe Ali would like to go up against Joe Bugner again. He's a big British, blonde heavyweight." King's voice was very low and I knew he wasn't too crazy about this idea because we did not do well financially on the Wepner fight.

"Why don't you noodle around with Herbert Muhammad while I meet with Ong in Vegas tomorrow to see if he has real money behind him. I'll let you know right away."

"Yeah man. Bugner fought Ali in a non-championship fight in Vegas February of '73. Ali won by decision but Bugner stood up the whole twelve rounds. Maybe we should think about this one." King seemed to be warming up to the idea.

Before leaving for Las Vegas to meet Ong, the Angels gathered some data on Bugner. It appeared that Joe Bugner was exactly what Ong was looking for, a Hungarian-born Adonis-type who became the handsome loser following his previous fight with Ali. We could give Bugner another chance.

Connie came along with me to Las Vegas. She loved to play blackjack. Caesars Palace casino didn't have the ambiance of the White Elephant in London, the swanky private club where all the women wore evening gowns and the guys were in tuxedos. Connie lost her "virginity" upstairs at the White Elephant and maybe she could win it back at the blackjack tables at Caesar's Palace.

Mike Ong Phoot Aun turned out to be the special business coordinator for Tinj Dunla Sendirian Berhad, a private company supported by the Malaysian government. We met in the casino. After a drink at the bar, I invited him to join me at the elite blackjack tables behind closed doors.

I sat down at one of the high stakes tables and threw a chip at the croupier before the deal.

Ong filled me in on the back-story of how he became involved in the fight. He rattled off a list of names you don't hear often in the western world.

"You know Hank, our government hasn't held a professional boxing match since the Japanese occupation. Before the war, professional boxing was very popular in Kuala Lumpur. Datuk Harun Bin Haji Idras asked me to put this together. He is the Minister of the State of Selangor, one of the fourteen states in our country."

"I'm guessing that Malaysia is a Muslim country." I signaled for another card.

"Yes, yes. Datuk Harun, besides being the Chief Minister, is also supporting the Tingu Duna Group, a private company, that is a syndicate of several money men who will promote this fight," Ong continued.

"Are you the business coordinator putting this together for the syndicate?"

"Yes, yes. But it has to be Ali. Because he is a Muslim… he could bring boxing back to our country."

"One more." I signaled the croupier. I was on a roll.

"I guess, from your perspective it would look good if a big white country boy from England lost to a Black Muslim."

"Yes, yes. You've got the picture." Ong was obviously pleased that I had picked up on the angle. I looked at my cards, which were face down on the blackjack table.

"Does the syndicate want to handle just the financing or do they want to be the promoter?"

"Yes, yes. They will also be the promoter; the same way the government of Zaire was the promoter of the Ali-Foreman fight."

"OK my friend, if I arrange a championship fight between Ali and Bugner, will your group give me an agreement to manage the whole event as well as the broadcast and worldwide distribution rights?" I was watching Ong's eyes to see whether he was over-reaching his authority to negotiate with me.

"Yes, yes. We will give you a management agreement and the TV production and distribution contract."

"You know we had a little problem with the tax authority after Foreman-Norton. The fighters and their managers were put under house arrest until some hot-off-the-press tax was levied. The Malaysian government could screw everyone when the cash leaves your country."

"Never! Never would the Malaysian government tax you or the fighters or do anything that would create income in the US. We are very clear on your reasons for holding these fights offshore." His face was somber, as if he had been insulted. I made a mental note to make sure that any contracts entered into with these guys would have a protective paragraph that kept us from having any income tax ramifications.

"Let me make some telephone calls. We'll see if we can get Bugner to fight Ali again in Malaysia. My vice president, Don King, will talk to Ali's manager." Ong was almost jumping up and down as we said good-by.

I flipped my cards. Blackjack! The croupier scooted a big stack of chips in my direction as I threw another one her way. I won $11,000 while I negotiated the deal with Ong. Nice work if you can get it.

CHAPTER 3
HANK DEFENDS HIS TITLE

King and I spent the next two days in Las Vegas convincing Ali to sign for a title fight with Bugner. When I got back to New York Herbert Muhammad called me.

After the usual pleasantries Herbert said, "Hank, you have helped several black fighters get a big leg-up in the boxing world so I thought I should tell you that Don is trying to tie up another championship fight between Ali and Smokin' Joe. I knew that Don eventually was going to run around behind your back and work an angle," he said.

"Don is always lookin' out for himself," I responded.

Herbert continued, "Bob Arum has had his hooks in Smokin' Joe for years and Don said that if I could work something out with Arum we could get to work on a third fight. I think you need to be careful Hank… when he is talking there is no mention of you and Video Techniques. It's all about him and his production company." Herbert had read the tea leaves better than I.

I discovered that King talked to Mike Ong and then bent Herbert's ear. King's plan was to get Ali to take the championship fight in Kuala Lumpur and then immediately defend his title in a rematch against Frazier. I got on the phone with King right away.

"Don, if we're going to put this fight together between Ali and Bugner we need to talk to Mickey Duff, Bugner's manager." I assumed that Duff had been involved in the previous fight with Ali. "But if we get Ali first, it will be pretty easy to get Bugner to sign. So now we have to see how this sits with Herbert and how much Ali wants. Then we reach out to Mickey Duff."

"Brother, I can get both fighters to your desk. Just write up our standard championship fighter's contract and I will make it fly."

King used the word "our" when referring to the contracts. He seemed to be assuming an attitude of ownership. Instinct told me that King thought he knew everything he needed to know about the fight business. He was trying to force his way up the ladder into the limelight.

By the beginning of April, three executed contracts found their way back to my desk. They were between the Malaysian promoter and Ali, Bugner, and Video Techniques, respectively.

"Karen, these contracts with the fighters have been redrafted." She came over to look at the documents. "The ones we prepared provided that Video Techniques would act as the general manager and we were assigned the television production and distribution rights. On these copies the first page has been reworked so that Video Techniques and Don King Productions are acting jointly as the general manager. And look at the last page—it's signed by Don King Productions as co-general manager. He also signed for Video Techniques as its vice president. The address for Video Techniques and Don King Productions is here—39 West 55th Street. How the hell did this happen?"

"You're kidding," Karen said, looking over my shoulder. "Why did he do this?"

"Get Don over here right away so we can figure out what's going on."

It took two days to find King and get him to my office.

"Hank, I am aware of what the documents say, what is your problem?" he mumbled when he finally showed up and sat across from my desk.

"Don't pull that crap with me, Don! How the hell could you sign these agreements acting as the representative of your company and then signing again as the vice president of Video Techniques? I never agreed to split the revenue with you. And we have never discussed you acting as the general manager for the Ali-Bugner championship. What the hell are you doing?"

King shifted in his chair as I continued to question these bullshit moves. He would not make eye contact with me and mumbled something unintelligible.

"Don, you have taken this way too far. Be honest with me… you did not have the authority to cut yourself into these deals." Don had reached out to Ong and worked his own deal behind my back!

"Hank, it's time to bring Don King Productions to the front of these new deals. I need to open an office in New York City so that my company can start putting the deals together." His overriding self-interest started to show itself. "Hank, you taught me most of what I know about the boxing business. But we always discussed that Don King Productions would remain an independent operation."

He had run his own numbers operation very successfully in Cleveland and I should have known that he would eventually want to spin out on his own.

"Don, I have always dealt with you fairly and honestly."

King rolled his eyes. "Yeah, yeah. But I gotta build my own business and, brother, I will take you along with me…"

This statement totally pissed me off.

"Bullshit!" I exploded, "You will never take anyone along with you. You don't even think that way, Don."

King had a personality that always wanted the spotlight on him. Most of what came out of his mouth was half the truth. He said whatever he needed to say to keep the conversation moving along, and focused on his own interests.

I looked past King to the posters on the wall behind him advertising the events that we had staged during the three years we had worked together. When I first joined forces with him I needed someone who could form a relationship with the fighters while I reached out to governments and the private funding groups. We had worked well together. On the flip side, King was using me to supply the technical skills for the television broadcast while he built up Don King Productions. The difference between us was that I thought of our professional relationship as a partnership and he considered it an educational process that he would eventually graduate from. I never once considered using what I learned from him to cut him out of the game.

"Don, as a vice president of Video Techniques, you cannot sign a contract for Don King Productions while working out of my offices. Do you know where we are right now?"

"Yeah man, we're headed to Malaysia for this fight," he said.

"That's not what I'm talking about. Where are we sitting right now?"

King smiled, "We're sitting in your office on West 55th Street."

"Take a look at the last page of the contract, Don. How could you sign that contract for both Video Techniques and Don King Productions at 39 West 55th?"

Don had allowed our partnership to fall apart. I was staring at him to see if he could face the truth. "You keep telling everyone, including the media, that you are acting as Don King Productions. You don't even mention Video Techniques anymore. This has really become apparent as we have put together the fight in Malaysia. You are pushing yourself out front. You're saying that Don King Productions is putting on this fight instead of Video Techniques or Telemedia. And now you are trying to take credit for the broadcast and distribution of these events worldwide. That is bullshit! You are breaking up the team, Don. That's OK, but you cannot pitch it both ways. If you are going to establish Don King Productions in New York and you want to distance yourself from Video Techniques, you better find your own office."

"OK. Maybe that's what we should do," King said. "If I can't run my business out of Video Techniques' office, help me find an office in Manhattan so I don't have to fly back and forth from Cleveland. I've got to find a high-class joint."

"While we're in Malaysia we can figure out what you want to do with your company. We will work together as two separate companies."

"Yeah, Hank, that sounds good."

"OK, I will help you get an office here in New York but you can't work anymore as my vice president. We have to operate totally separately. You go your way and Video Techniques will walk down its own path."

King visibly reacted and got very quiet. He did not like the idea that he was out of Video Techniques.

I continued, "After the Ali-Bugner championship is signed, anything you bring to the table that needs television production, high-tech communications, satellites, microwaves, marketing, or raising the money; we will work out a separate arrangement between Don King Productions and Video Techniques."

I stood up and walked out of my own office. I called back, "Let's see how this is going to work out—Don King Productions working independently." King shook his head as he tried to put a positive spin on being fired.

Ali signed the contract to fight Bugner in Kuala Lumpur on June 30, 1975 for an initial, non-refundable $100,000 from

Tinju Dunia Sendiran Berhad and a letter of credit issued for $1.9 million. Bugner signed for $50,000 and a letter of credit for $450,000.

My next move was to find an office for Don King Productions. I called a guy, who was married to one of my Angels, to see if he could help us out.

"Hi there, Mike. Don King is moving to Manhattan. He wants a small brownstone somewhere on the East Side," I explained.

"Are you nuts? You think the realtors up there will let a black guy move into their neighborhood?"

"We can't think that way Mike. Besides, he's not just any black guy. He's a black guy with a lot of money and a big mouth with a direct line to the media. This kind of up-scale neighborhood would not want any negative press."

"Every newsman doing a story about a couple boxers will always shove in a couple of lines about Don King."

"If Video Techniques is going to continue in the boxing game, Mike, I need Don King in my corner. He asked for my help."

Mike found an older guy who was divorcing a younger wife and needed to get rid of a brownstone on East 62nd Street.

King checked out the neighborhood and the house. He liked it and was already imagining what it would look like furnished.

"Do you and Connie have any extra furniture you are not using that Henrietta and I could use to fill up this place?"

"We've got a 28-foot long couch that has a lot of turns and twists in it that we just replaced with something a little more modern. We'll see what Connie says about it."

"My man. Did you see the separate entranceway, where you walk down a couple of steps and go into a finished basement?"

"I don't think they call it a basement in this neighborhood, Don. Those are the housekeeper's quarters."

"Yeah, maybe the young chick that guy was married to started out as the housekeeper," he laughed. Then he came up behind me and gave me a jab in the ribs. "How would you and Connie like to take that finished basement and use it as your in-town apartment?"

"You should discuss this with Henrietta and we'll see how Connie feels about it."

Getting King a fancy office in the middle of Manhattan was a little tougher. Mike and I looked at three high-end spaces but decided that the only one King should look at was a group of offices in a suite on the 67th floor of 30 Rockefeller Plaza, two floors above the Rainbow Room. It was expensive but good value for the dollar.

"Man this is gorgeous. Who had this place before?" King was practically salivating.

"We don't know who had it before; I can check it out. Do you want to move into this place or not?" I said.

"My man, this is definitely worth the money."

"Don, you know that office to the right when you walk in? It's about one-third of the total space. You lease this place and I get that office… that will finalize matters between you and me."

"What do you mean finalize matters?" King asked as he was looking at the view. You could see all of lower Manhattan when the skies were clear.

"If you want to keep the lines of communication open so that Video Techniques can produce and distribute the events you promote, we have got to have a formal working arrangement." I interjected.

King stopped looking over Manhattan and we walked out onto the huge balcony that was attached to the office I had claimed for myself. The wind blew through the space between us and we locked eyes. He knew that he had advanced the visibility of Don King Productions ahead of Video Techniques in every interview given to the media for months. It was quiet for about five minutes. A pigeon flew down and landed on King's shoulder. So I addressed the pigeon.

"Do you know whose shoulder you are sitting on? He is a guy that can only say 'Don King Productions.' He has forgotten how to say 'Video Techniques.' He used to be my vice president."

The pigeon got scared and flew away.

"Hank, what are you complaining about? You know it's my ability to talk to and my relationships with the fighters that gets these deals done," he said as he brushed his shoulder to make sure that the pigeon left nothing behind.

"The pigeon didn't leave anything on you… but Don, you did shit on Video Techniques and Telemedia."

"OK, let's stop this crap." He was calming down. "You've got the office. If I'm no longer the vice president of Video Techniques, maybe you should become the vice president of Don King Productions." I looked at my right shoulder to see if the pigeon dropped anything on me but I was clean as far as I could see.

I checked out the office once again and surveyed the balcony that we were standing on. It was true we had drifted apart and there was certainly going to be a power struggle as to who was going to be the guy on top. Even so, I felt like we could work it out. The office was much bigger than Video Techniques present location. And how about this balcony?

Don and I were moving in the right direction based on our different personalities and strengths. But if we were going to continue working together in the future we had to be very clear about who did what and how we were compensated.

"Video Techniques has got to get the TV production and the international distribution rights to every event you promote, under separate contracts."

"Yeah, yeah, OK man. You got the office. You got the balcony. If we work together long term, what's the difference whether I'm the vice president of your company or you're the vice president of my company."

I just nodded, knowing it wasn't going to be easy keeping Video

Techniques on the front burner after we shifted positions.

The lease was drawn up by the building manager's lawyer and reviewed by King and one of his attorneys. It was signed and submitted to Rockefeller's property management office.

"Hank, that lease we sent over to be signed, they're sending it back unexecuted," Mike told me.

"What! Why? It had a certified check with it, properly executed by Don King Productions."

"Racism would sum it up in one word," he explained.

"Let me see what we can do about this. Give me the name and number of the guy that called you."

Starting with the on-site manager at Rockefeller Center, I worked my way up the ladder to one of the Rockefeller family members involved on the real estate side of their business.

"Let me explain to you what will appear in the newspapers if Don King, a black American independent business man, is unable to lease an office in your building. First, it will be reported that, after earning the respect of his colleagues at Video Techniques, he set off to expand his own company in New York. But he was treated very poorly, by Rockefeller Center. It is only a matter of time before the television media are on your doorstep seeking a comment."

That conversation had its intended effect.

"OK Don, you can move into 30 Rockefeller Center in about four weeks, as soon as the old tenant cleans out the place."

"Man, that's great."

"Don't forget, my office is the one on the right with the balcony."

Hank's Angels and I moved to 30 Rock. The Angels were pleased with the new arrangement. Their new office was much larger than the one on West 55th Street. I sat in my new office, behind my fancy new desk, on my big Zairian chair with buffalo horns protruding from each side. I looked out over the clouds and thought about how far we all had come.

The Angels, Don King, and I had risen to the top of 30 Rock.

CHAPTER 4
ALI-BUGNER IN KUALA LUMPUR

June 30, 1975

The fight was to take place in Stadium Merdeka, an outdoor stadium that sat on a hilltop in the middle of Kuala Lumpur, the picturesque capital city. The stadium had the usual deficiencies in structure and technology, but the preparation was relatively easy compared to our previous sites.

We needed to build another roof to brace for the possibility of rain. Ong provided me with a contractor to build a translucent roof over the center of the stadium.

Since the ring would be set up in the middle of the stadium's field, we needed to build five tall platforms, all at different angles, on which to mount our cameras. "Yes, yes, just a little bit of work," Ong said.

When Singapore became independent, no updated satellite dishes or links remained in Malaysia that could broadcast video signals out of the country. We worked it out so we could send a microwave signal to Singapore in order to broadcast from there.

The heat was the most overwhelming problem in Kuala

Lumpur. It was difficult to work during the day because the sun heated the air like a pressure cooker. It was much hotter under the translucent roof. We were not looking forward to 10 a.m. on July 1st, when 36,000 Malaysians would sit in the torrid heat to see Ali defend his title.

We had other setbacks as well, but Ong was very cooperative. He was always smiling and nodding. It was refreshing to have a competent local partner.

Everyone involved seemed enthusiastic and entirely at ease in spite of the fact that no one in Malaysia had ever been remotely connected to a boxing event before. Malaysians love sports but, up until this point, they were never exposed to *"tinju,"* their word for boxing.

In Zaire the people loved Ali because he emphasized his African-American heritage with enormous enthusiasm. In Malaysia, it was different, but very much the same. As Ong had informed me, Malaysia had a large Islamic population and the people did not view Ali as African or American, but Muslim. They adored the fighter who switched his name and faith and became the heavyweight champion a second time. Whereas in Zaire he represented his African heritage, now he was representing his faith. Ali was the people's champion wherever he went.

Ali and Bugner arrived three weeks before the fight. They both trained in the ring under the new roof, dividing the day in half between the two camps. It was unbelievably hot and humid and both fighters lost weight in the weeks before the fight because they were expending so much energy—and calories—as they trained.

Local fans were allowed in the stadium to watch the fighters train. Thousands came every afternoon to see the most trivial activities, like Ali being rubbed down with abalone cream to make him comfortable and prevent his skin from burning.

We were concerned about Ali and the heat. He was 33 years

old and some argued that he was past his prime. One particularly oppressive day I asked him how he was feeling. Dripping with sweat, he looked over and said, "It's bad to have a reputation because every young man is out to shoot you down."

Ali was thinking that his younger opponent might be better able to take the heat. Ali may have been feeling that he had been outclassed.

"Muhammad, Bugner is not going to take you down."

Ali leaned over the ropes and looked down at the group of journalists that were standing behind me and said, "He's going up, while I'm coming down." It came out as singsong and Ali resumed his comedy act.

"You know man, if Bugner wants to follow my advice, he shouldn't show up. I'm just following the rules of the M.B.F.," Ali said, referring to the Malaysian Boxing Federation. "Somebody better be telling the M.B.F. rules to Bugner."

"What does that stand for?" somebody hollered out.

Ali shuffled his feet in the middle of the training ring and said, "Murder Bugner Fairly." Everybody laughed.

Ali played with the newsmen while sweat poured off of him. The amount of water that came out of Ali's body during training was impossible to believe. But he never stopped his banter with the journalists who stood around the ring while mopping their own brows.

"Ain't that something? You ever seen water pouring out of a man like what is pouring off me? And I'm an African. Bugner, he's just a white man, like a safari leader on a visit. I'm used to heat. My home town is Miami Beach where it gets hot all the time," Ali said while singing and dancing and hollering. He continued tossing out lines as he sparred with one of his trainers.

An American journalist hollered back, "Hey Muhammad, you used to live in Louisville and your home town is in Chicago, not in Miami! Is the heat getting to your brain?"

Bugner was experiencing the same problems—nearly slipping

on the puddles of sweat under his sneakers as he moved around the ring. Andy Smith, Bugner's trainer, had sent Bugner to an RAF jungle warfare base in England for twelve days. It was supposed to prepare him for the blazing, sub-tropical summer weather conditions in Kuala Lumpur. Nothing could have prepared him for this.

Ali and Bugner both knew that the temperature was going to be a major influence on the outcome of the fight. The heat would factor into the endurance each fighter had and how long they could continue throwing punches.

A couple days before the fight Ali was holding court with the media after a three-round sparring session. As he talked about how he would beat Bugner, Joe Frazier walked into the arena.

King had gone behind my back and negotiated an agreement with Ali and Frazier for their next championship event. We were in a situation similar to the one when Foreman fought Norton while already having an agreement to a fight with Ali. This new match was dependent upon a Bugner defeat so that Ali would retain the heavyweight title.

Smokin' Joe arrived in Kuala Lumpur and went directly from the airport to the stadium. It was very unusual for Ali to lose the attention of the media. Ali was normally the instigator who showed up at fights to taunt his future opponents. But when Frazier walked in all eyes shifted to him. Ali was literally speechless. Caught off guard, Ali searched frantically for a flippant response to the intrusion. He did not look comfortable in this role reversal.

Frazier walked up to the ring, pointed his finger at Ali, and said, "I want ya. I want ya, like hogs want slop. I want ya. You're scared, scared to death by the white Bugner that nearly beat you into slop."

Ali found his voice and screamed, "Joe Frazier! Throw him out of here! Joe Frazier! Throw him out!"

Smokin' Joe smiled, turned his back on Ali and walked out of the stadium.

Although the fight was a considerable event for Malaysia, it was not a big money-maker for us. Many of the seats in the stadium were empty because the fight was broadcast throughout the country and people preferred to stay in the cool and watch from their homes. Those without TV sets rented them or watched in the homes of their friends or at a local coffee shop. Others listened to the live broadcast over Radio Malaysia. The quality of our broadcast was good and the reception was better than what the locals were used to.

Malaysia was almost at a standstill before, during, and after the fight. The streets were deserted and not a single share was bought or sold in the first hours of trading on the national stock exchange. Office workers, factory workers, laborers, and school children were glued to their TV sets watching the live broadcast. Schools in Kiang reported an absentee rate of more than 70%. The children were with their parents at home watching the fight.

The heat made Ali move slowly. One of his corner men was shouting, "Force yourself, Ali. Force yourself. You're fighting for a cause. Don't let him take the title from you." Ali was visibly affected by the punishing heat. As the rounds progressed the force in his punches gradually declined.

The fight lasted the full fifteen rounds and Ali won a unanimous decision. After Ali cooled down and cleaned up, he met with the media.

"Joe Frazier didn't give me as rough a time as you did," he said looking over at Bugner, who was also at the press conference. "Foreman, early in the morning in Africa, and Norton, when he broke my jaw, didn't give me as rough a time as you did, Bugner." Ali was happy it was over.

"I'm in good shape," he continued. "I'm gonna prepare for my next fight against Joe Frazier in Manila. I'm gonna stay here and train. I will send most of my people back to the US and keep one or two trainers here to help me stay in good shape. I'm in good shape now but if I go home, I'll get out of condition. I'm too old to get away with doin' the things I shouldn't do. It's best for me to stay here in Kuala Lumpur to get ready to beat down that ugly gorilla Joe Frazier."

Ali knew how to keep himself in the newspapers. After cooling down for a minute he was ready to heat things up again.

CHAPTER 5
THE THRILLA IN MANILA

September 30, 1975

Ali had once again coined a phrase that the media jumped all over and it became the name by which the fight was known throughout the world—The Thrilla in Manila.

By the time of the Ali-Frazier fight in Manila, Don King had effectively hijacked the event and established himself as the promoter of the fight. We were sharing the beautiful new offices at 30 Rock, but the tables had turned.

"Come on, Hank," King said. "Arum and I worked out the championship event in the Philippines. Now it's time for you to do your part of the job."

Ali-Frazier III was scheduled for October 1st, 1975 in the Araneta Coliseum near Manila and it was getting close enough for the Video Techniques production staff to start moving our cameras and microwave equipment into Manila.

"The production expenses and the payments to the fighters will be coming out of Ferdinand Marcos' pockets so you don't have to worry about that." Ferdinand Marcos was the president of the Philippines and he was funding the fight. I was completely out of the loop on the details of the financing. "You've got to go down there and put the communications infrastructure together," King said with a smile, knowing I had a hell of a job in front of me. His teasing grin, in addition to the fact that he was throwing his weight around giving me instructions, really started to bother the hell out of me. The power had totally shifted.

"Listen partner, you're lucky you got this fight together with all the problems between you and Bob Arum," I said, trying to push back. King and Arum were both very strong personalities accustomed to making the decisions and running the show. This led to a great deal of friction in the weeks prior to the fight.

"I have a flight to the Philippines tomorrow and I'll try to pull all this together once I meet with President Marcos and the government officials that are involved."

The Philippines is far more interesting than Malaysia. Connie decided to come with me and spend a few weeks there while we rebuilt the network.

"Why are you working as the vice president of Don King Productions?" Connie asked while we packed our suitcases.

"You know that my high-tech expertise is essential to the financial success of the event. I am best known in the sports world for the hard stuff that is needed to bring the television revenue in. It doesn't really matter which one of us is the president and which one the VP, as long as we keep the team together and produce the right result."

I would have felt better if the Thrilla were being promoted by Video Techniques. All the fights we had done so far had been promoted through my company.

"Don is full of shit and playing big ego games," I explained to Connie. "Let's forget about it and have some fun. Let me get my crew situated with the new equipment. Once they're set we can go out into the night and pretend we are Nick and Nora

Charles."

Connie smiled at me and that was the last time she asked anything about the nature of my working relationship with King.

Once we arrived at the Manila airport and started to unload the TV equipment, a large flat bed truck pulled up next to us. Accompanying the truck was a military unit on motorcycles with M16 rifles hanging off their shoulders. Someone had ordered the convoy to ensure the safe transportation of the equipment to the Araneta Coliseum, which was about eight miles out of Manila in the city of Quezon.

"Are you going to get shot at again?" Connie asked as she observed the military escort.

"I hope not," I said.

I knew, before we left the US, that we were going to a country with social and economic issues. Unfortunately, it was nothing new for us. We had worked in politically volatile conditions in Jamaica, Caracas, and Zaire.

"Why all the soldiers with guns?" Connie wondered.

"President Marcos has placed this part of the country under martial law. He's using a lot of his personal money to finance this event."

The imposition of martial law was helping Manila become a "must-see" tourist destination. Because of the incredibly high cost of travel to Tokyo, Hong Kong, Singapore, and other Asian capitals, tourism in Manila was growing. Martial law gave tourists the impression that they were safe from thieves and scam artists.

Once the equipment was unloaded, fifteen soldiers were left behind as guards to make sure nothing was tampered with or disappeared. The equipment was safe under their protection. A curfew was in effect. After 9 p.m. only members of the press were allowed on the streets.

CHAPTER 6
THE THRILLA IS GONE

October 1, 1975

Connie and I arrived at the hotel and found ourselves in a junior suite next to a much larger suite occupied by Ali. We didn't know where Frazier was staying with his entourage but everyone knew Muhammad Ali was staying at our hotel.

Ali arrived with his entourage and was greeted at a press conference that was set up by President Marcos and the Philippines' First Lady, Imelda. Ali had traveled with a pretty model that he had met in Zaire during the Rumble in the Jungle. She was very attractive and she and Ali looked good together. In fact, the President and First Lady greeted her as Ali's wife.

"Your wife is very good looking," President Marcos told Ali.

"She sure is," Ali responded.

The journalists and photographers covering the press conference immediately reported this news worldwide. When the news reached Chicago, Ali's wife Belinda was furious.

Around 10:30 that night, Connie and I retired to our suite. The thin wall between our suite and Ali's gave way to a ruckus.

We heard furniture crashing, glass breaking, and high-pitched shrieking coming from next door.

"Connie, call the front desk and tell them something's going on next door. Find out if they know anything about it," I said.

"Are you kidding? We don't want to make a bad situation worse. They will calm down soon, I'm sure."

We sat in bed, listening to objects smash against the wall. Finally I picked up the phone. "We seem to have a little noise next door to us," I told the front desk manager.

"Ah, Mr. Schwartz, a woman claiming to be Muhammad Ali's wife arrived and went upstairs to see him before we could even call up to ask if he wanted to see her."

I turned to Connie. "Holy shit, Belinda knows that Muhammad has been traveling around with Veronica."

Connie looked at me and suddenly both of us realized what was going on in the next suite. Connie's eyes were also giving me the message, *Don't interfere.*

In the hotel dining room the next morning we learned from the waiters that Belinda arrived in Manila, stormed into Ali's suite, and flew into a destructive rage. She ripped the drapes off the windows and physically fought with Ali, scratching his back and his face. No one knew what she did to Veronica. By the time we heard the news, Belinda had whizzed around and boarded a flight back to Chicago.

Later that day a journalist asked me, "How are Muhammad Ali's personal issues going to affect his fight against Frazier?"

I said, "Ali is OK. His mind is focused on this championship fight and he is in great shape."

Doctor Ferdie Pacheco was in a better position to answer the question. Pacheco was a skilled doctor who had been traveling with Ali for years and knew him well. He told me all about Ali's physical condition but mentioned nothing about his marital troubles and how they might affect his performance. We would just have to wait and see.

Frazier, on the other hand, was as focused as he had ever been. Many people knew that when Ali was suspended for refusing induction into the Army, he was broke and without a source of income. Frazier supported Ali's attempt to have his boxing license restored. Frazier had found it unforgivable when Ali later taunted him in such a disrespectful manner. For instance, Ali had effectively renamed Smokin' Joe the "gorilla in Manila." At a press conference before the fight a large rubber gorilla doll sat next to Ali, who kept punching the Frazier stand-in. Ali spouted many times during the press conference, "It's going to be a chilla, and a killa, and a thrilla, when I get the gorilla in Manila." Though he had helped Ali periodically, now Frazier only wanted to get into the ring to unleash his anger and dethrone Ali to recapture the heavyweight crown.

We had a fight to produce, which is never easy when you're working with a military-based government. Although it was not as difficult as the stadium in Jamaica, it was no small task getting the communication network connected and sending a signal out of the Araneta Coliseum. My crew, by this time, had a lot of experience rebuilding facilities to make them ready for broadcasting. The only difference was that they were working for Don King Productions *and* Video Techniques now.

At fight time our questions about the fighters' condition would be answered. Both fighters were entering the twilight years of their ring careers. This fight would be very different from their first fight in Madison Square Garden. Could Ali-Frazier III deliver the magic of the previous fights? Would they both go for knockouts? Did they have the stamina to fight for fifteen rounds? Would Ali's marital troubles affect his performance? Both fighters were super heavyweight champions who had contributed so much to boxing history. Frazier had won the first fight and Ali the second.

The referee for the fight was Carlos Padilla. Once the fight started Padilla's main job was to separate Ali from hanging on to the neck of Frazier while Ali's gloves pounded his body.

"Take your glove off the fighter's neck," Padilla hollered at Ali repeatedly.

"Joe, Joe, too low," he hollered at Frazier to keep his short blows where they belonged. Padilla was doing his job and making the fighters look good.

Ali was hitting Frazier's head and Frazier was mostly connecting short blows to Ali's body. The fighters alternated winning successive rounds. They were hurting each other. They were exhausted. By round nine, Ali looked swollen and bruised and weary. Angelo Dundee, his trainer, looked concerned. Each time Ali came back to his corner he looked worse.

Frazier's face was battered and weary and by the thirteenth round he started to catch more shots from Ali. It looked like Ali had more stamina but Frazier was still standing. He still had plenty of guts.

At the beginning of the fourteenth round, Ali reached into his drained, sweat-ridden body and fired nine straight bull's eyes at Frazier's head. Bull's eye after bull's eye after bull's eye. Frazier's eyes glazed and his legs trembled but he still made it through the fourteenth round. Ali was showing that he was the consummate heavyweight professional, knowing his job and maintaining concentration, but Frazier wouldn't go down.

"Joe, I don't want you to go any further," said Eddie Futch. Futch was the graying, 64 year old trainer for Frazier. "Your eye is swollen closed and you can't even see the punches coming."

"I'm alright, I'm alright," Frazier mumbled back. "I want him, Boss." But Futch couldn't be persuaded. It was the responsible decision and probably the most significant of Futch's career.

"It's all over. No one will forget what you did here today," Futch said to Frazier as he signaled the referee to come over. "Hey ref, it's over, it's over. Frazier can't go on. He has one eye closed and can't see what's coming. We've gotta call this done."

At the end of the fourteenth round the fight ended with a

TKO. Ali was sitting in his corner wondering how he would be able to continue. When the call was made that there would be no fifteenth round, Ali's entourage climbed through the ropes and filled his corner. Ali collapsed on the canvas. He had retained his heavyweight championship title.

A microphone picked up Ali's mumbling above the screaming crowd that surrounded his limp body.

"I felt like quitting, I felt like quitting," he said. "This was my toughest fight so far." But nobody was listening. They were screaming and dancing and jumping all around him.

I left the studio trying to get closer to Ali or Frazier, but there was a crowd of people around both of them. I finally found Frazier, his face battered, sitting in his dressing room with no one dancing around him. He sat and stared in painful seclusion. He looked at me with the one eye that was functioning.

"I was almost there, wasn't I?" he mumbled. "That reach he has… did somethin'… you can't do nothin' about." Frazier looked down at the floor.

"Smokin' Joe, you were great. Some things just happen that way." I tried to comfort him as much as possible. He still fought like a champion no matter what. "Listen to me. Futch was right not letting you get out there for the fifteenth round."

"Yeah, yeah, but I could have won in the fifteenth if I had a longer reach." He was still mumbling at the floor. There wasn't much more that could be said to him.

In Ali's dressing room, he was surrounded by journalists. Ali looked worse than I had ever seen him. His face was swollen on one side. He wasn't signing posters or programs. He wasn't indulging in his playful banter describing his clever techniques. He looked hurt. No one had ever seen him so subdued and so drained.

"He could have whupped me," Ali said to Gene Kilroy, who was standing between him and the group of journalists that were shouting out questions.

"Come on guys, let Muhammad alone for a moment." Kilroy turned to face the pack of reporters and motioned to the dressing room's door.

"How did you stand up to those shots to your head?" someone asked.

Kilroy sought out the journalist who had asked the question so he could throw him out. Ali was quiet and exhausted. The reporters started to drift out of the room so they could get on their telephones and fax machines.

To my amazement, Ali said, "My arms are sore. My legs are sore and the rest of my body…" The newsmen turned around and started to push back into the room. Ali's voice slowly became stronger and louder. As he saw the group coming back in and surrounding him, he reverted to his standard media pitch.

"It was a heck of fight wasn't it? Smokin' Joe took a lot of my punches but it was kind of close because I almost wasn't able to take all of Joe's punches."

A yell came from the pack of reporters saying, "When you talked to me a couple days ago you called Joe an ugly gorilla."

This time Kilroy found the guy and threw him out of the dressing room. Ali didn't acknowledge the statement.

"Joe took a lot more punches from me," Ali added, hoping that when the journalists reported the fight throughout the world, he would come out looking like he was in good shape. Ali switched to a low voice so most of the guys leaving the room didn't hear his final comment, "I never really thought of Frazier as being an ugly gorilla."

Then, instantly, he reverted to the more familiar Ali. Loudly he stated, "I withstood Joe Frazier's best shot and remained the world heavyweight champion."

Kilroy finally got the media people out of the dressing room. Ali still looked really bad. He was black and blue and his right eye was swelling the whole time he spoke. After reminding everyone there was an after-fight party thrown by the First Lady,

I left. It was tough seeing Ali and Frazier beaten up so badly. I think they would still be in the ring fighting if Futch had not put a stop to it.

CHAPTER 7
STEPPING ON IMELDA'S SHOE
(SHE HAS MORE)

What a night! After Ali's victory over Frazier in what turned out to be one of the most brutal fights ever seen, the First Lady hosted a lavish after-party at the president's residence, the Malacañang Palace.

Imelda Marcos was not your typical First Lady. She was very active politically and very pretty. I had been told at least a dozen times that Imelda was a former beauty queen and she still looked it. It was reported that she had an estimated 2,700 pair of shoes. The shoes became a symbol of the Marcoses' gross indulgences of material objects at the expense of the Filipino people. As we walked into the palace, it was obvious that Imelda had ostentatious taste.

When the enormous doors opened to the party, soft music drifted in from the terrace where a group of Filipino musicians played. Connie and I were having a great time. We had filled our champagne glasses at least four times when Muhammad Ali walked in. The First Lady met him and led him by the hand up the red-carpeted staircase to show off to everyone that he was her guest.

Ali had to pause as he took each step up the winding staircase. The First Lady guided him carefully into the palace ballroom. When Ali reached the huge buffet table, ornamented by an enormous crystal candelabrum, the flickering light illuminated Ali's battered face, revealing his bruises, swollen eyes, and pained expression.

Imelda filled Ali's plate from the buffet table and kept whispering into his ear. Ali could not lift the fork to reach his bruised pink lips. Imelda was caring for him like a helpless child.

"This scene with Ali and the First Lady doesn't seem real to me. Watch how he moves," I said to Connie.

Connie shook her head, "His eyes have always darted around and he has always looked so alive. Usually his face seems… how can I explain this… his eyes have lost their childlike wonder. His face looks like a mask."

Connie could not take her eyes off Ali. "He looks like he has drifted away. He doesn't look present. I think he is hurt badly," she said.

Ali was clearly not himself. He didn't want the hundreds of guests to see how his face had been worked over by Frazier.

"Where's Frazier?" Gene Kilroy asked as he looked around.

"He's not coming," I said. Eventually someone from Frazier's entourage said, "Oh man, they invited him but he ain't coming. He's a couple of miles from here by now. When I went to his room he was lying on his bed and couldn't even see me. He started to yell 'I can't see, I can't see. For Christ's sake turn on the lights,' and he still didn't see me. He was breathing real heavy and he just rolled over on his pillow and said, 'God damn. I hit him with punches that would have brought down the walls of Jericho', and then Smokin' Joe closed his eyes and went to sleep."

By this time the musicians were playing music that sounded a little bit more like what we were used to.

"Here comes Marcos to ask you to dance, Connie." I smiled at Connie as the president of the Philippines whisked her onto the dance floor.

Ali had moved away from the First Lady. This was an opportunity for me to ask Imelda to dance. I walked over and said, "First Lady Marcos, would you dance a foxtrot with me?" She smiled and held out her arms but her eyes never left Ali as we moved slowly around the dance floor.

I broke her lock on Ali by accidentally stepping on her left shoe. She turned and glared at me for being such a lousy dance partner.

"Oops, I'm sorry," I said. Our dance together ended about thirty seconds after that. What a night.

Connie was giggling when she got back to me after her dance with President Marcos. I guessed that he had not stepped on her shoes.

Three days later we got on a plane to New York and we ended up in first class. I suggested that we go upstairs to the bar and have a cocktail.

We sat down in the comfortable lounge seats with our martinis and Frazier just happened to be sitting right across from us. He didn't look any better now than he did three days before. His face was so battered that no amount of patching up could fix him. Only time could heal his wounds.

Frazier smiled at me and put out his hand for me to help him get up from his lounge chair. He went over to look out the window.

"Man, he is a great fighter," we heard him mumbling about Ali.

"You are a great fighter too," I said. "Are you going to fight Ali again?"

"Hank, I don't want to fight again at all. Ali should quit too," Smokin' Joe said as he looked out the window. I had the feeling he was saying goodbye to Manila, to Muhammad Ali, and to the ring.

PART 7

THE FINAL ROUND

CHAPTER 1
REGINA V. HENRY SCHWARTZ

Five months after the Thrilla in Manila I was on trial in the Queen's Court in London, supported by my solicitor, Anthony Leader, and Queen's Counsel, John Bull. It was Friday of the third week of the trial. When we were dismissed for the weekend I was exhausted. I walked out of The Old Bailey, and, supported by my date, walked to the club where I had arranged to take my date. We took a spin on the dance floor during cocktails and then enjoyed a very romantic dinner by candlelight. I invited my date back to my hotel room. She eagerly agreed it was time to go. Just as we stepped inside the suite, the phone rang.

"Mr. Schwartz, you have a woman in your room and you should make her disappear immediately," said a woman on the other end of the phone.

"Who the hell is this?" I asked.

"This is Sergeant Heatherton, the head of security for the hotel."

"There is no woman in this room that does not belong here,"

I assured her.

"Mr. Schwartz, I hear the woman giggling in the background. I am sure that it is not from the television."

Well, she was right. There was a very pretty, partly naked woman in my bed, listening to my side of the conversation and laughing hysterically while trying to be quiet.

"Sergeant, I repeat, if there is a woman in this room she is perfectly entitled to be here."

"Mr. Schwartz, we uphold the highest moral standards at this hotel and are vigilant on these matters in order to maintain our fine reputation. If you do not get that woman out of your room immediately, we will have to extricate her."

Turning to Connie, I hung up the phone. "Do you think this is funny?" She laughed loudly now.

Standing in my BVDs, refilling our wine glasses, I heard a knock on the door. Suddenly the door flew open. I was face-to-face with Sergeant Heatherton, a small woman in a stiffly starched security uniform accompanied by a 6 foot 2 burly man who I knew was the janitor. I jumped back under the covers with Connie. They had opened the door with a master key. They frowned at us as they walked to the foot of the bed.

"Mr. Schwartz…" Sergeant Heatherton growled in an accusatory tone.

"Hold on, Sergeant. There are two passports on the credenza over there, one for me and the other for this woman, who has flown in from the United State today. You will see that she is my wife!"

Sergeant Heatherton picked up the passports. While keeping an eye on both of us, she looked them over thoroughly. Her fair white face flushed a rosy pink.

"I am so sorry, Mr. Schwartz, Mrs. Schwartz, I really didn't know. Mrs. Schwartz, why didn't you check in today when you arrived?"

"I came in on a very early flight so that I could see my husband before he left for the court," Connie said, trying to suppress the giggles.

Connie had been taking the red-eye on Thursdays so that she could get to Heathrow early enough to see me on Friday mornings before I left for the Old Bailey. I thought I was above suspicion, but evidently not.

Both Sergeant Heatherton and the janitor bowed sheepishly as they backed out of the room. As soon as the door closed Connie screamed in hysterics. I put the double lock on the door and returned to be in bed between the sheets.

Every time I came to London there always seemed to be some kind of incident.

At 8 a.m. the next morning there was another knock on the door. This time Connie and I both had our clothes on. In rolled a fabulous breakfast with a bottle of icy cold champagne and a bouquet of roses; a gesture of atonement from the hotel. We popped the cork on the cold champagne and toasted a successful conclusion to my legal troubles in London.

Richard Saul and his company were suing me for losses he allegedly incurred from the fight in Caracas. Saul, and his company InstantVision, had provided a letter of credit in the amount of USD $140,000 for the UK license to broadcast the Foreman-Norton Heavyweight Championship fight into theaters in the UK.

When Foreman developed a bad knee on the day of the fight and claimed he couldn't proceed, the press around the world reported that fact through their print and broadcast media. Because the UK is six or seven hours ahead of Caracas time, a significant number of fans who were going to watch the fight in Saul's theaters canceled their tickets. By the time Foreman "recovered" and the fight went on at the time originally scheduled, there was not enough time to get the word out to the ticket holders. Saul lost money because of cancellations and a complete absence of walk-ins. Some enterprising attorney had told him that under English law he stood a good chance of getting back whatever amount he had lost.

Saul also claimed that he signed and paid for an option for the UK rights to the Rumble in the Jungle. Saul had lied through his teeth. This second agreement never existed.

In his sworn affidavits, he referred to this non-existent agreement between Video Techniques and InstantVision, and claimed he saw both fighters' signatures on it. This was the basis of my arrest at the Grosvenor Hotel during the meeting with the Zaire team, and why I spent that fateful night in the slammer.

Now I found myself in Courtroom 7 of the Old Bailey, finishing the third week of "Regina vs. Henry Schwartz." I was directed to stand in the defendant's box, in the middle of the courtroom, facing the magistrate who sat on a tall bench. In front of the magistrate stood my lawyers, wearing curly white wigs and flowing black robes that swirled when they turned around to pose a question to the witness. The jury was to the right of the witness box.

Over the first two weeks, Saul had been questioned multiple times by my legal team. His answers were completely inaccurate. I would write notes indicating the discrepancies and pass them to Leader. He would pass the note on to Bull who would read it and judge whether it was relevant. If the point had merit, he would pass the note on to the head counsel to use in the questioning.

Several non-British citizens were involved with contracts for Ali and Foreman or the contracts for the video production. They were invited to appear as a witness on my behalf. The most crucial of these was Don King, who had actually helped to obtain the fighters' signatures on the contracts.

Despite repeated requests, Don King did not appear to testify in my defense. His testimony was vital to support my side of the story and verify the facts to counter Richard Saul's claims. There were hundreds of thousands of dollars on the line, yet he just fucking did not show up.

What saved me, I think, was Foreman's attorney. Steve Bomse who flew in from San Francisco to testify on my behalf. He was the guy who helped prepare the fight contract and provided the text that appeared ahead of the signatures on the three blank pages signed during the infamous walk in the parking lot. He was the attorney who actually negotiated with me to create the fight contract.

"Mr. Bomse, had you full knowledge of the agreement between Telemedia de Panama and George Foreman?" my counsel asked.

"Absolutely!" Bomse said.

"Tell us more about that."

"The draft of the agreement for Foreman to fight Muhammad Ali was sent to my office in San Francisco from Telemedia de Panama and executed by their legal agent, Henry Schwartz."

"And what was your role?"

"George Foreman agreed to all its terms. When Don King visited George while he was training, George put his signature on three blank pages, signing one on the top, one in the middle, and one on the bottom. He sent those signed pages to me so that I could complete the agreement and the signatures would be properly printed on the correct pages," Bomse stated with certainty.

"And just to be clear, who signed the agreement with George Foreman?"

"It was signed by Telemedia de Panama's legal agent, Henry Schwartz."

"Do you know of any other contract signed between George Foreman and Video Techniques for his championship fight with Muhammad Ali?"

"No sir, I do not."

"Have you ever heard of any such agreement between George Foreman and Video Techniques?"

"No sir, I never saw one, I never heard about one, nor have I any knowledge about one. If there was an agreement, it would have been given to me to prepare or approve the terms as required by George Foreman. No such contract, to the best of my knowledge, has ever been prepared."

"Thank you Mr. Bomse."

It was getting close to lunchtime after Bomse's testimony. The magistrate looked at his watch and stood up.

"Is Mrs. Schwartz here?" he called out, scanning the audience.

Connie, sitting several feet to my right, did not want to answer but reluctantly raised her hand and said in a wavering voice, "Yes sir. I'm over here."

The magistrate smiled at her and said, "We're getting close to the end of this trial. Take your husband to lunch but make sure you are back here no later than 1:15. Please be sure not to discuss the trial with anyone."

They opened the exit door from the defendant's box and I walked over to Connie.

"What's going on?" she asked.

"I don't know, honey." I had asked Connie to bring the check for $140,000 in case I lost and had to settle, but now I was having different thoughts.

"You have the certified check in your bag?"

"Yes, yes. I have it."

"Hold on to that pocketbook real tight. Even if I lose this trial and end up in the hoosegow, I want you to take the check home and put it back in the bank. I have done nothing wrong." I was still wondering how this absurd situation would end.

"The magistrate took a risk letting us go out to lunch." I laughed to keep Connie relaxed.

The Old Bailey was on the edge of a neighborhood that had a large Jewish population. Three blocks from the courthouse, we found a delicatessen that looked like what we used to go to on the lower East Side of New York. I wanted some pastrami but it didn't go by that name in London. Connie searched through a cardboard menu that was stained with oil spots.

"I think they call pastrami 'salt beef' here," she said.

"OK, let's have the salt beef and enjoy ourselves… as long as we get back to the courthouse on time."

"Don't worry, honey. I think everybody is starting to realize that this lawsuit against you has no truth behind it at all."

"Well, I'm glad that you're seeing it that way. But remember, take that $140,000 back to New York, no matter what happens."

"OK, OK."

The salt beef tasted more or less like pastrami. We ate our lunch without much conversation. Both of us were wondering what might be coming next.

We arrived back in the courtroom on time. All the players resumed their positions. Several documents were read, and at 2:30 in the afternoon, the magistrate stood up and faced the jury.

"Gentlemen of the jury, you have reviewed the testimony and documents from knowledgeable and engaged witnesses indicating that there are no viable claims against Henry Schwartz, Video Techniques, or Hemdale Leisure Corp. Regarding the execution of a valuable security that was claimed by Mr. Saul to have been entered into through deception or false representations, as claimed under this suit against Henry Schwartz contrary to section 20 (2) of the Theft Acts of 1968, these allegations have not been proven. Under English law we find no misconduct. Therefore this case is hereby dismissed."

As the magistrate dismissed the charges against me, there was a modest round of applause coming from the balcony that surrounded the back of the courtroom.

My lead counsel shook Bull's hand and Bull shook his hand, and then I was released from the defendant's box for the last time. They all came over and shook my hand. Bull said, "Let's go upstairs and have some tea in the cafeteria."

The cafeteria was filled with older men, who, Bull explained, were retired businessmen who spent most of their time in the audience of courtroom proceedings. Some of the retirees were jostling each other and I heard some English that was tinged with Jewish vernacular. A few of them walked over to me as I finished my tea.

"What took them so long?" said one of the men with a heavy Jewish accent. "What's wrong vit that bunch of schlecht people that brought this to a court?"

Another elderly man sporting a gray van dyke put his two cents in. "This should have been done in tre days."

"Thank you gentlemen," I said. "I hope you had a good time watching all the dreck."

Bull stood up, took off his white wig and put it on my head.

"A gift for you, Henry."

CHAPTER 2
EVICTED FROM 30 ROCK

Saturday, after we returned home from London, I went to my office at 30 Rockefeller Plaza. I tried my key in the door and it did not work. I went down to the building maintenance office and found one of the cleaning women who knew me well. She unlocked the office with her key.

My office looked like a moving company was expected any minute!

My relationship with Don King was over. Someone else had taken up residence in my office. My desk and horned chair from Zaire had been pushed into a corner. My books and files were heaped in a messy pile that would take days to sort out. Don King had replaced me while I was on trial in London.

I called the real estate guy that had helped me find the office space for King.

"There is space available at 150 East 58th Street," he told me.

The Angels and I moved into the new space, but it was far

from the luxury we had enjoyed at 30 Rockefeller Plaza. My horned chair, which was an important visual reminder of what I had accomplished in Kinshasa, did not fit anywhere in the new office. I ended up bringing it home, where it stands now in front of one of Connie's paintings.

From King—I never heard a fuckin' word.

CHAPTER 3
ALI'S LAST HURRAH

October 2, 1980

We had no difficulty rebuilding Video Techniques and attracting consulting work in satellite communications. After four years King called me one day, out of the blue.

"Is my man in?" King asked Karen.

Karen now sat next to my desk. She waved the phone at me. "Hank, it's Don King."

"No shit. He still remembers me?" I said, wondering what he wanted after all this time. I picked up the phone. "Don, where the hell have you been?"

"I have been so busy with all the fighters I have under contract now. I am running a fight for Muhammad Ali." I knew he was promoting an unimportant fight between Ali and Larry Holmes in Las Vegas.

Within the span of seven months Muhammad Ali won and lost the heavyweight title from Leon Spinks. Spinks had been a professional for thirteen months and had only eight fights on his record. He wasn't anywhere close to the fighter Ali had been.

People in the business were getting very concerned about what they were seeing in the ring. Teddy Brenner, the matchmaker at Madison Square Garden, said he didn't like what Ali looked like and told Herbert Muhammad privately that Ali should retire. Even Ali's doctor, Ferdie Pacheco, knew that Ali's body was not responding well to the commands from his brain.

It was 1980 and Ali had been away from boxing for two years.

"Hank, meet me for dinner tonight near my office in the 80's and Madison," Don suggested.

"Who's paying?" I asked. I still had no idea why Don was reaching out to me.

Later that night, we sat down for dinner at one of the local steakhouses. Don got right down to business. "Hank, I got a problem," he said. "Maybe you can help me get out of it."

Sitting next to each other in that booth, we were as comfortable as we had been six years earlier. We reminisced for a few minutes and laughed as we looked back over the years when he worked for Video Techniques and the short period I worked for Don King Productions. His personality was still overbearing but he was full of compliments. King could be very charming when he needed something.

"Hank, you know I have been using our old buddy Jack Murphy to oversee and organize the Ali fight in Vegas."

"Well Jack was always good when he was on my production team… what's your problem?"

"Man, he's having some issues. He doesn't show up when he's supposed to, I think he might be hitting the juice a little too hard… the cameramen and lighting guys don't want to take instructions from him."

"You know he was sitting next to me when Mobutu had the Minister of Communications shot to death. He must have fallen apart after that."

King looked at me with a blank stare, trying to put together what happened in Kinshasa. I had never told King the whole story of the events that led up to the fight. "Hank, Ali is fighting Holmes at Caesar's Palace and I need you to help me pull the production together."

"OK, let's work out a contract. Get me a ticket and I will fly out there and see what I can do. When is this fight going to happen?" I asked.

"It is scheduled for October 2nd."

"Don, that's only three weeks from now. Why didn't you bring me in two weeks ago?"

"We weren't having the issues then. I thought Murphy could pull it off."

"OK, get the ticket. I'll take a look and see if I can turn it around."

I got to Las Vegas and found Murphy in the bar. "Jack, what's the big problem? Why are you so out of control?"

Jack said, "Frank Sinatra is coming in to do a show here. They decided to turn the parking lot next to the hotel into a temporary stadium so they can pack it with the mobs of people that will come to see Frank."

"Are they going to put the fight in the stadium as well?" I asked.

"Yeah, and there isn't much of a gap between the two events. Everything is in shambles out there."

"Let's go check it out. We should call a meeting immediately with the contractors that are building the bleachers in the parking lot."

The arena was being constructed out of aluminum sections with rows of seats going up about forty feet around the ring. The structure was totally unstable. They had not contemplated secure locations solid enough to mount the lights and cameras. We called a meeting with the contractor to look over the construction plans.

"We'll have to add four platforms that won't tremble or

shake the television cameras so the picture comes out alright," I explained to him. "Let me work with your engineers so we can redesign the interior of the arena and isolate the camera platforms from the stadium seats. That way when the people in the audience stamp their feet or jump up and down, the vibrations won't be transmitted to the camera platforms and then up to the camera. Do you understand the extent of the problem we have to solve?"

"Yeah, yeah. I see what you're saying." The head of the construction crew was very cooperative. We got the camera stations designed and built.

"Jack, get a couple of our cameramen to jump up and down on the rows of the seating close to each camera while I get the TV picture up and running in the mobile studio."

The test delivered a steady picture, good enough to be transmitted through a mobile uplink. We were ready to roll. It felt great solving production problems again.

Even though the cameras were ready and steady, Ali looked shaky just two days before the fight. The odds were in his favor, but the spread was very close. Holmes had been one of the best sparring partners in Ali's camp, and he knew everything about Ali's style.

Ali's age and long career had taken its toll. Dr. Pacheco thought that Ali's kidneys had been affected when he endured the "Rope-a-dope" punishment and took so many blows in the midsection from Foreman in Zaire. Dr. Pacheco, Herbert, and the Nevada boxing commissioner decided to send Ali to be examined at the Mayo Clinic in July before the fight.

The Mayo Clinic's overall report was favorable, but Ali seemed to be losing his agility and motor skills. The lab reports indicated that Ali appeared in general good health. However, a report from Dr. Frank Howard indicated that a CAT scan revealed a small hole in the membrane covering Ali's brain. Perhaps the most disturbing signal of his deteriorating health was his difficulty coordinating the muscles that controlled his speech.

The Nevada State Athletic Committee granted Ali a boxing license based on the clinic's report. After reviewing all of the reports and talking to Herbert and Dr. Pacheco, I suggested that the fight be canceled. I thought this would allow Ali to retire with dignity and in relative good health. Ali insisted on proceeding as planned.

The day before the fight, the betting odds in the casino leveled. Just before the fight the odds were nearly even, but most commentators were picking Holmes to win.

King was quoted as stating, "Ali is the greatest of all time, but he will meet his Waterloo in Holmes. This will be Ali's last hurrah." Generally, promoters shouldn't comment on the fight's outcome.

When the fight started the temperature was over 100 degrees in Las Vegas, and even higher in the ring because of the hot lights. I looked at Ali's face through the camera and saw that it was a death mask. He was expressionless. In the early rounds he had no power behind his punches and with each bell he slowed down. It was devastating to watch him come out round after round more exhausted each time. All of the spirit and the energy was drained out of him. I could see on the monitors that Holmes started to pull his punches so as not to hurt Ali any further.

I had seen Ali at his very best, and on this day I feared I was seeing the worst. By the tenth round, Angelo Dundee called to the referee. "This ball game is over," he said. "I'm the chief second here, and I'm stopping the fight." Ali had fought sixty fights up to that point, wining fifty-six and losing only three. This was his fourth loss.

Ali would return once more in 1981 to fight and lose to Trevor Berbick. Shortly after the Berbick fight, Ali learned he had Parkinson's disease, a movement disorder that affects the central nervous system. The symptoms had started to show before the Holmes fight. His slowness of speech. His hesitation of movement. There are conflicting reports as to when this debilitating disease seized control of his nervous system, but it was clear, following the Berbick fight, that Ali was experiencing increased symptoms. These last two fights should never have happened.

After the Ali-Holmes fight, I knew that the Golden Era of heavyweight boxing had passed. I had taken enough of a beating myself and it was time for me to move into the next generation of communications technology and see what I could stir up with this new thing called the internet.

EPILOGUE

THOSE PRECIOUS HANDS

One day I was surprised to hear from one of my Angels that Ali was on his way up from the lobby to see me.

It had been twenty-three years since Ali had sat next to me at my side of the desk in my office on West 55th Street, asking me to believe that he could regain the heavyweight title. I knew back then that the lives of Frazier, Foreman, and Ali would cross in an ever-shifting battle for the championship. I had become a part of it. I uniquely created the technology to broadcast unquestionable gifts of these three men to the corners of the earth. I had delivered the brute force of George Foreman, the dazzling brilliance of Smokin' Joe, and the unspeakable beauty of Muhammad Ali to the world from the many satellites that hovered high above the earth's equator. And now here Ali was again.

I dropped the papers I was reading and went to greet him. He shuffled slowly down the long hallway. He was mumbling something and stroking his face with trembling fingers. I got close to him and tried to understand what he was saying. Ali smiled at me and motioned to get closer.

"Hank, I'm still pretty ain't I?" Ali whispered in my ear. I stepped back and smiled at him so he would know I heard what he was saying.

"Muhammad, you are still pretty."

Ali was quiet. He kept smiling as we locked eyes and he sucked energy from me through the intensity of his gaze. He had propelled himself to the top drawing on the energy of others.

"Muhammad, there were three great champions: you, Joe Frazier, and George Foreman. You had to challenge both of them to win back your championship title. In the process you became an icon—the most recognized face on the planet."

Ali's eyes started to tear up and so did mine.

"You are a poet. You are a devotee of Islam and you have the blessing of Allah. You are adored and respected by millions of people around the globe, no matter their religion or nationality. Muhammad, you are and always will be the *people's champion.*" Ali put his quivering hand forward and I took it in mine. "You aren't just pretty Muhammad, you are beautiful." I felt the uncontrollable shaking of his fingers in mine. I flashed back to the image of Angelo taping these broken hands after Dr. Pacheco shot them full of Novocain to deaden the pain. I held this precious hand, in full understanding of the power it once held.

We stood there without saying another word.

I let go of Ali's hand. His smile still worked as his tears rolled down his face. He turned and shuffled back to the elevator. His driver was waiting to help him into the elevator.

I stood in the hallway for a few moments with a blurry view of the posters that decorated the wall. I recalled when Muhammad Ali arrived in Zaire on a dark evening and was greeted by miles of adoring Africans who lined the road to N'Sele, holding torches that pierced the surrounding jungle's midnight canopy.

I knew my work was done. I signed off on the broadcasts of the Golden Era of the Heavyweight Championship that was part of the greatest story ever told, one which embraced Muhammad Ali and could never become a fading myth.

ABOUT THE AUTHOR

Henry A. (Hank) Schwartz, born in Brooklyn, is an expert in video communications technology and was involved in the broadcast, promotion, and distribution of notable boxing matches involving Muhammad Ali, Joe Frazier, and George Foreman during the 1970's. An authority on microwave and satellite technology, Schwartz utilized his expertise to telecast major boxing events such as "The Rumble in the Jungle" in Zaire, "The Thrilla in Manila" in the Phillipines, as well as other major events in Kingston, Jamaica; Caracas, Venezuela; Kuala Lumpur, Malaysia; and Madison Square Garden in New York. Hank has designed systems for E.I. Dupont, Western Electric, Bell Telephone, Westinghouse Electric, Revlon, RCA, and others. He also installed and designed the first cyclotron monitoring equipment for Columbia University's School of Engineering. From 1974 to 1978 Schwartz served as Minister of Communications for the former Republic of Zaire.

In January of 1973 he produced the first championship boxing event ever broadcast from a foreign country for distribution by the INTELSAT satellite system. The championship fight between Joe Frazier and George Foreman was sold to HBO and became the first pay-per-view sports program on cable TV. His technical innovations have generated millions of dollars for cable companies and program owners such as ESPN, FOX, and HBO. Schwartz holds a number of patents and patent applications in the electronics and visual communications fields.

He served in the US Army in WWII and then attended Brooklyn Polytech, from which he received his Bachelor of Electrical Engineering degree (BEE). In 1999, he was inducted into the Golden Jubilee Society.